D1084032

The Chances of Explanation

PAUL HUMPHREYS

The Chances
of Explanation

Causal Explanation in the Social, Medical, and Physical Sciences

PRINCETON UNIVERSITY PRESS

PRINCETON, NEW JERSEY

Copyright © 1989 by Princeton University Press

Published by Princeton University Press, 41 William Street,
Princeton, New Jersey 08540
In the United Kingdom: Princeton University Press, Oxford

Library of Congress Cataloging-in-Publication Data

Humphreys, Paul.
The chances of explanation : causal explanation in the social,
medical, and physical sciences / Paul Humphreys.
p. cm.   Bibliography: p.   Includes index.
ISBN 0-691-07353-8 (alk. paper)
1. Causation. 2. Chance. I. Title.
BD541.H78 1989   122—dc20   89-10269

Publication of this book has been aided by the Whitney Darrow
Fund of Princeton University Press

This book has been composed in Linotron Times Roman by J. Jarrett Engineering, Inc.
Clothbound editions of Princeton University Press books
are printed on acid-free paper, and binding materials are
chosen for strength and durability. Paperbacks, although satisfactory
for personal collections, are not usually suitable for library rebinding

Printed in the United States of America by Princeton University Press,
Princeton, New Jersey

Designed by Laury A. Egan

TO MY PARENTS

William Edward and Florence Christina Humphreys

who contributed more than I shall ever know.

C O N T E N T S

PREFACE   ix

CHAPTER ONE. Traditional Causation   3

§1   Scope of the Work   3

§2   Methodology   4

§3   An Example   6

§4   The Multiplicity of Causes   7

§5   The Incompleteness of Causal Knowledge   8

§6   The Principle of Causal Contribution   9

§7   Sufficiency Theories of Causation   9

§8   Sine Qua Non Analyses of Causation   12

§9   Why Sine Qua Non Analyses Are Inadequate   13

§10 Indeterminism   16

§11 Chance and Cause   18

CHAPTER TWO. Probabilistic Causation   22

§12* Ontology   22

§13* Assumptions for Quantitative Probabilistic Causality   26

§14 The Binary Case   34

§15 The Contrast Case   37

§16 How This Affects Relative Frequentists   45

§17 A Tripartite Distinction   46

§18 Passive Empiricism and the Trivialization Problem   47

§19 Antiformalism   53

§20 Experimental Contexts and Regularities   55

§21 An Argument for Unobserved Structures   58

CHAPTER THREE. Cause and Chance   61

§22 Chance   61

§23 Common Causes and Structural Stability   66

§24 The Probabilistic Case   70

§25 Mill's Unconditionality Requirement   72

§26 Consequences   75

§27 Further Discussion   80
§28 The Scope of the Theory   88
§29 Causation as Inductively Defined   89
§30 Contributing Causes and Necessary Conditions   93
§31 Counteracting Causes   94
§32 Are Processes or Mechanisms Necessary?   95

CHAPTER FOUR. Scientific Explanations   98
§33 Introduction   98
§34 The Canonical Form for Linguistic Explanations   100
§35 Explanatory Ontology   103
§36 The Deterministic Case   104
§37 Detailed Specification of Events   107
§38 Why Probability Values Are Not Explanatory   109
§39 On the Very Possibility of Explaining Chancy Events   117
§40 Testing the Account   118
§41 The Pragmatics of Causal Explanations   126
§42 Why Ask Why-Questions?   132
§43 Explanatory Knowledge   138

APPENDIX ONE.* Covariance Measures   143
**APPENDIX TWO.* Extension of the Basic Quantitative
Theory**   145
APPENDIX THREE.* Transitivity and Negative Links   153
REFERENCES   158
INDEX   167

PREFACE

This book had its genesis in a comment made to me in 1977 by the late J. L. Mackie, when he suggested that despite their technical interest, existing theories of probabilistic causality had thus far managed to avoid addressing all the important philosophical questions of causation. He was right, as always. Things have improved markedly over the intervening decade in that respect, and the present work is an attempt to draw together most of what I see as the important insights gained to date in the area. What emerges, I think, is that probabilistic causality is not, at root, all that different from deterministic varieties of causation, and in linking it with more familiar traditions of causation, perhaps philosophers who hitherto have viewed probabilistic causality as a somewhat esoteric subject will find that they share more common ground with the topic than might appear at first sight. Indeed, we shall see that probabilistic causality is not actually probabilistic at all.

I hope that some of this book will be of use to scientists, especially in the social and medical sciences. Much philosophical discussion of causation must seem remote from their interests, and I have attempted to make at least some of the examples representative of reality. But this is a philosophical book, not a treatise on methodology, and it must be read with sympathy for that end. The sections that are primarily of technical interest are indicated in the table of contents by asterisks and need not be read by those whose interests lie elsewhere. Those readers who are unfamiliar with probabilistic causality or with causal models would do well to move straight from chapter 1 to chapter 4, returning thereafter to those sections of chapters 2 and 3 that have particular relevance to their interests.

Most of the book is about causation, but its real subject is explanation. The kinds of explanations with which I am concerned tell us about the causes of phenomena, about the rich panoply of influences which affect even commonplace features of the world and which the methods of science gradually uncover for us. The account of explanation I have to offer is, I think, rather different from others that have been put forward (unlike the theory of causation, which is a synthesis of existing ideas) and may seem a little too directly causal for some. In evaluating its worth, one must keep in mind that its scope is that of causal explanations discovered by science, and not about other forms of explanation. I make no claims of universality here, only of truth.

Over the years I have had invaluable help of various kinds. Wesley Salmon has spent innumerable hours discussing explanation and related matters with me, and I have profited enormously from his help. It is true to say that without his pathbreaking work on explanation this book would not have existed. James Woodward provided me with many detailed and helpful comments on the penultimate version of the manuscript, thereby greatly improving the final product. Hubert Blalock kindly read the sections concerning causal models and provided generous help with constructive criticisms, resulting in the avoidance of a number of errors. Others who have been of particular assistance are Patrick Suppes, who aroused my interest in probability and causality and whose voice seems always to be at my ear urging greater rigor upon me; James Fetzer, who has been an endless source of lively discussion on all matters contained herein, especially single-case propensities; Alan Ryan, for contributing the perspective of a Mill scholar and social philosopher to the final version; Ken Olson, for drawing my attention to the wonderful Austin quotation in §19; and of course all those whose contributions to the subject are reflected in the text and references.

Financial help was provided by the National Science Foundation, the Center for Advanced Studies at the University of Virginia, and the Center for Philosophy of Science at the University of Pittsburgh, and it is gratefully acknowledged here.

Scattered sections of this book draw on a number of my previously published articles, parts of which are reproduced here with the permission of the publishers: "Aleatory Explanations Expanded," in *PSA 1982, Volume 2* (Philosophy of Science Association, 1983); "Quantitative Probabilistic Causality and Structural Scientific Realism," in *PSA 1984, Volume 2* (Philosophy of Science Association, 1985); "Causal, Experimental, and Structural Realisms," in *Midwest Studies in Philosophy,* vol. 12, edited by Peter French, Howard Wettstein, and Theodore Uehling (University of Minnesota Press, 1988); and "Scientific Explanation: The Causes, Some of the Causes, and Nothing but the Causes," in *Scientific Explanation. Minnesota Studies in the Philosophy of Science,* vol. 13, edited by Philip Kitcher and Wesley C. Salmon (University of Minnesota Press, 1989).

Gratitude of a special kind does not fit easily into a preface, and I do indeed owe more than I could possibly say to my wife, Diane, whose patience and understanding made completion of this book possible.

Charlottesville, Virginia
January 17, 1989

The Chances of Explanation

CHAPTER ONE

Traditional Causation

§1. Scope of the Work

Ontology, epistemology, and conceptual analysis constitute the great philosophical triad of causation. When pursuing ontological issues, we try to provide an account of the nature of causation: what differentiates causal relations from noncausal relations and what causal relations, as part of the world, are like. Epistemological interests, in contrast, focus on how causal relationships are discovered, how hypotheses about causal relations are tested and confirmed, when it is justifiable to assert a causal claim, and what kinds of causal inferences might be valid. Conceptual analyses, finally, are concerned with what a term such as 'causes' means, with constructing definitions of 'cause' and related terms, with their use in language, ordinary or technical, and with providing rules for the correct employment of such terms. A similar tripartite division can be made in the areas of probability and explanation, even if one of the divisions is considered to be empty, as, for example, those who have denied the existence of objective chance have held. Philosophical work in each of these areas is entirely legitimate, and the divisions cannot be entirely separated, yet confusion can easily arise if arguments that are based primarily on evidence from one of these areas are used as reasons to accept or reject a position in another area without this move being explicitly noted and justified. So it is as well to state right at the outset the orientation of this work. In each of these three areas—causation, probability, and explanation—my primary interest will be ontological. A moderate amount of attention will be paid to the epistemological, and the least attention will be devoted to conceptual analysis.

This ontic orientation may seem peculiar in the case of explanation, for explanation has traditionally been taken to be squarely in the realm of epistemology, with conceptual analysis contributing as a source of useful insights. The reasons for my own orientation will become clear as we proceed, but it derives from two axiomatic theses. The first is that an inviolable requirement of a satisfactory scientific explanation is that it be true. In the case of causal explanations this means that explanations must accurately capture the causal structure of systems and their interactions. False explanations, however psychologically beguiling and however widely accepted in a scientific community, are incapable of producing genuine understanding of the way the world works. The second axiom is that scientific methods, especially experimental methods, have been successful in discovering at least some of the causes that operate in the world and that they are more successful at this than are unsystematic, nonexperimental methods. We thus need to address and answer the philosophical question, "Why are experimental methods superior to non-experimental methods in discovering and establishing the existence of causal relations?" The answer to this second question will move us away from a traditional kind of empiricist epistemology toward one that, although still empiricist, allows for a good deal of realism about unobserved entities, especially unobserved causes. This causal realism then allows us to address explanations as features of the world that one can discover, rather than construct, and the linguistic explanations that have been the focus of so much philosophical inquiry must be seen merely as flexible devices that convey the essential causal content from individual to individual, when required.

§2. Methodology

The avoidance of conceptual analysis mentioned above has a specific reason and a specific consequence. The consequence is that we should not be primarily concerned with what is said in ordinary language(s) about causation or forced to square our theory with every construction in English that appears to have causal content.[1] The reason is this: there is no ground for supposing that languages which have evolved over the centuries in response to various needs, most of them noncausal and unscientific, should contain within them a coherent representation of causal truths, even at a nonsuperficial level of linguistic structure. One of the more remarkable features of the literature on causation and scientific explanation is the frequency of appeals to what we should ordinarily say about various cases. There is an important difference between our knowing that certain relations are elementary cases of causation and what we should ordinarily say about such cases, other than that they are causal.

The linguistic situation is even worse when we enter the realm of probabilistic causality, especially when, as we often shall be, we are concerned with causal relationships between quantitative variables. Most ordinary talk, and most classical philosophical terminology, is oriented toward deterministic

---

[1] In a curiously uncharacteristic concession to informal concepts, Suppes ([1970], p. 11, also pp. 7–8) motivated his theory of probabilistic causality by an appeal to ordinary language: "The deepest and in many ways the most substantial reason [for defining casuality in terms of probability] lies in the wide use of probabilistic causal concepts in ordinary talk." Nevertheless, this stated motivation seems to have had little effect on the theory itself.

causal relations between qualitative events. This presents anyone who is concerned with providing more than a purely mathematical or logical theory of causation with a potentially serious difficulty, akin to the difficulty that the early advocates of the Copenhagen interpretation of quantum mechanics noted. They claimed that because our epistemic access to quantum phenomena was ultimately made through the medium of experimental apparatus at the macroscopic level, and the conceptual apparatus at that macroscopic level of observability was thoroughly infused with classical mechanical modes of thought, it was profoundly difficult, and perhaps impossible, to construct a satisfactory mode of description for nonclassical quantum phenomena. Whether or not they were correct about that issue, we have to face a similar predicament in providing an understanding within the confines of ordinary English of a theory of probabilistic causality and explanation that is applicable to quantitative scientific contexts.

Fortunately, the structure of these more complex causal and explanatory systems lends itself to a method that to a large extent avoids these difficulties. One of the principal themes of this work is that our understanding of probabilistic causation comes from principles that also apply to nonprobabilistic causation. A second theme is that causal knowledge comes from something like an inductive definition, with simple base cases of causation being used to discover knowledge about more complex cases, and that this base knowledge is nonlinguistic, perhaps even prelinguistic. These two facts about causation mean that one can appeal to clear cases of traditional causation as examples and then argue by analogy, via explicit connecting principles, to the probabilistic case. We can also, it transpires, apply pieces of standard talk about causes to the new cases. There are limits to this, and when there is a conflict between the consequences of a systematic philosophical theory of causation and casual talk of causation, it is the latter that has to give. This strain of revisionary metaphysics is explicit throughout the book, and I consider it to be an important contribution that philosophy can make, in conjunction with science, to our understanding of causation.

Our use of examples is also affected by these concerns. There is a perfectly legitimate tendency in philosophy to use the simplest examples that will illustrate the point at hand, with resort often being made to artificial and artificially simple examples. Yet a characteristic feature of science is its attention to the importance of detail—as noted in §4, the world is a complex place, and part of science's success stems from not ignoring that complexity. One consequence of the use of simple examples in the philosophical literature has been the almost total lack of consideration of quantitative examples, or of how causation and explanation operate with quantitative variables. So most of our examples will be at least moderately sophisticated real examples that reflect the detailed character of science. On occasion, however, everyday and simplified examples will be used where this will not prove misleading.

§3. An Example

In 1981, physicians in Los Angeles and New York began to notice an unusual cluster of cases of formerly rare symptoms—Kaposi's sarcoma, *Pneumocystis carinii* pneumonia, and other opportunistic infections, primarily in young men.[2] At that time no specific etiology for the symptoms was known, and the repeatedly raised question, "What is the explanation of this man's illness?"[3] set in motion a standard scientific procedure. The search for an explanation brought to bear segments of scientific methodology that are designed specifically for the discovery of causes, in this case epidemiology to identify risk groups, theories in molecular biology to identify possible causal factors, and controlled experimentation to isolate the specific causal factors that were responsible in each case. What this systematic search for an explanation was seeking was not a linguistic entity (such as an argument or a speech act) but a real thing, a cause or group of causes of the disease. As we now know, an explanation was found that included, among other causative factors, a group of retroviruses that cause AIDS. Subsequently, and only subsequently to this discovery, were the investigators in a position to answer why-questions, what-questions, or how-questions, and gradually to fill in the causal story so that groups with different interests—homosexuals, intravenous drug users, public-health officials, biomedical researchers, and so on—could have described to them the parts of the explanation in which they were most interested. Most notably, an explanation could be given even though it was incomplete. It was never claimed that there were no factors involved other than the retroviruses, factors that increased or decreased the risk for an individual, only that part of the internal causal mechanism leading to the illness in each case had been found, and a mechanism of transmission found that was causing the cluster of cases.

Any adequate philosophical theory of scientific explanation should be able to provide an acceptable account of such a case as this. Yet existing theories are all defective in one or more ways. For some, the causal theory that lies behind their presentation of causal explanations proves inadequate when there are multiple probabilistic factors at work. Others are so idealized that claims to have an explanation when we know some, but not all, of the causes influencing the phenomenon violate their criteria of adequacy for explanations. As we shall see, once we move beyond simple, idealized examples, the features of multiplicity, insufficiency, and incompleteness of causes is normal, rather than unusual.

[2] See Gottlieb et al. (1981), Masur et al., (1981), and for an early survey, Gottlieb et al. (1983).

[3] Here and occasionally elsewhere I use the definite article for convenience. As we shall see below, the indefinite article is greatly to be preferred in order that we escape the prejudice that there is a unique explanation for any given phenomenon.

§4. The Multiplicity of Causes

The world is a complex and messy place. If it were not, if it consisted solely of medium-sized atoms that were causally independent of one another, say, we should not need science to discover its structure.[4] But the world is not self-presenting in that way. As the early natural philosophers slowly solved the problem of the difference between appearance and reality, they realized that theories about the immediately accessible parts of our world were generally either banal or false. At least as early as Galileo, scientific investigation was found to proceed most efficiently when investigating artificial phenomena produced in the clean and austere conditions of the laboratory, when only a single causal influence was at work. But science is also frequently called upon to investigate naturally occurring phenomena such as epidemics, tree diseases, rainfall distributions, migratory patterns, rainbows, the nonexistence of higher forms of life on Mars, and planetary movements.[5] It is nowadays also often required to explain the results of applied science, such as rocket explosions, holes in the ozone layer, the properties of artificial elements, the effects of plastics on the environment, and presidential campaigns.[6]

A characteristic feature of these natural and unnatural phenomena is that they are usually the result of multiple causal influences. For example, the rate of enzyme-catalyzed reactions is affected by the enzyme concentration, the substrate concentration, the temperature, the pH of the substrate, oxidation of the sulfhydryl groups of an enzyme, and high-energy radiation; the first two increasing the rate of reaction, the last two decreasing it, while the actions of the third and fourth have maximal points of inflection at optimal temperature and pH, respectively.[7] The occurrence of familiar, everyday phenomena is also characterized by this multiplicity. Successively adding (1) a smoking level of twenty cigarettes a day, (2) medium-high blood pressure (140/88), and (3) medium-high serum cholesterol levels (250 mg/dl) increases the probability of having a heart attack within the next twelve years for a forty-six-

---

[4] In such a world it is highly improbable that humans would exist to invent their kind of science, as various anthropic principles have noted (e.g., Barrow and Tipler [1986]). But some other kind of intelligent entity might exist in a slightly more complex world; perhaps a huge abacus.

[5] By 'natural' here I mean the world as it would be without scientific intervention, and this may be interpreted so as to include much of social and behavioral activity as well as the traditional realm of the 'natural sciences'.

[6] 'Applied science' covers the engineered world, which is either artifactual or manipulated to artificial ends. *Results* of applied science may, of course, be unintended and not themselves part of applied science. Furthermore, application of science to the world is not coextensive with applied science, for that application may be purely predictive in form.

[7] See Harper (1975), pp. 139–42. I am, of course, supposing for the purposes of illustration that these factors are genuine causes.

year-old man from .03 to (1) .05, (2) .075, and (3) .15.[8] The flight of any commercial airliner is the result of many causal factors: the thrust from the jets, uplift from the airflow over the wings, tail and head winds, downdrafts, thermals, and so on. Some of these are more important than others, and some aid the flight whereas others hinder it, but for a full understanding of the flight as it actually occurs, they must be identified and listed. Such multiplicity of causes is commonplace in the social sciences, where for practical, ethical, or theoretical reasons, many phenomena occur in nonexperimental contexts, and the frequent use in those areas of multifactorial models is a direct consequence of the need to represent the numerous and distinct causal influences affecting such phenomena.

A number of different things may be meant by 'multiple causation', among which are:[9]

1. That specific effect E was produced by specific causes A and B, both of which were present, and each of which separately contributed to E.
2. That specific effect E was produced by the interaction of specific factors A and B, both of which were present.
3. That effects of kind E can be produced, as a kind, by either kind-A or by kind-B causes.
4. That a specific event E was overdetermined by specific factors A and B, both of which were present.

Case 1 is the one that our theory covers, and it will apply to probabilistic as well as to deterministic cases, to quantitative as well as to qualitative factors. Cases 2 and 3 concern, respectively, causal invariance and causal generalizations, which are both discussed in §25. Case 4 precludes us from calling either factor a cause, and will be discussed in §7.

§5. The Incompleteness of Causal Knowledge

A common epistemic consequence of the multiplicity of causes is the incompleteness of our knowledge about them. Rarely are we in a position to provide a complete list of all the influences that affected a given outcome. Hence if those causal influences constitute the explanation of that outcome or are an integral part of its explanation, we have two options open to us. We can either allow that an incomplete specification of explanatory causes does provide explanatory information and that cumulative additions to our knowledge of the causes is a common feature of scientific explanatory procedures, or we

---

[8] Figures are from Truett et al. (1967), p. 511.

[9] I have given the definitions for the case of two causes only. The generalization to N causes is obvious.

can require that a complete specification of the causes is necessary for an adequate explanation. The second of these options is, I think, to be avoided if at all possible. In both the AIDS example and the enzyme-catalyst reaction example, there is no pretense that a complete explanation of the respective phenomena has been discovered. Yet we have good reason to suppose that what has been offered as an explanation is true and explanatorily informative. Successive supplementation of such partial explanations does not undermine the accuracy of the previous explanations. Yet, as we shall see (§38), many contemporary models of explanation have the consequence that they cannot separate true from complete explanations, and I take this to be a serious defect in those accounts.

We begin, then, with the fundamental notion that many scientific explanations consist in a specification of the causes of the phenomenon to be explained, that those causes will be numerous, and that our knowledge of them will ordinarily be incomplete. We now need to examine various types of causes in order to assess their suitability for inclusion in causal explanations of this kind.

§6. The Principle of Causal Contribution

Underlying various accounts of causation in terms of sufficiency, of necessity in the circumstances, of INUS conditions, of probabilistic relevance, and so on seems to be this general principle:

> PRINCIPLE OF CAUSAL CONTRIBUTION. A factor X is a cause of another factor Y if and only if X's existence contributes to Y's existence.

As a schema, rather than a fully interpreted generalization, this principle is, obviously, too broad. For, casually construed, it would allow the middle third of a tub of lard (X) to be a cause of the whole barrel (Y). By variously, but specifically, interpreting 'factor' and 'contributes to', however, one can see identifiable accounts of causation emerging from this very general principle.

§7. Sufficiency Theories of Causation

It was once common to hold that a cause is a factor which is sufficient for its effect. Thus, according to a naive application of our principle, if X is sufficient for Y, X contributes to Y's occurrence in the strongest possible way, for it makes the occurrence of Y inevitable, inescapable. So, it is said, a force of twelve tons causes an extension of 0.03 inches from the unstretched position in an aluminum bar with a cross section of one square inch, since, by Hooke's law, the force is sufficient to produce, and hence contributes, exactly that extension. The attraction of the sufficiency approach runs deep, often because underlying it is a strong psychological attachment to determinism, and with it a marked reluctance to accept that anything less, especially chance, constitutes a strong enough contribution for genuine causation.[10]

Despite its appeal, however, it is now generally accepted that sufficiency by itself cannot serve as an acceptable basis for causation, and one can see this in terms of a correct application of our principle. The most common reason for rejecting mere sufficiency is its inability to deal with overdetermining causes. Such cases involve two factors X_1, X_2, both of which are present, and each of which is, individually, sufficient for Y. Example: Two thumbs simultaneously press a button detonating a charge. Which thumb pressing caused the subsequent explosion, given that the pressure from each alone would have been enough to set it off? It seems wrong to call either event of thumb pressing a cause of the explosion, since each such event violates our principle. Given the existence of the first thumb's pressure, the second thumb's pressure contributes nothing to the effect's coming into existence, and similarly, mutatis mutandis, for the second thumb's pressure.[11]

Adherence to the principle also explains how other supposed examples of overdetermination work. Consider the classic case of two bullets that simultaneously strike a man in the heart. It would seem, prima facie, that neither is, individually, a cause of the man's death, even though each was sufficient for it. However, one tends to feel about this example and many others like it that if the effect was described in more detail, described as it actually occurred, in full and pathological detail, then each bullet would be seen to contribute something to the effect, for the manner in which a death occurs by virtue of two bullets is different in detail than one produced by a single bullet, in which case each bullet is a contributory cause of the death as it actually was. (A small-caliber bullet, however, could pass cleanly through a death wound produced by a larger-calibre bullet, leaving no trace, but then the small-caliber bullet would not be a cause of the death.) There is thus reason to believe that genuine overdetermination cases are rare and that many such examples gain their plausibility by underdescription of the events in-

---

[10] For reasons why this commitment to determinism is misguided, see §10.

[11] Devices such as this have sometimes been used in executions to obscure the attribution of causes and hence of blame. It is worth noting that resolution of overdetermination cases such as this one is not a matter of merely philosophical interest, for important issues can sometimes rest upon a correct resolution. In a famous murder trial of the 1970s involving Charles Manson, one of the defendants, Leslie van Houten, claimed that she was guilty of stabbing one of the victims, Rosemary LaBianca—but only after LaBianca was already dead. Quite clearly, if this had been true, then van Houten could not have been said to have caused LaBianca's death because, deplorable as the action was, it contributed nothing to the death. This was not a case of simultaneous actual overdetermination but one of potential overdetermination, where the principle to be applied is that nothing can contribute to something that has already occurred.

volved or, less contentiously, because we group a diversity of events under the same event type. Strychnine and cyanide administered simultaneously to an individual by different malefactors can produce only one death, but it is relatively easy to distinguish such a death from one due to either poison administered in isolation.

In contrast, situations involving probabilistic causation are often free from this characteristic feature of distinguishing marks. According to current theory, there is no difference between the radiation produced by spontaneous and by induced emission. Nor, as far as I am aware, is there a difference betwen the radiation produced by thermionic emission and photoelectric emission. This, again, is a reason to prefer real examples of causation to hypothetical cases. With real examples, all the detail is there and can, at least in principle, be known. With hypothetical examples, all one has is the usually sketchy description provided by the inventor. This would be acceptable if one were able to restrict oneself to that minimal information, but many causal theories require other information, such as which laws of nature apply or what would have happened in a counterfactual case, and then underdescription becomes a serious problem.[12]

In contrast to simultaneous overdetermination cases, when one overdetermining cause occurs earlier than the other, the inclination is to identify the earlier event as the cause and to reject the later. Why? Because as soon as the earlier has happened, the effect is guaranteed to occur, and from that time on, no other event can contribute anything to the effect. This inclination needs, I think, the caveat that if a process leads from the earlier event to the effect, it must arrive at the effect earlier than any process leading from the later event. If I first light a long fuse leading to a bomb and you shortly thereafter light a much shorter fuse that burns to completion first, it was you and your fuse that caused the explosion, not me and mine. Here, presumably, an application of the earlier argument to the last part of the processes, together with an appeal to the transitivity of causation, will give us the right result. That is, one must work backward in the completed process that leads from cause to effect in order to arrive at the correct attribution, rather than forward.

We may allow, however, that, rare as they may be, overdetermination cases do illustrate that mere sufficiency cannot serve as a foundation for a causal account. These arguments do not establish, of course, that there are no sufficient causes, nor do they deny that when they *are* causes, it is their sufficiency that qualifies them as such (although as we shall see, there are good reasons to believe that there are also insufficient causes). They indicate, however, that what makes a factor a cause is something logically separable from its sufficiency; it is the contribution that the factor makes to the effect's coming

---

[12] James Cargile has convinced me over the years of the dangers of underdescribed philosophical problems, especially with respect to certain 'paradoxes'. See his account of the original Newcomb problem (Cargile [1975]) and of the Surprise Test Paradox (Cargile [1967]).

about, and it cannot make that contribution in the presence of other sufficient conditions.

§8. Sine Qua Non Analyses of Causation

Overdetermination cases such as those described in the previous section (and other reasons) led philosophers to move to the requirement that a cause must be necessary for its effect, either in the circumstances or generally. This seems plausible because, for example, in order for my car to start, each of the following three factors at least must be present: there must be an inflammable gas in the cylinders, there must be a source of ignition at the cylinder heads, and the pistons must be free to move in the cylinders. Employing our principle of causal contribution in these cases of necessary conditions, the contribution that each necessary causal factor makes is that it renders an effect possible. Without each of the causes, the effect is impossible: each factor's existence contributes to the effect's occurring by removing a source of (physical) impossibility. Often, in order to retain the commitment to sufficiency, such analyses are embedded within a framework that takes the joint occurrence of the factors as sufficient for the effect, and hence their joint contribution is also present in addition to their separate individual contributions, but the essential contribution of necessary conditions as causal factors is as I have stated, since none of them is, by itself, sufficient for the effect.

Because it is rare that a factor will be necessary under all circumstances for an effect, contemporary theories emphasize the necessity of causal factors in the particular circumstances, and these theories are of particular interest because of their potential to be employed in indeterministic contexts.[13] These contemporary causal theories are generically known as the *sine qua non approach*.[14] Although there are many variants of this approach,[15] they have the

---

[13] Lewis (1973) explicitly restricts himself to deterministic situations, whereas Mackie (1974) does not. Mackie's account of the directionality of causation in terms of fixity in fact requires a degree of indeterminism. Although he subsequently conceded that his fixity account was defective, arguments such as those in Beauchamp and Rosenberg (1977) can be modified to show that his theory is still committed to indeterminism. Bunzl (1979) has argued that Lewis's denial of certain counterfactuals to avoid preemption problems violates the determinism in terms of which his original published theory was formulated. However, in section B of "Postscripts to 'Causation' " (Lewis [1986b], but stated in n. 3 therein to be based on a treatment arrived at in 1973), Lewis extends his account to indeterministic contexts. Most other advocates of sine qua non accounts (e.g., Loeb [1974], Swain [1978], Goosens [1979]) have, implicitly or otherwise, stayed with deterministic worlds.

[14] Sine qua non accounts should not be identified with counterfactual accounts, although they often are. Counterfactual analyses make essential reference to nonactual states of affairs, usually as contrast cases, and they need not require that something would have been the case if the cause had not occurred. Appeals to counterfactual states can and should allow terms such as 'might have been' and 'probably'.

[15] See principally Mackie (1974) and Lewis (1973, 1986b).

following features in common: (1) Causation holds between specific events in particular circumstances, in the sense that it is singular causal claims which are primary, rather than causal regularities;[16] (2) an event A is a direct cause of an event B if and only if both A and B occurred and the counterfactual conditional 'if A had not occurred, then B would not have occurred' is true; and (3) an event A is an indirect cause of B if and only if there is a chain of events connecting A and B, each event in which is a direct cause of its successor.

There is no doubt that sine qua non theories capture a great number of cases where causal attributions are possible, and they are impressively well supplied with detail. Of course, there are profound issues involved in the enterprise of providing a set of truth conditions for the counterfactuals (indeed in the question of whether such truth values even exist) and with the question of whether the theories are too broad.[17] My concerns are of a rather different kind, for they focus on the question of whether the sine qua non theories are too narrow. We must ask whether there are interpretations of our principle that are wider than those which insist that contributions must make an effect possible. It is inherent in any sine qua non account that it cannot provide a treatment of multiple causal factors whose presence contributes to an outcome already made possible by other factors. Because of the prevalence of such multiple factors in many contexts, we must look closely at this issue.

§9. Why Sine Qua Non Analyses Are Inadequate

What caused you to fall in love with your spouse? One would have to be a peculiar perfectionist to assert that eye color was a necessary condition without which, in the circumstances, marriage would not have taken place, yet such a factor is often a contributing cause, sometimes even a significant one. Would you have married her had she not liked Beethoven? Or never been attracted had he not shared your views on labor unions? Some factors may be necessary, such as being of the right gender, but many can contribute without being indispensable.[18] Informal examples can, as we said, be misleading, but scientific examples are not lacking.

---

[16] See, e.g., Mackie (1974), p. 80; Lewis (1973), §2.

[17] See Kim (1973b) for criticisms of this kind. Lewis's theory is also open, in my view, to the serious problem that he has to deny the truth of certain counterfactuals in order to solve the asymmetry and 'epiphenomena' (joint effects of a common cause) problems. That denial appears to many to be not only ad hoc but wrong.

[18] I take it here that such factors are not (noncausal) reasons. Those readers who believe that ratiocination about such matters is de rigueur should keep in mind Kant's fate: as a result of his

EXAMPLE 1. Under the classical theory of statistical mechanics, a beaker of water has an exceedingly small but nonzero chance of freezing spontaneously. (This probability is so small that such an event is unlikely to happen in the lifetime of the universe, although given the relevant laws, it is nomologically possible.) I put this beaker in a flash-freeze unit and observe shortly after that the water is frozen. Suppose that the placement in the flash-freeze unit is (practically) sufficient to freeze the water. Was it necessary in the circumstances to place the water in the freezer in order for the water to freeze?

Clearly not, given the laws of statistical mechanics, and hence the counter-factual "If that beaker had not been placed in the freezer, the water would not have frozen" is not true.[19] Thus, according to sine qua non theories, the placing of the water in the freezer is not a direct cause of its freezing. Nor can we fill in a sequence of intermediate states of the gas to construct a causal chain in order to make the placement in the flash-freeze unit an indirect cause. For if it were said that by following the evolution of the gas at the molecular level, a fine-grained analysis of the internal energy states would allow a sequence of counterfactuals of the form 'If the gas had not been in state S_i, it would not have been in state S_j', where the sequence of states $[S_i]$ forms a connecting process from the initial to the final states of the gas, then one should properly respond that the correct fine-grained analysis should employ the states described by quantum thermodynamics, whose energy exchanges would not always satisfy the counterfactuals.[20]

Yet it seems correct, prima facie, to attribute the freezing to the placement in the freezer unit. Why? Because the placing of the water in the freezer contributes a (here substantial) increase in probability to the effect's occur-rence. This appeal to an increase in the probability of the effect is the starting point of all theories of probabilistic causality. Noting that what is produced is not directly the effect, or changes in it, but a change in its probability, I propose that we take this idea seriously—in fact, literally—and see what ensues. That is, let us allow provisionally that the chance of a phenomenon is measurable, and moreover something which can be increased or diminished

---

deliberating at great length about whether to marry, two potential brides grew weary and left, never to return.

[19] This claim requires that scientific laws are inviolable. Lewis's assertability conditions for counterfactuals lift this restriction occasionally (see Lewis [1979]). Despite my profound ad-miration for Lewis's work, his view that the age of miracles is still with us is not one I share.

[20] This example is, if the action of the freezer is a sufficient condition for the water's freezing, structurally identical to Mackie's chocolate machine M ([1974], pp. 41–42), of which he asserts that it is in principle undecidable whether the nonspontaneous factor was a cause. For a detailed discussion of Mackie's claim, see §32.

in value by changes in certain properties. Then using our basic principle, we have as a preliminary working hypothesis that a factor X is a (probabilistic) contributing cause of a factor Y if and only if X's existence contributes to the chance of Y's existence.[21] Here 'contributes to' means that the chance of Y is deterministically increased by the presence of or occurrence of X, and 'factor', in its most general sense, is taken to be the value of a quantitative property. What happens after that chance has been increased is acausal—after the causal factor has increased the chance of the outcome, that outcome either just happens or it just does not happen. In this modified sense, the traditional reluctance to attribute causal efficacy to chance itself is correct; the causing is not in the chance itself but in the relation between the cause and the chance.

This characteristic of a probabilistic cause is as yet devoid of details and needs fleshing out, but we can see how it applies to another case.

> EXAMPLE 2. A laboratory mouse is given a diet containing both gyromitrin and diazonium metabolite and contracts a stomach tumor. Neither substance is sufficient to produce tumors at low dosages, but each individually has been shown to increase the incidence of tumors in laboratory mice.[22] Neither substance was necessary in the circumstances to produce the tumor and thus is not a cause under sine qua non accounts. Should we call such carcinogenic factors contributing causes in the production of tumors?

Presupposing that the statistical associations involved here are representative of the true chances (an issue that we shall have to examine later), I think that we should judge such factors as causal and for the same reason that we cited in Example 1, which is that each factor contributes an increase in probability to the outcome, even though neither factor is sufficient for the effect. In doing so, we follow a widespread epidemiological and biological practice.

> EXAMPLE 3. An azo–dye is fed to a laboratory rat, and selenium is introduced into the diet. The latter substance reduces the probability for cancer from .90 to .14.[23] Is its administration a counteracting cause of cancer?

According to the sine qua non account, it is not a cause of any kind, because even without the selenium, there is a nonzero chance (of .10) that the rat will not have cancer if the selenium is withheld.

However, according to our principle, the ingestion of selenium contributes to the chance of nonoccurrence of cancer, or, equivalently, diminishes the

---

[21] A forewarning—chance here is not to be construed as a relative frequency, a fact that is essential for the use of the biconditional here.

[22] Sources for this claim are *J. Agri. Food Chem.* 31 (1983):1117; *Carcinogens and Mutagens in the Environment,* edited by H. F. Stich (Boca Raton, Fla.: CRC Press, 1984), pp. 99–108.

[23] See *Cancer Letters* 9 (1980): 299.

chance of cancer's occurrence. This last example brings out the need for a distinction between two different kinds of cause. Let us, generalizing our principle, preliminarily characterize a factor X as a *contributing cause* of Y if and only if the occurrence of X results in an increased chance of Y; and characterize a factor Z as a *counteracting cause* of Y if and only if the occurrence of Z results in a decreased chance of Y. This distinction is one that cannot be captured by sine qua non accounts. To see why, note first that a contributing and a counteracting cause, either of which is sufficient to, respectively, produce or prevent the effect, cannot be present together, because nothing can counteract what is inevitable, nor can anything contribute to what has been rendered impossible.[24] Thus the simultaneous presence of a contributing and counteracting cause must allow that the effect is neither guaranteed nor precluded.[25] But then we cannot truly assert, in cases such as the above, that if the counteracting cause had not occurred (in the circumstances, which include the insufficient contributing cause), the effect would not have failed to occur, because of the insufficiency of the contributing cause.

Although, as mentioned above, many sine qua non analyses have restricted themselves to deterministic contexts, the arguments just given show that they cannot be extended directly into the realm of indeterministic phenomena. This is, prima facie, a serious difficulty, because by insisting that what is important about causation is the necessity, rather than the sufficiency, of causal factors, it appears that sine qua non accounts should be ideally placed to provide a theory that encompasses both indeterministic as well as deterministic causation, if the former is in fact a genuine possibility. Our next task, then, is to see why indeterministic causation should be seriously considered.

§10. Indeterminism

One frequently finds, although perhaps with diminishing frequency, that the very idea of indeterminism arouses resistance. Although the general theory of causality and explanation expounded here does not presuppose indeterminism, the probabilistic form of it does. It would be unfortunate if a psychological prejudice in favor of determinism prevented an objective evaluation

---

[24] I note here a minor caveat that will recur throughout the book. Under measure-theoretic and relative-frequency interpretations of probability, a probability of 1 does not guarantee that the effect will occur and is thus slightly weaker than a sufficient condition. Analogously, a probability of 0 does not ensure that the effect will not occur and is thus slightly weaker than the absence of a necessary condition. Where I intend sufficiency (or necessity) I shall say so, and similarly for probability 1 or 0. The difference is sometimes important, and it is good to be clear on this.

[25] 'Counteracting' and 'contributing' are interpreted here in an actualist sense—a contributing cause, for example, must actually, rather than potentially, contribute to its effects.

of the present theory, and so a few words to lessen the pull of that attitude are required here. I must emphasize that this is not an argument but a polemic designed to undermine deterministic prejudices.

As a psychological habit acquired from everyday experience, a belief in universal determinism is peculiar in the extreme, because events in the ordinary world are neither sufficiently predictable nor sufficiently under our control that an inference of inviolable regular succession would be warranted from our experiences. Consider a man who, on a whim, takes an afternoon's motorcycle ride. Descending a hill, a fly strikes him in the eye, causing him to lose control. He skids on a patch of loose gravel, is thrown from the machine, and is killed. This sad event, according to the universal determinist, was millions of years beforehand destined to occur at the exact time and place that it did. Billions of generations of flies and aeons of air currents have inexorably led to this precise fly's being there and then. The invention of motorcycles and gravel-covered tarmacadam, the rider's decision to go out for a spin, his failure to wear goggles, and the accumulation of stones in that exact spot—all these inescapably were to come to pass. This claim, when considered in an open-minded way, is incredible. Whatever the fact of the matter about universal determinism, it is not a thesis that carries with it a high initial plausibility. Nor is this implausibility confined to single events. The economy of any large industrial nation or primitive agricultural society bears not even the slightest resemblance to a deterministic system. Its course cannot be predicted with anything like certainty, it cannot be controlled with anything like certainty, and in the case of industrial societies, even the task of listing the factors which influence it cannot be carried out with anything like certainty.

So where does this common belief in favor of universal determinism come from, if not from everyday experience? I take it that it is no longer convincing to claim that the thesis of determinism is an a priori truth. Yet an appeal to fundamental science for support of the thesis is also no longer possible. There is now good empirical evidence to suggest that not only might the thesis of universal determinism not be necessarily true, but that in certain special but well-defined microsystems, the weight of evidence is in favor of indeterminism.[26] Furthermore, it has only been proved that classical mechanical systems (which were always cited as paradigms of determinism) are deterministic in certain extremely simple cases.[27] Hence, at the very least, the reader should

[26] For a detailed analysis of Bell's inequality and experimental tests of it, see Redhead (1987), chap. 4.

[27] See Montague (1962). Traditionally, the case has been based upon a belief that classical mechanics was a deterministic theory, together with a reductionist view that any theory could in principle be reduced to classical mechanics or cast in a form which was structurally similar. There is no reason to believe that either of these claims is true. Earman (1987) contains a survey of technical results relating to these areas.

be open to the possibility that indeterministic sequences of events occur. In fact, the claim of universal causal determinism is so strong, claiming that for all types of systems, over all histories of those systems, not a single event was lacking a sufficient causal antecedent, that the burden of proof must be on those who claim that it holds.[28] Indeed, it should be mentioned that the simple dichotomy of systems into deterministic and indeterministic is far too crude for our purposes. It is the intermediate cases between determinism and pure indeterminism (where nothing influences the chance of the outcome) that need to be examined—i.e., the realm of probabilistic causality.

§11. Chance and Cause

Any theory that allows causes which are not sufficient for their effects must reconcile causation with chance. To many, any such attempt to do so is doomed to failure because the essence of something's happening by chance is that "it just happens."[29] This informal way of putting it has the advantage of conveying what lay behind the long-standing reluctance to allowing that chancy phenomena could be caused or that they could be explained. Nothing causes them, people would say; they just happen, inexplicably, for no reason, and so they have no cause and, a fortiori, no causal explanation. On this view, sequences of chance occurrences are quintessential examples of what Hume had argued for in the deterministic case: the events in the sequence are truly 'distinct existences', and there is no real connection between them—they simply succeed one another.

[28] Those who think that indeterministic contexts are far removed from everyday life and do not influence it to any great degree should have been acquainted with my paternal grandfather. In the early days of Britain's national lottery using Premium Bonds, winning numbers were selected by a random-number generator named ERNIE (Electronic Random Number Indicator Equipment) that was based on a physically indeterministic process. Not a wealthy man, he won a considerable sum of money as a result of this device, thus significantly altering his later life for the better. Much earlier, during World War I, a sniper's bullet missed his head by a couple of inches when he foolishly lit a cigarette in the trenches at night. Were his survival and the writing of this book determined? At the very least I should need to see a convincing deterministic theory of the sniper's muscle tremors. My father, an intermediate link in my own casual chain, was himself involved in such a fortuitous event. Trapped in France after the fall of Dunkirk, his unit was split into two by its commanding officer. On the toss of a coin his half was sent to the port of Saint-Malo; the other half went to the port of Saint-Nazaire. My father's half was evacuated safely; the second half perished in a sea of burning oil when the *Lancastria* was hit by a bomb. I leave a deterministic reconstruction of this sequence of events to any as yet unconvinced readers.

[29] "If constant conjunction be imply'd in what we call occasion, 'tis a real cause. If not, 'tis no relation at all, and cannot give rise to any argument or reasoning, . . . 'tis impossible to admit of any medium betwixt chance and an absolute necessity" (Hume [(1739–40) 1888], p. 171).

Given this attitude, it is not surprising that most early attempts at combining cause and chance either concluded that it was hopeless or tried to employ purely statistical techniques to ground probabilistic causal relations. It is also significant that the first cases of irreducibly probabilistic phenomena examined late in the nineteenth and early in the twentieth century were usually described as 'spontaneous'. To the pioneer workers in the area, the most interesting aspect of radioactive decay was the inability to alter the decay rate by means of any existing physical or chemical means, and they concluded that the half-life, or equivalently the probability of decay per unit time, was an intrinsic, fixed property of the atoms, immune from change by any known causal process, and hence analogous to fundamental physical constants (although varying between elements). In this way it was similar to the classical view of gravitational attraction, which is unaffected by any external changes that leave the masses and geometrical relationships unchanged. Temperature, pressure, magnetic fields, and so on all leave the attraction the same. Thus, at best, all that could be done with indeterministic phenomena was to give the probability distribution that covered the phenomenon and to use this to derive the probabilities that attach to specific events. This approach, where the laws governing the phenomena are probability distributions and no causal intent is conveyed by the law, clearly underlies many early and contemporary approaches to probabilistic explanation. Indeed, as we shall see in chapter 4, these approaches, within which to explain an indeterministic phenomenon is to attribute to it the correct probability value, still have a pervasive influence on accounts of statistical explanations.

We have seen, however, in §9 that it is possible to say more about the relation between cause and chance than simply that the phenomena in question have certain specified probabilities, in that what is crucial is a change in the probability, rather than its mere value. To see why the value itself cannot be a measure of the degree of causal influence, consider the following cases.

It will be generally conceded that the event of one's having a cup of tea at noon today (event B) makes no difference to the event of a uranium atom in Nevada decaying before noon today (event A). That is, the degree of causal influence of B upon A is 0. Furthermore, the chance for that atom to decay before noon today is unaffected by whether or not it is conditioned upon B, so that $P(A/B) = P(A/-B) = P(A)$. This last chance is the physical probability for spontaneous decay, which is nonzero. Hence neither the conditional physical probability $P(A/B)$ nor the absolute probability $P(A)$ can measure the degree of causal influence of B upon A. Consider also the situation with counteracting causes. Giving a man an antivenin serum after a rattlesnake bite reduces the chance of his dying from the value that it would have without administering the serum, i.e., $P(D/S) < P(D/-S)$, and allowing that the antivenin causally affects that chance, the serum is a negative, or counteracting, cause of his dying. Hence $P(D/S)$, which of course is positive, cannot possibly be an adequate representation of the degree of negative influence which S has on D.

One final point needs to be made in this context. There may be a lingering suspicion in the reader's mind that although changes in the value of the chance are important, the value itself must have something to do with producing the effect, because the higher the chance, the more likely it is that the effect will come about. For example, in the case of the radioactive decay mentioned above, one might say that, after all, if the atom did decay, the chance for spontaneous decay was present, and this fact cannot be ignored in describing the causal situation. But this kind of argument conceals a potentially serious confusion. The temptation to attribute causal properties to the chance alone must be resisted because it amounts to hypostasizing chance and elevating it to the status of a universal causal power. One of the pitfalls of engaging in an abstract philosophical analysis of chance and causation and of trying to ascertain which features are common to all causal relations is that there is a natural tendency to slip into a mode of description which makes it appear that there is a universal type of chance entering into any probabilistic causal situation.

This point is elementary, and I do not believe that anyone overtly makes this mistake, but there does appear to be a tendency to view propensities in just that way, in part because the propensity value is automatically a by-product of a complete specification of the causal influences on an effect. Chance by itself has no causal properties or powers, just because there is no such thing as a universal property of chance in the world, any more than there is a universal deterministic tendency in the world. There are particular kinds of physically grounded probabilities, just as there are particular kinds of forces, but in the absence of a successful unifying program, there is no reason to suppose that there is a universal theory of propensities or causes. That sort of modern Platonism must be resisted. Once we have specified the structural basis of the particular propensity and cited all the concrete factors which affect the conditional propensity value, there is nothing else. That is all there is to indeterminism. In a sense clearly analogous to what Hume had in mind for the deterministic case, and even more clearly, after all has been said, things just happen. Of course, all that can be said is often a great deal, even in the spontaneous case. By specifying the structural features of uranium, we can explain why it can decay and why, for example, a lead atom cannot. Reference to these structural features is, after all, exactly what 'spontaneous' means. This does not mean that everything has a cause, even a probabilistic cause, and hence we are not committed to a principle of universal causation, even in a weakened sense. But these considerations do seriously weaken the idea that the propensity value has any causal force. Thus if asked whether probabilistic causality is primarily probabilistic (in that the causal relations can be analyzed in terms of probabilities) or is primarily causal (in that the probabilities are grounded on causal relations), I should say that neither is correct. Specific causes operate on the structural bases of physical chances, but the chances are themselves acausal.

The considerations raised in the last three sections provide some motivation for expanding the scope of our basic principle to cover contributions to the chance of an effect or to the chance of its absence. Rather than developing a theory ab initio, however, we shall show that existing theories of probabilistic event causation follow naturally from a small set of basic assumptions that concern causal relations between quantitative variables. This will not only provide a natural link between philosophical theories of probabilistic causality (which have almost all been qualitative in character) and quantitative theories of causal modelling that have been developed in the social sciences, but it will allow us later to demonstrate the advantages for causation and explanation of taking a quantitative approach. Our method of procedure will be first to develop the theory rather abstractly and then to examine various components with an eye to their philosophical justification and consequences.

CHAPTER TWO

Probabilistic Causation

§12. Ontology

The following entities are proposed as the basic objects of study:

1. A system S.
2. Properties of, and relating to, S.
   A. A set of state properties for S, characterizing the state that the system is in either before, during, or after a trial.
   B. A set of properties not possessed by S.
      i. Properties (changes in) which can causally influence either the state of S or properties of kind ii below.[1]
      ii. Properties which are effects of (changes in) the state of S or of properties of kind i above.[2]
3. A trial T, performed on S.

The system S could be an atomistic individual with no internal structure, a complex object with structural relations between its parts, a closed system upon which no external influences operate, or an open system which is not shielded from outside causal influences. The characteristic which makes it a system is that it persists through changes which are classified as causal according to our criteria given later in the book. Well-known cases of such systems and their properties are atoms and their structural relations, chemical compounds, genetic structures, stellar structures, family relationships, status structures in small groups, economic organizations such as commodity markets, and so on. I want to emphasize that these are real structures, and although abstract characterizations of them by means of various forms of mathematical and conceptual models are a useful way of representing substructures of actual systems, the causal and explanatory claims concern the influences on the

---

[1] These are standardly but variously called 'causal variables', 'independent variables', or 'exogenous variables' in the causal modeling literature.

[2] These are, again, standardly but variously called 'effect variables', 'dependent variables', or 'endogenous variables'.

structures themselves and are not solely about the models.[3] The relationship between the model and the real structure is captured in the usual way, by an isomorphism between the model and some substructure of the real system.

The difference between properties that characterize the system and those that are included under (2A) is that the former properties are essential to the system's existence and hence are such that the system would no longer be the same system were any of these properties to change, whereas properties in (2A) can change in value or be present or absent without the system itself thereby losing its identity. Examples of the former are (*a*) possession of a Y chromosome in male humans,[4] (*b*) the existence of a market operating independently of the state in a free-world economy, (*c*) having exactly one proton and one electron in its atomic structure in a hydrogen atom. Examples of (2A) are (*a'*) possession of secondary sexual characteristics, (*b'*) having a GNP of N units of currency, (*c'*) being bound in a water molecule.

Although there are deep issues about the nature of natural kinds that underlie such a division, from our present perspective it is irrelevant how the distinction between essential properties of a system and nonessential properties of a system is made. Our causal apparatus applies whether one believes that essential properties are theory relative, with the proviso that the theory be true, or intrinsic to the systems themselves.

Not all properties involved in a causal relation are properties of the system S. An increase in the frequency of incident radiation can cause an increase in the number of electrons emitted from a metal, but the change in frequency is not a property of the metal itself; it is a change in an external factor. The reason for requiring a distinction between the two kinds of property is that, because sequences of direct causal relations can occur in causal chains to create indirect causes, unless we allow this separation between external properties and state properties, the limits of what counts as a system property would increase without bound. States of S can act as causes or effects, as when an increase in the internal temperature of a metal causes an increase in the number of electrons emitted by thermionic emission. They may also play a passive role, as when a system acts as a catalyst. Because of this potential causal role by some systems' states, we shall make no distinction in notation between the three kinds of properties noted under (2). Properties may be qualitative or quantitative, but we shall consider the former a special case of the latter.

Finally, it will often be the case that replicas of S exist, so that an ensemble

---

[3] As, for example, seems to be common in the social science literature. See, for example, Simon (1953), p. 51; Blalock (1962), p. 183.

[4] Where sex here is chromosomal sex, rather than gonadal or phenotypic sex. If one wishes to unify these, then a more detailed structural analysis, involving segments of the Y chromosome to account for such variants as 46,XX (gonadal) males, would be required.

of trials on S-type systems can be made or so that repeated measurements on S itself can be made over a period of time (although we want also to be able to make causal claims about unique system states). These replicas need not be perfect replicas, however, merely similar in the properties that are under investigation. Hence we have (3), a trial T, which may be an experiment, an observation, or a sampling.

Our conception of the relation between causal variables and structural chances can be represented schematically as:

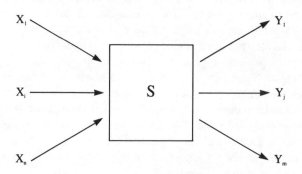

S is the system containing the structural basis upon which the chance is based. The connections between X_i and S, and S and Y_j, may be either deterministic or indeterministic. Associated with S is a probability distribution for the endogenous variables Y_j, which depends upon $\{X_i\}$.

The basic notation for events is then $\langle S, Z, T \rangle$, which represents the presence of, or change in, property Z with respect to the system S on trial T. It is not required that S itself possesses Z, however. For example, an external humidity level of 98 percent can, coupled with a temperature of 111°F, contribute to violent behavior in an individual, even though that individual never possesses either of those values of the properties. It should be noted that changes in properties, which are usually represented by $Z_i(t') - Z_i(t)$, where t', t are times, can equally well be represented by a single property $Z_i(T)$, where T is a trial. We now define:

> An *event* is a change in, or possession of, a property in a system on a trial.[5] *Event types* are events considered without regard to the trial—$\langle S, Z \rangle$.

[5] In connecting these primitives with probabilistic apparatus, we depart from the standard framework for probabilities, which is based on the apparatus set out by A. N. Kolmogorov in the 1930s. Although Kolmogorov himself placed some emphasis on the experiments which generate the events accorded probabilities by his theory, subsequent presentations, in their efforts to make the theory as general as possible, have abstracted from that aspect. Thus, the standard

Events and event types are thus what might be called in other theories *aspects* of (spatiotemporal) events. Thus, for example, the property of achieving a score of 151 on a particular administration of the Stanford-Binet IQ test by a given individual is an event in our ontology, as is a change in the pressure of a sample of oxygen on a particular experimental trial. It should be noted that what are ordinarily termed 'states' or 'standing conditions' are included within the category of events here. Unless otherwise noted, specific events, i.e., possession of specific values of a property on a given trial by an individual system, will be denoted by A, B, C, etc., whereas an event variable, i.e., a specific system and trial, but with an undesignated value of the property level, will be denoted by $\mathfrak{A}, \mathfrak{B}, \mathfrak{C}$, etc. Ruled out as causes and effects are (1) facts (as linguistic descriptions of events), (2) objects, and (3) unactualized possibilities. (1) is ruled out because of our desire to stay in the material mode. (2), although attributed causal and effectual efficacy in ordinary talk, as in "The car demolished the wall," invariably sharpens into some property or behavior of the object being the cause or effect: "The high momentum of the car caused the collapse of the wall" (clearly it was not the car per se, for a car parked touching the wall has no effect). To take a more scientific example: it may seem that it is the absence of electrons in a semiconductor lattice ("positive holes") that allows the flow of electrons from electron-rich to electron-deficient regions. But what is actually a contributing factor (via the absence of a counteracting cause) is the absence of a negative charge at the site, rather than the absence of an electron per se.[6] (3) is eliminated because only actualities can be causes and effects in specific instances.

---

apparatus has probability spaces, consisting of a set of outcomes; an algebra of subsets of the outcome space, called 'events' (usually given the structure of a Borel field); and a probability measure on that algebra. Random variables, representing real-valued quantitative properties, are then defined on the algebra. Systems are never mentioned in this apparatus. Two things are needed to remedy this omission. First, any member of the outcome set, w, is taken here to be a function of the system, property, and trial, $Z(S, T)$. Second, the real probability, the feature of the system which is associated with the causal properties of the system, is also taken to be a property of Z, S, and T, and not, as the Kolmogorov probability measure is, a property of sets of outcomes. This will make the connection between substantive scientific theory and the universal, content-neutral apparatus of probability and statistics easier to make and will help to keep in focus that the causality is located not in the probabilistic apparatus but in the concrete systems it represents. Events that serve as the relata of causal relations are thus not the same as events that serve as the basis of abstract probability theory. Taking events as set-theoretic entities, however advantageous it may be for purposes of measure-theoretic probabilities, is a disadvantage for causation at least because (1) The 'events' are, in the discrete case, ordinarily disjunctive occurrences of basic outcomes (thus the 'event' of getting an even number on a die is actually a disjunction of the basic events 'two' 'four' 'six'); (2) allowing Boolean operations in set-theoretic events allows spatiotemporally widely separated disjuncts and conjuncts in unions and intersections of events.

[6] This could be rendered entirely free of particle language by the use of quantum-field theory,

§13. Assumptions for Quantitative Probabilistic Causality

The assumptions laid out in this section have a twofold purpose. The first is to provide a minimal basis from which much of the apparatus of linear causal models can be derived. This explicit basis should make it easier to assess the sense in which this apparatus is indeed a causal apparatus and to answer criticisms that the apparatus is ad hoc. I do want to stress that the assumptions which appear here may well not represent the motivation which many workers in the field bring to causal modeling, which is often success in predicting and reproducing observed correlations. Although it is not always possible to separate assumptions which are made for the purposes of statistical estimation from substantive causal assumptions, those given here are oriented almost exclusively toward the latter, even if they happen also to be useful in applications of particular estimation techniques.

The second purpose of the assumptions is to show how, by embedding the philosophical theory of probabilistic event causation within the more general framework of quantitative probabilistic causality, we can explain why the former is indeed a theory of causation and what the appropriate structure for the theory should be, and we can appraise it from a more general perspective, rather than resting its merits on an appeal to intuition and examples. As a side benefit, the apparatus here should enable proofs to be carried through more easily in the event case. (For an example, see appendix 3.) In what follows, I shall move back and forth between mathematical representations and the real properties they represent, assuming that the reader will make the required adjustments in interpretation.

Let Ω be an outcome space from a trial on system S, and let $X_1, \cdots, X_m$, $Y_1, \cdots, Y_n, U_1, \cdots, U_p$, etc. be real-valued random variables defined on $\mathscr{B}$, where $\mathscr{B}$ is a sigma algebra generated from Ω. The random variables will be measured on at least an interval scale of measurement.[7] Let E be an

---

although the lattice would remain as a permanent system even in that mode of representation. It is worth noting that the resistance of semiconductors is often extremely sensitive to temperature, typically decreasing by 4 percent per degree Celsius increase around the region of room temperature, thus making temperature an additional causal factor.

[7] There is some dispute in the econometric literature over whether it is appropriate to consider the exogenous variable(s) as random variables. The reasons for this involve the use of regression equations for estimation purposes: if the values of X are fixed values, whereas the values of Y vary stochastically, as for example they would be in an experimental situation in which X was a controlled variable, then estimating values of X using $E(X/Y = y)$ is claimed to be meaningless (Maddala [1982], p. 99). However, since estimation issues are not our primary concern and since a random variable is any measurable function from (subsets of) the sample space into the real line, constant functions are included under this category. Of course, to assume that exogenous variables are actually constant in experimental situations is an idealization—all controlled variables in real experiments fluctuate around the supposed fixed value—but a similar idealization

expectation operator, and we shall assume that the expectation is defined over all Borel functions of the random variables. a_i, b_j, etc. will denote constants for the system S. We assume that all exogenous variables are measured without error. A brief survey of the covariance measures that underlie the causal theory is contained in appendix 1.

Our first assumption follows from the multiplicity of causation discussed in §4. The presence of these multiple causal factors requires that the models be multivariate in form. Furthermore, following the indeterministic considerations of §10 or the incompleteness argument of §5, those factors which are included in the model will rarely determine the outcomes, either because of omitted or uncontrolled factors which influence those outcomes or because the relation between some of the X_i's and Y is genuinely indeterministic. Rejecting the traditional division of theories into those which are purely deterministic and those which are purely indeterministic as too crude, we allow our structures to occupy a position between the fully deterministic extreme of a simple, isolated, classical mechanical system and the fully stochastic statistical models of coin tossing and urn selection. Let us then postulate:

> ASSUMPTION 1. The value of a variable Y is the sum of a traditional deterministic functional of the variables $X_1, \cdots , X_m$ and of a stochastic disturbance term U. Hence $Y = f(X_1, \cdots , X_m) + U$.

Assumption 1 provides us with part of our conception of probabilistic causation, in that Y is the result of both a deterministic influence and a separable purely chancelike component. U is uncontrolled, uncontrollable, unobservable, and unpredictable, except in a purely post hoc manner.[8]

What constraints can be imposed on the functional f?[9] Our second assumption, which is a special case of an invariance condition on causation that

---

is followed here in assuming error-free measurement of exogenous variables. (This issue was brought to my attention by James Woodward.)

[8] Within much of the causal-modeling literature, U is taken as containing the residual causal influences on Y which have not been included in the model. Some of these models are committed to determinism, so that U has no purely stochastic component, whereas others allow that U may have such a component. Although, as I said earlier, I prefer to view these assumptions as describing real phenomena rather than models, those who are interested in modeling may make the appropriate changes in interpretation, as long as U behaves as if it were at least partially indeterministic. Because even within the deterministic construal of models, U is observable only post hoc and is uncontrollable; it is a classic example of a variable whose only purpose is to preserve a prior commitment to determinism.

[9] The comments of Hubert Blalock and James Woodward on an earlier version of the manuscript have led to substantial improvements in the rest of this section, as well as elsewhere. In particular, their remarks forced me to reconsider the need to require additivity and hence prevented me from maintaining a seriously wrong view about quantitative causation.

is discussed more fully in §25, entails that f is additive.[10] This consequence will no doubt seem unduly restrictive to many, who would prefer to view additivity as a convenient but conventional simplifying assumption, rather than as a necessary consequence of a fundamental causal principle. This less restrictive view holds that nonadditive relations between variables are consistent with those variables having a causal role, as in the classical gravitational relation $F = Gm_1m_2/r^2$ where it seems legitimate to allow changes in the mass of either body or in the distance between them to cause a change in the gravitational force between the bodies. This more general position of allowing nonadditive factors seems to be prima facie correct, and so we must explain why the more restrictive assumption is made here. The first reason is that our goal is to recover the theory of (linear) causal models, and since these are additive, we may restrict our assumptions suitably. The second and more interesting reason is as follows. When we require that a cause contributes to an effect, we can mean one of two things. We can mean that the cause in question contributes a precisely characterized quantitative amount to an equally precisely quantified effect variable. Or we can mean merely that the causal factor contributes to the effect rather than counteracts it (or is irrelevant). In the present context we must be concerned with the first of these meanings because the quantitative models wish to represent accurately the exact contribution to the effect of each causal factor.

So suppose that we take a quantitative approach to causation and claim that a unit change in a variable X_i caused a change of y units in Y when all other factors X_j were constant. Then that change of y units must occur irrespective of the particular level at which the other X_j happen to be. For if not, it was not the change in X_i that caused the change of y units in Y but the change in X_i together with the prevailing level of the X_j's.

Putting this invariance condition as an assumption, we have:

ASSUMPTION 2. The contribution of an individual variable X_i must be the same at whatever level the other variables are held constant.

Assumption 2 can be interpreted as requiring that $\partial f/\partial X_i = g_i(X_i)$ for any i. This then restricts f to an additive form:

$$(1) \qquad f(X_1, \cdots, X_m) = \sum_{i=1}^{m} h_i(X_i) + h_0 .$$

PROOF. We must have $f(X_1, \cdots, X_m) = h_1(X_1) + h'(X_2, \cdots, X_m) + h'_0$ from the constraint $\partial f/\partial X_1 = g_1(X_1)$ (where h'_0 is an

---

[10] Although 'additivity' here means scalar additivity, what is crucial is the separability of causal influences, and similar arguments to those given below could be used to support other additive representations, such as vectors and elements of tensor product spaces.

arbitrary function). We assume that no X_i is a function of any other X_j, $j \neq i$, otherwise it is impossible to change X_i while holding all other variables constant. Then, we must have $h'(X_2, \cdots, X_m) = h_2(X_2) + h''(X_3, \cdots, X_m) + h''_0$ from the constraint $\partial f / \partial X_2 = g_2(X_2)$. By iteration, we have the required result.[11]

The argument given above for the assumption is an adaptation of one constructed by J. S. Mill. In following Mill on this issue, I am not thereby endorsing Mill's other views on causation: in particular I have explicitly rejected his deterministic position, and his famous Methods of Experimental Inquiry are clearly too simplistic from a modern standpoint. His argument for the unconditionality of causes is, however, independent of those other positions.

Now consider the situation where what is of interest is whether an increase in a causal variable produces an increase or a decrease in the effect variable. One can see in the example of the gravitational force, $F = Gm_1m_2/r^2$, that an increase in the mass of the first body results in an increase in the gravitational force, irrespective of what value the other causal variables (m_2 and r) have, but the value of that increase is clearly not independent of the values of those other variables. Hence if we are concerned solely with the claim that an increase in m_1 contributes to the value of F, the invariance condition is satisfied, but if we were dealing with the issue of whether it was the given increase in m_1 that contributed the precise increase in F that occurred (when the other variables are fixed at some level), the argument given immediately preceding Assumption 2 above shows that it was not. This distinction between qualitative and quantitative contributions to an effect explains, I think, why one can allow nonadditive relations as causal in qualitative assessments but not, I think, in specific quantitative claims of causal contributions unless one has effectively turned a nonadditive relation into a (degenerate) additive relation by holding constant all but one variable, thereby implicitly relativizing the causal claim to a specific set of contextual factors. A similar distinction between qualitative contributions and quantitative contributions is important for our explanatory theory and is discussed in §36.

I note here that the invariance assumption used here is weaker than the full invariance assumption discussed in §25, because there we require that a cause produce its effects not just when other factors are held constant but under all circumstances. Recalling that our present task is to recover the basic apparatus of causal models, it is preferable to use the weakest principles consistent with that aim, even though, obviously, the stronger version of §25 could be used

---

[11] I owe the method here to a suggestion from Jean Paul van Bendegem.

to derive Assumption 2 as a special case. The fact that the apparatus of causal models can be based on the weaker invariance principle is a consequence of the fact that the models are intended to provide a theoretical apparatus that replicates for nonexperimental phenomena a methodology based on experimental controls, the ultimate goal being to isolate the separate causal threads in a complex web and to provide a numerical value of their contribution. This last task can be achieved only if the values are not confused with the contribution of other factors—hence the ersatz experimentalism that underlies Assumption 2.

Are there further constraints which could be placed on the h_i? Not ones that can be motivated on purely general causal grounds. It is a matter of contingent fact how the X_i's affect Y. In order to simplify the discussion and to connect the assumptions with the scientific literature, we shall adopt the auxiliary assumption of linearity in Assumption 2a below, in part because all the causal models we shall discuss are linear (in both the coefficients and the variables). One could change any invertible function of X_i into X_i itself by a suitable transformation, or simply define $Z_i = h_i(X_i)$ to arrive at a linear form for f artificially, but to do so would distort the interpretation of the variables in many cases, and hence this should not be adopted as a general strategy. Furthermore, we note that all covariance measures of association give misleading results when the relationship between variables is nonlinear. For example, any symmetrical function (e.g., $Y = X^2$) together with a suitably symmetrical probability distribution will yield a zero covariance, even though there is a clear functional relation between X and Y. For these reasons, I shall focus only on the case of $h_i(X_i) = b_i X_i$ in order to recover the linear models, while recognizing that this is a special case of causal relations. Hence:

ASSUMPTION 2a. In (1) above, $h_i(X_i) = b_i X_i$, where by convention $h_0(X_0) = a$.

We thus have from Assumptions 1, 2, and 2a that, for the theories considered here,

$$Y = \sum_{i=1}^{m} b_i X_i + a + U .$$

In keeping with our focus on systems, the b_i are also properties of the system. They are not properties of populations. The probability values and variables which determine the value of the expectation also are all properties of the system under consideration.

The status of the linearity assumption is quite different from that of the invariance assumption. The latter allows, for example, that the functional relationship between two exogenous variables X_1, X_2, and an endogenous variable Y can have the form $Y = X_1^7 + X_2^{15}$, and X_1 and X_2 would still count as contributing causes of Y because their contributions to Y are additive. Hence violations of linearity do not themselves preclude quantitative causal attributions, and Assumption 2a clearly does have a conventional role in our theory. In contrast, our earlier discussion of additivity and nonadditivity has shown that the invariance condition has a fundamental causal justification.

The third and final assumption gives some weight to the deterministic leanings which many have. It attempts to conform to the widely held precept that our scientific theories should be such as to account for the regularity of phenomena as far as is possible while remaining consonant with the facts and, allied with this precept, that our theories should be as predictively accurate and as explanatorily complete as is possible. We thus have:

ASSUMPTION 3. The functional f should be that which minimizes the contribution of the stochastic element U to changes in Y.

This assumption should not be viewed as an attempt at legislative metaphysics (for I know of no convincing argument which establishes that the world must be such as to be minimally indeterministic), but rather should be viewed as a selection procedure for choosing that theory, among all those consistent with the data, which satisfies this principle. The precise sense in which the contribution is minimized will be stated in the proof below.

It is worth noting that none of the assumptions depends in any way upon the form of the particular probability distribution under which the variables fall. The only requirement is that in calculating covariances, the variables must have a joint distribution. The form of the distribution is often important when estimation techniques are employed, especially the frequently used assumption of normally distributed error variables, but again, this issue is not a causal one.

There is one further assumption that is standardly made for causal models, which is that the X_i and U are mutually probabilistically independent or, more weakly, uncorrelated. This assumption is discussed in detail as Assumption B of appendix 2. For the purposes of Theorem 1 we can avoid making this assumption because, when X_i has a fixed value x_i, it automatically has zero correlation with any other variable (see appendix 1). It should be stressed, however, that in general one needs to make this independence assumption, and it is a particularly problematical one—in part because it is so strong, in part because it is impossible in practice to test. (In addition to appendix 2, the reader is referred to the discussion of ceteris paribus conditions in §41.)

THEOREM 1. The functional f is such that $f(x_1, \cdots, x_m) = E(Y/x_1, \cdots, x_m)$ for every value $x_1, \cdots, x_m$ of the variables $X_1, \cdots, X_m$.

PROOF. Denoting the vector $x_1, \cdots, x_m$ by $\mathbf{x}$, we have from Assumption 1 that $f(\mathbf{x}) + U = Y$. Thus

$$
\begin{aligned}
E(U^2/\mathbf{x}) &= E((Y - f(\mathbf{x}))^2/\mathbf{x}) \\
&= E(Y^2/\mathbf{x}) - 2E(Yf(\mathbf{x})/\mathbf{x}) + E(f^2(\mathbf{x})/\mathbf{x}) \\
&= E(Y^2/\mathbf{x}) - 2f(\mathbf{x})E(Y/\mathbf{x}) + f^2(\mathbf{x}) \\
&= (f(\mathbf{x}) - E(Y/\mathbf{x}))^2 + E(Y^2/\mathbf{x}) - E^2(Y/\mathbf{x}) \\
&= (f(\mathbf{x}) - E(Y/\mathbf{x}))^2 + \text{Var}(Y/\mathbf{x}) \ .
\end{aligned}
$$

Then interpreting Assumption 3 as asserting that, for any specific value of $\mathbf{x}$, the stochastic contribution to Y is minimized in the sense that the left-hand side of the above equations is minimized, since only the first term on the right is dependent upon f, we have that $E(U^2/\mathbf{x})$ is minimized when $f(\mathbf{x}) = E(Y/\mathbf{x})$, giving us the required result.

From the discussion of Assumptions 2 and 2a, we required that f be a linear function of the X_i's. To be clear about the relation between the constraints imposed upon f by Theorem 1 and by Assumptions 2 and 2a, we note that Theorem 1 requires that, for every fixed value of $\mathbf{x}$, the spread of values of Y for that fixed value has a mean which is equal to the systematic contribution of $\mathbf{x}$. Furthermore, we see from the last line of the proof that when $f(\mathbf{x}) = E(Y/\mathbf{x})$, the variance of Y for any given value of $\mathbf{x}$ is entirely due to the residual stochastic element U. The constraint imposed by Assumption 2a does not relate to stochastic fluctuations around a fixed value of $f(\mathbf{x})$ but requires that the systematic contributions (and hence by Theorem 1 the conditional means of Y) satisfy a linearity condition which holds across all values of $\mathbf{x}$. We thus have:

COROLLARY 1. $E(Y/\mathbf{x}) = \displaystyle\sum_{i=1}^{m} b_i x_i + a$

It is then possible to show that the coefficients of this systematic contribution satisfy a standard definition for regression coefficients:

THEOREM 2. For each variable X_j, the coefficient $b_j = \text{Cov}(Y, X_j)/\text{Var}(X_j)$.

PROOF. Since Corollary 1 holds for all values of **x**, denoting as usual by $E(Y/\mathbf{X})$ the conditional mean for an arbitrary value of **x**, we have $E(Y/\mathbf{X}) = \sum_{i=1}^{m} b_i X_i + a$. Letting E_X denote expectations with respect to **X**,

$$E_X(E(Y/\mathbf{X})) = E_X(\sum_i b_i X_i + a),$$
$$E(Y) = \sum_i b_i E_X(X_i) + a$$
$$= \sum_i b_i E(X_i) + a .$$

Thus, substituting for a in the generalized form of Corollary 1,

$$E(Y/\mathbf{X}) = \sum_i b_i X_i + (E(Y) - \sum_i b_i E(X_i)),$$
$$E(Y/\mathbf{X}) - E(Y) = \sum_i b_i(X_i - E(X_i)) .$$

Hence, multiplying through by $(X_j - E(X_j))$, and taking conditional expectations with respect to X_j, holding all other X_i constant, we have:

$$E_{j.\ i \neq j}(E(Y/\mathbf{X}) - E(Y))(X_j - E(X_j))$$
$$= \sum_i b_i E_{j.\ i \neq j}(X_i - E(X_i))(X_j - E(X_j)) ,$$
$$E(Y - E(Y))(X_j - E(X_j))$$
$$= b_j \operatorname{Var}(X_j) \quad (\text{using } E_{j.\ i}(E(Y/\mathbf{X})X_j) = E(YX_j).)$$

Hence $\operatorname{Cov}(Y, X_j) = b_j \operatorname{Var}(X_j)$, giving us the required result.

Further development and interpretation of this quantitative apparatus is contained in appendix 2, which should be read after the philosophical development of causation contained in the body of the book. For the present, we turn to the simplest form of discrete causation, causal relations between events that are considered only with respect to their occurrence or nonoccurrence. This binary situation is the one that has been discussed almost exclusively in the philosophical literature, and our task is to show how that simple situation is a special case of the apparatus we have just developed.

§14. The Binary Case

As we saw in §9, a key measure for binary-event causation is the difference that the presence of the putative cause makes to the chance of the effect, compared with the absence of that putative cause.[12] Let us call the measure $P(A/B) - P(A/-B)$ the *relevance difference,* and denote it by $R(A, B)$. Allowing for the moment that our three assumptions of §13 apply to these binary situations, let I_A be the indicator variable for the event A, so that $I_A = 1$ if A occurs, and $I_A = 0$ if A does not occur.

Now take the indicator variables I_A, I_B for the events A, B respectively. Recalling that $E(I_A) = P(A)$ and similarly for B, we have that $\text{Cov}(I_A, I_B) = P(AB) - P(A)P(B)$. Using the definition of relevance difference, by simple algebraic manipulations and the use of the theorem on total probability, we have that $R(A, B) = (P(A/B) - P(A)P(B))/P(B)P(-B)$. But for dichotomous variables, $P(B)P(-B) = \text{Var}(I_B)$, and hence we have that $R(A, B) = \text{Cov}(I_A, I_B)/\text{Var}(I_B)$, giving us from Theorem 2 the central result:

The relevance difference is the regression coefficient of the indicator variable I_A on the indicator variable I_B.

We thus have $I_A = R(A, B)I_B + P(A/-B) + U$.[13]

Now suppose that I_B changes from 0 to 1 (i.e., the situation changes from

[12] Much of what is said here about the binary case can be extended to the case of nondichotomous discrete variables by use of the technique described in Hanushek and Jackson (1977), §4.7, which relies on considering discrete variables with n levels as a set of $n - 1$ dichotomous variables. For caveats about the use of binary representations of fundamentally nonbinary properties, see the next section and, for technical issues, the next note.

[13] An important side remark must be made about this result. Ordinarily, in order to use covariance measures, variables must be measured at least on an interval scale, as we originally assumed, yet indicator variables (often called "dummy variables" in the causal-modeling literature) are, on one view, simple new names for nominal variables. There is, however, a well-established tradition that dummy variables can legitimately be viewed as two-valued variables upon which expectation operators can be used. More directly, all that is needed in the demonstration of the central result is that the elementary operations of multiplication, subtraction, and expectation can be given a meaningful interpretation for the indicator variables, and this is the case. It must be kept in mind in general that care has to be taken in derivations involving indicator variables to avoid nonsensical consequences.

James Woodward has raised this issue about the legitimacy of applying regression methods to dichotomous variables (Woodward [1988], p. 267 n. 9), referring in particular to Humphreys (1985), in which occurs an essentially similar treatment to the one given here. His objection has two parts: (1) when the endogenous variable is dichotomous, several of the assumptions underlying ordinary least-squares estimation techniques will not be satisfied, and one will arrive at biased estimators; (2) even if it were permissible to view dichotomous variables as a special case of linear models, the probabilistic interpretation does not seem to generalize to interval-valued variables. The first point is quite correct if one is concerned with regression techniques as a method for estimating the parameters in regression equation. This is how Woodward himself

$-B$ to B because B occurs). Then there is a contribution of $R(A, B)$ to I_A which is added to the base-level chance of $P(A/-B)$, this contribution being due to the occurrence of B. This purely formal fact can be interpreted within our approach in terms of the effect that the change from $-B$ to B has on the propensity of the system to produce A. The change deterministically produces an increase in the propensity from its base level of $P(A/-B)$ to a new value $P(A/B)$ by virtue of the contribution $R(A, B)$. Assuming that this change in I_B is the only change which occurs prior to the consequent change in I_A, we can assert that the increase in the propensity is caused by the change in I_B, i.e., the change from $-B$ to B, which in the case at hand, is the same as the occurrence of B. Thus far, everything has been couched in terms of a recognizable contributional account of causation. At this point, however, after the contribution of B has been taken into account through its effect on the propensity, it is a matter of sheer chance whether or not A occurs, i.e., whether I_A takes on the value 1 or 0. U then represents the de facto contribution of chance to the eventual outcome, and the representation we are using here makes quite explicit the peculiarity of the indeterministic case, because chance must "top up" the propensity value to unity, or "drain" it to zero. Events come in ontological chunks, and this all-or-nothing feature of the discrete case might make it appear that chance is cooperating with the causal factor to ensure that exactly A or exactly $-A$ always occurs.

Yet this is, I think, a rather misleading way of putting it, because once we have described the contribution of B to the occurrence of A, there is no further explanation of the occurrence of A to be had. After citing the causal factor (here the change in I_B), the event A either just happens or just does not happen.

---

construes them ([1988], especially p. 256), but as I stated in §13 above, my project is to show how causal models in general, and regression equations in particular (see appendix 2 for the relations between these), can be given a coherent causal interpretation, and for this purpose I am considering regression equations as a theoretical device descriptive of a homogenous population. This fact that Woodward's approach is data driven, whereas mine is not, accounts for many of the differences between our conclusions. I think that we would agree that many uses of regression methods (of either kind) are inadequately justified. However, as I try to show in subsequent sections, the frequency-based approach assumed by Woodward and many others is the wrong choice for probabilistic causality, and I view his conclusions about data-driven regression as further reason to adopt single-case probabilities rather than relative frequencies.

As to point (2) above, I hope that the arguments given throughout this and the next two chapters will persuade the reader that there are significant connections between the discrete and continuous cases. (I should note that Woodward did not see the manuscript of the book until after writing his article.) In a personal communication, he has also pointed out, quite correctly, that although dichotomous exogenous variables can be used without serious difficulty, when a dichotomous endogenous variable is used, one may arrive at estimates for the expectation of that variable which are greater than 1 or negative and hence are not interpretable as probabilities, necessitating the use of logit or probit analyses. Although this is true when one has continuous exogenous variables linked to dichotomous endogenous variables, it is not a difficulty for the particular result shown in the text, where all variables are dichotomized.

That is the nature of chance.[14] There might still appear to be something odd about the situation, because although the increase in the propensity means that the propensity for A to occur is now closer to 1 than before B occurred, it looks as though we have to resort to some metaphorical language to the effect that this increase makes it "easier" for chance to move I_A up to 1 than down to 0. But we should resist this further causal talk and remain with the idea that once the contribution of B to the propensity has been cited, there is nothing more to say that is genuinely causal—it is simply that the higher the value of the propensity, the more likely A is to occur.

This is an appropriate point at which to emphasize that one must not impose requirements on probabilistic causation that are at variance with its peculiar and special nature. James Woodward (personal communication) has raised this issue in a very clear way. Consider, he suggests, the example that I used in §9 of the mouse exposed to two carcinogenic chemicals. Given that the mouse develops a stomach tumor and that each chemical increases the chance of contracting such a tumor, he suggests that this information alone does not discriminate between the following three possibilities: (1) the tumor was entirely caused by the first chemical, (2) the tumor was entirely caused by the second chemical, (3) both chemicals contributed causally to the tumor. That is, because we know that on other occasions the first chemical alone has led to (has caused) a tumor, why should the present case not be one of those occasions? (And analogously for the second chemical.) Woodward was motivated to make this argument by a distinction drawn by Eells and Sober ([1983], but much more explicitly in Sober [1985]) between population-level (or property) causation and individual-level (or token) causation, and the conclusion that one is expected to draw from this example is that some kind of connecting process is the key to individual-level causation, rather than increases in probability. I shall discuss connecting processes and negative links in, respectively, §32 and appendix 3, but we do not need here the arguments in those sections.

The correct response to the example is this: probability is construed here in terms of single-case chances, grounded in structural bases and affected by multiple exogenous factors. In particular, probability is not reducible to relative frequencies. In the example at hand, the situation with both carcinogens present *is* different from the situation with only one—the chance is higher than with either alone because both chemicals have contributed to the value of that chance. And that is all there is. To think otherwise is to conceive of the example in terms of a deterministic image where the tumor was "entirely caused" by the first chemical and the second chemical was thereby irrelevant.

[14] Compare Hume: "It is universally allowed that nothing exists without a cause of its existence, and that chance, when strictly examined, is a mere negative word, and means not any real power which has anywhere a being in nature" ([(1748) 1955], §74).

But that is not the situation. The second chemical is not irrelevant on this (or any other occasion) for it contributes to the chance on this occasion, as does the first chemical, and after they have done this, *nothing else causal happens.* It is, as I have said, a matter of sheer chance whether the tumor occurs or not. To raise the image of something else occurring after the chemicals have interacted with the cellular structure and changed the chance is to reify chance into a non-Humean chancy connection, a view for which I find no support whatsoever (see §22 for further criticisms of such a view).

Everything that has been said thus far is in terms of actual changes. There is a comparison of $P(A/B)$ with $P(A/-B)$, but in the binary case this is a comparison of an actual value with an actual value, since $-B$ was the case before B occurred and the change in propensity value also actually occurred. In the next section we shall see that this simple expedient of comparison between the present actual and the prior actual does not carry over into cases beyond the binary-event situation, and a more careful account of the contrast case will be needed there.

One further result in the dichotomous case is worth noting. As we saw earlier, the function which minimizes the indeterministic contribution to the outcome variable is the conditional expectation. In the dichotomous case, this will be $E(I_A/I_B) = P(A/I_B)$. Now suppose that we take a predictivist interpretation of the equation. Then because the regression function is the best predictor of I_A, we have that when B occurs, the best predictor of whether A will occur is $P(A/B)$, and when $-B$ occurs, it is $P(A/-B)$. This fact is worth keeping in mind when we discuss the virtues of various theories of explanation. At one time, it was a highly controversial issue as to whether explanations and predictions had a parallel structure. Given that the relevance difference is central to causation, whereas the conditional probability alone provides the optimal predictive base, there is reason to believe that causally based explanations are different from predictions (whether causally based or not), except perhaps in cases where $P(A/-B) = 0$. Moreover, in accounts of explanation where the probability value itself is taken to the central object of attention, the plausibility of this may arise from its optimality as a predictor, whether $P(A/B)$ is high or low.

§15. The Contrast Case

BOY: Father, I saved fifty cents today by walking to school rather than taking the bus.

FATHER: Congratulations son, but next time save five dollars by walking to school rather than taking a cab.

Contributing causes are contrastive: they make a difference between situations in which they are present and situations in which they are absent. But in which situations is the cause absent? Sine qua non counterfactual analyses (see §8) have taken a particular stand on this issue. Given that their primary concern is for causation in the circumstances, rather than with causal generalizations, the essential idea in the contrast case is to keep as much of these (actual) circumstances as is possible, consonant with the absence of the causal factor under analysis. This use of a contrast case thus has the flavor of a thought experiment, but one of a particular kind. Such contrast cases that focus on singular 'in the circumstances' claims usually only mimic those experimental situations in which the other causal factors that are operating in the circumstances are kept constant at the levels of contribution they had in those circumstances. (By 'kept constant', I do not mean that variables that changed value in the circumstances are literally held constant, but simply that any such changes also occur in the contrast situation.) Experiments in which the other factors are held constant at different levels than those they had in actuality or in which all causal influences are removed other than the one under investigation are difficult to replicate under this sine qua non method.

What constitutes the nonoccurrence of a causal factor is often hard to determine precisely, and the difficulties would appear to be compounded when the factor is quantitative in form. If a car had not entered a curve at 60 mph, what speed would it have had? Attempts to resolve such underdetermination have led to deeply pragmatic elements in theories of counterfactuals, elements that are best avoided in an objective theory of causation. What is the general form of the nonoccurrence of a causal factor when that factor is quantitative? The obvious candidate is what I shall call the neutral level of the variable— that level of the variable at which the property corresponding to that variable is completely absent. This concept of a neutral value is not circular, in that it does not require prior knowledge of whether or not that variable is a causal factor for the effect in question, although some causal knowledge of other kinds is ordinarily required because the measuring devices will frequently be causally linked to the factor under investigation. The detection devices for ascertaining when the zero level of a variable has been reached are ordinarily causally independent of the effect variable in which one is interested (a fact that results from the multiplicity of effects from the same causal variable), and the zero level is not defined as that level at which no causal influence is operating. Indeed, it would be unwise to identify the two levels, because there may be threshold effects below which no causal influence operates, even though the cause has a nonzero value. Furthermore, one should not assume that the effect will never occur when the causal variable is reduced to zero, for some spontaneous occurrences may still occur (there, however, it will not be caused).

Is there a universal causally neutral state? Almost certainly not, because in many cases the absence of something will itself have causal effects. For example, a vacuum, perhaps the quintessentially negative state, would not allow many of the systems which underpin our ontology to exist qua system type, this being most obviously true in the case of living organisms which are oxygen dependent. Furthermore, even speaking of a neutral *state* may be misleading, because the comparison case will sometimes consist of a neutral change, or nonchange. The selection of the neutral state or change will ordinarily also require some specific prior causal knowledge—a famous example here being the precautions needed to avoid the placebo effect in psychiatry and medicine. The nature of this kind of knowledge is taken up in §29. The neutral state will thus ordinarily be factor or system specific. To see how this works, suppose that we wish to assess the causal influence of current on heat generated in a circuit of fixed resistance. The zero level of current can be straightforwardly achieved by disconnecting the circuit or, if it were suspected that some spontaneous level of current would exist even then, could be checked with a galvanometer, the operation of which depends on the torque produced by current in a magnetic field, an effect that is causally separable from the heating effects of current.[15]

The situation with probabilistic causes is similar. As I have repeatedly stressed, the essential feature which distinguishes probabilistic causes from sufficient causes and necessary causes is that multiple probabilistic causes are frequently present. This entails that the absence of a probabilistic cause does not usually reduce the probability of the outcome to 0 and that the neutral value of the relevant variable is not necessarily that value of a variable which results in the lowest probability for the outcome, for negative values of a quantity may be a counteracting cause, when positive values are a contributing cause. Thus for the stochastic case we must consider a comparison with the state in which only the factor at hand is neutralized, in order that the effect of the other factors is taken into account and to ensure that if an interaction effect occurs with some other factor present, which for example converts what is ordinarily a contributing cause into a counteracting cause, this will manifest itself.

Some examples will illustrate the use of the neutral state. Consider a case of a car skid and the contributing factor of its speed. Let the neutral state be a speed of 0 mph. Suppose further that the actual speed of the car was 40 mph, that the posted safe speed for a dry road was 30 mph, that at or below the posted speed the probability of a skid is 0, and that above 30 mph the probability is a monotonically increasing function of the speed. Hence, relative to the neutral state, the speed of 40 mph is a contributing factor to a skid. The speed might have been higher, say 47 mph, and that too would have been a contributing factor had it occurred instead: indeed, any speed greater than 30 mph would contribute to a skid. This example is of course a simplified

---

[15] For a description of the operation of galvanometers, see, e.g., Bleaney and Bleaney (1965), chap. 7.

version of an ordinary phenomenon, and a parallel scientific example may thus be useful. Within rather wide limits, the probability of an electron's being emitted from a metal by thermionic emission is a function of the absolute temperature. The neutral state here will be at a temperature of absolute zero, at which temperature the probability of thermionic emission is 0.[16] Furthermore, for a fixed temperature, the probability of emission is also a function of the chemical potential for the metal involved. The neutral state for that factor is when the potential of the electron gas external to the metal is in equilibrium with the internal chemical potential, and hence any increase or decrease in that (zero state) equilibrium will be, respectively, a counteracting or contributing cause of an electron emission (see, e.g., Knuth [1966], pp. 114–118, 213). (Both of these last two examples involve a mixed ontology, where the effect is an event, and the cause a value of a variable, but in the general case, both cause and effect will be values of variables.)

It has been pointed out to me by James Woodward (personal communication) that one often ought to construe effect events as contrastive as well as causal events. As he notes, our car example of a little earlier could be given two different comparative effects. The first is that of a car rounding the curve and skidding, compared with the same car entering the same curve and not skidding. The second comparison could be between a car rounding the curve and skidding and the same car rounding a different curve and skidding. This point is quite correct and is intimately connected with the issue of whether explanatory questions are comparative in form, and if so, what the correct comparison case is. For the same situation could give rise to two quite distinct questions: "Why did the car skid on that corner rather than not skid?" and "Why did the car skid on that corner rather than on a better designed one?" I take up that issue in §41 but note here that one can preserve an exact parallel between cause and effect events. Effect events are also for us aspects of (properties of) spatiotemporal events grounded in specific systems, and there are neutral states of effect events just as there are neutral states of causal events. It should further be noted that when the effect in question is a change in a variable or property, there is one implicit contrast within the change itself, the contrast between the final and initial states of the system, but the correct contrast will be between the change and its neutral state—i.e., no change.

The objectivity of a neutral state will thus reduce to the question of whether

---

[16] The thermionic current I, from which the probability of emission per unit time can be calculated, is given by $I = 4\Pi em(kT)^2 e^{-w/kT}/h^3$, where w is the internal potential minus the zero-point energy. (See, e.g., Born [1962], app. 36.) An important caveat must be made here. In many derivations of quantum statistical distributions such as the above, Bose-Einstein or Fermi-Dirac statistics are used, with the attendant assumption of particle indistinguishability. Application of probabilities to individual particles seems to be precluded by this indistinguishability, and so single-case explanations will be difficult in these cases.

an objective criterion for a zero value for a quantity can be given. In order to have a unique zero value, the variables must be measurable on a ratio scale, rather than an interval scale. This is not quite so restrictive as it may seem, for usually the cause will be constituted by changes in a given variable, rather than by the values of the variable itself, and since interval-valued variables are unique up to positive linear transformations, null changes in such variables are transformationally invariant, even if the zero point is not. Thus, although it may make little sense to ask what the zero level of intelligence is in humans, it does make sense to posit that increases in intelligence contribute to increases in the speed at which standard problems are solved.

There are other candidates than the neutral state for comparison, but they all have serious drawbacks. Consider first the average value of the conditioning factor. It has often been noted in passing by various writers on probabilistic causality that the inequality (I) $P(A/B) > P(A/-B)$ in the definition of positive relevance is formally equivalent to (II) $P(A/B) > P(A)$ and also to (III) $P(AB) > P(A)P(B)$ (except when $P(-B) = 0$). In terms of interpretation, however, there is a great deal of difference between those formally equivalent definitions. Because the unconditional probability is given by $P(A) = P(A/B)P(B) + P(A/-B)P(-B)$, in (II) a specific conditional probability is being compared with a weighted average, whereas in our account we are comparing it with another probability conditioned upon a specific contrast case. Furthermore, once we move outside the simply binary case, the two kinds of comparison are no longer equivalent.

The equivalence runs into difficulties as soon as we move to a tripartite partition of conditioning events (C_1, C_2, C_3). Then it is easy to show that

$$(1) \; P(E/C_1) - P(E) = \sum_{i=2, 3} P(C_i)(P(E/C_1) - P(E/C_i)) \; .$$

Suppose that we were interested in deciding whether C_1 was a contributing cause of E, according to the two comparisons suggested above. Equation (1) clearly allows $P(E/C_1) < P(E)$, $P(E/C_1) > P(E/C_2)$ but $P(E/C_1) < P(E/C_3)$. Consider a concrete example. E is recovery from an illness, C_1 is administration of a moderate dose of drug X, C_2 is administration of a placebo, and C_3 is administration of a heavy dose of X. Because the drug is effective but has unpleasant side effects, we perform a random drawing to determine which of C_1, C_2, C_3 occurs. Hence each of the probabilities in (1) is objective. Let $P(E/C_1) = .4$, $P(E/C_2) = .2$, $P(E/C_3) = .9$, and $P(C_i) = .33$ for each i. Now suppose E occurs and was preceded by C_1. Is C_1 a contributing cause of E? Elementary calculations give $P(E) = .5$, and hence according to criterion (II) above, administering a moderate dose of X is a prima facie counteracting cause of recovery since $.4 < .5$. This appears to be an incorrect assessment because C_1 contains an effective agent for producing recovery and surely contributed to the latter event. Not as much as would have C_3, admittedly, but we are not interested yet in the magnitude of the contribution. More important is the fact that whereas in the pure binary situation (i.e., where negations are taken as not open to further analysis) the contrast case in the second kind of comparison is immediately given by the complement of the putative cause, as soon as we consider any more detailed analysis of possible causes, whether or not C_1 is a contributing cause will depend, within a generalized comparison of the second kind—$P(E/C_1)$ versus $P(E/C_i)$—on what we choose as the contrast event. Relative to C_2 (the placebo), C_1 is a contributing cause, but relative to C_3, a heavy dose of the drug, C_1 is a counteracting cause of recovery. Using the neutral state of the variable C—i.e., C_2—gives the correct answer.

This kind of example, where problems occur in nonbinary cases because of using the mean value as the comparison case lies behind an argument given by Davis ([1988], p. 147) against the transitivity of probabilistic causal generalizations. He uses the example that

(1) having only a small hole in a tire (A) causes the driver to hear a characteristic hissing noise immediately (B); (2) Having only a small hole and hearing a characteristic hissing noise immediately (AB) causes the driver to have the tire repaired immediately (C); and (3) Having only a small puncture (A) causes the driver to have the tire repaired immediately (C). While seldom heard, a small leak does raise the probability of hearing the noise characteristic of a small hole; so $P(B/A) > P(B)$. And obviously, $P(C/AB) > P(C)$. So assuming no screening factors, our theories rule that (1) and (2) are true. Nevertheless, since other types of damage are more noticeable, having *only* a small puncture actually reduces slightly the likelihood that the tire will be repaired immediately; hence $P(C/A) < P(C)$. So (3) comes out false.

But the correct comparison case in the last inequality is not $P(C)$ but $P(C/A_0)$, where A_0 is the neutral state of escaping air, i.e., no hole at all. Then the chance of one's repairing the tire given *any* combination of factors and only a small puncture is greater than the chance given that same combination of factors and no hole at all.[17] The trouble originally arose because of averaging over all other kinds of damage conditions to get $P(C)$, rather than using the neutral contrast case.

There are two further arguments against using the average value. The first is that the average is usually a group property and not an individual property, and hence when considering causal properties of an individual via a propensity, we would be comparing an individual property with a group property.

---

[17] These factors must be compatible with having only a small hole, of course. Thus large gashes are ruled out, for example.

Of course, by taking a time average, rather than an ensemble average, this problem may be avoided, but this will not avoid the second problem, which is that there is nothing about the mean that guarantees it will be causally neutral. The average level of smoking in the United States is approximately one pack of cigarettes a day, hardly a neutral level of a contributing factor to diseases that kill more people than car accidents and gunshot wounds combined, and a similar point may be made about individual averages.

In using covariance measures to develop our quantitative theory, we did, of course, use an apparatus that takes deviations from the mean as the measure of variation. However, when the variables are measured on at least an interval scale, the covariance measures are invariant under linear transformations of the variable (see appendix 1), and hence the zero point of the variable can be substituted as the point away from which variations take place.[18]

A similar objection to that made against using the mean value can be raised against taking the normal state of affairs[19] or the natural state of affairs[20] as the contrast case. The natural level of radiation exposure to a human in the U.S. resulting from solar, cosmic, geological, and other sources is approximately 0.06 person-rems per year. For the majority of the population who do not live or work near sources of artificial radiation, this is also close to the normal level. (This natural level is almost 4,000 times the amount received from nuclear energy sources).[21] But it would be foolish to hold that this natural level does not causally contribute to levels of cancer in the U.S. or that these normal levels of cancer do not need to be explained. To take a happier example, it is normal, and natural, even in countries with high rates of fetal mortality, for a fertilized human egg to develop into a baby. Those who believe this needs (or has) no explanation or that there are no causes of this must be exceptionally jaded.

A third possibility is a comparison with the negation of the event. As we saw, the negation of an event is often a highly underdetermined entity, but there is a different problem in probabilistic causality. If B is a prima facie positive cause of A, then it immediately follows that $-B$ is a prima facie negative cause of A, in all theories that use the negation of the event as the contrast case (assuming that $--B = B$). On our theory, however, this does not follow if $-B$ is the neutral state. To see this, consider the well-known

---

[18] Our comparative measure $R(A, B)$ is always greater than $P(A/B) - P(A)$ unless $P(-B) = 1$, in which case $P(A/B)$ is undefined. Hence for practical purposes, the comparison we suggest will often be easier to detect than the comparison with the mean.

[19] This comparison is used by Hart and Honore (1959) in their pragmatically oriented treatise on causation in the law.

[20] As in Toulmin (1961), chaps. 3–4; also Gorovitz (1965).

[21] Figures are from 1978, from *Summary of Work Group Reports of the Interagency Task Force on Ionizing Radiation* (Washington, D.C.: Department of Health, Education, and Welfare, 1979), p. 20.

example of syphilis and paresis. The presence of syphilis is a contributing cause of paresis in a given individual S. Is the absence of syphilis a counteracting cause of paresis in S? Given that syphilis is the only way to contract paresis, the absence of syphilis is not counteracting anything, because it cannot lower the probability from a value that is already 0.

There are what appear to be counterexamples to using the neutral state as the contrast case. It is said that the cause of a flame's going out is the absence of oxygen. Yet because the absence of oxygen is the neutral state for that factor, we shall have to contrast the neutral state with itself, precluding the absence of oxygen from counting as a cause. But this example is misleading. "The flame's going out" is a change from the flame's burning to the flame's not burning, and the cause of that change is not a static state of absence of oxygen but a change from the presence of oxygen to its absence. The neutral state of that is a nonchange from the original state, and in comparison to that, the cited change is a cause of the flame's extinction. Are there any examples of a neutral state that can plausibly be considered causes and are not simply confusions along the lines just discussed? There may be, and if so they would be a difficult problem for our theory, but I myself have not seen or been able to invent any convincing cases.

There is an important logical point that must be made about the contrast case when A is an event of the type described in §12: (S, X, T). The usual Boolean operations must not be assumed to apply here. The 'negation' of A is (S, X_0, T), where X_0 is the neutral state of X. Then, if A_0 is a candidate for a cause, the contrast state will be itself, i.e., $(A_0)_0 = A_0$. If a causal factor is a compound event, as it often will be, so that a cause of $(S, Y = y, T)$ is $(S, X_1 = x_1, T)$ together with $(S, X_2 = x_2, T)$, $(S, X_3 = x_3, T)$, and so on, which compound cause would ordinarily be represented by the conjunction $B \cdot C \cdot D$, the contrast case is not the negation of the conjunction but $(B \cdot C \cdot D)_0 = B_0 \cdot C_0 \cdot D_0$, i.e., each of the causal factors has been reduced to its neutral state. The reason for this is that the comparison must be made with a state that is completely neutral, and it could well be that one of the causal factors, say C, is the absence of some factor.

To illustrate this point, recall that a cause, to contribute its effects invariantly, cannot be counteracted in a way that destroys its causal nature, in the sense that, were the counteracting cause to be removed, the previously contributing cause would no longer produce the increase in probability. So, for example, if the presence of an overly acidic soil contributes to the death of a plant, then there cannot be present an alkaline substance that would react with the acid to neutralize it permanently. Hence, the contributing cause of death in this case will be, say, "presence of acid X at level x together with the absence of lime." But what now is the contrast case to this? If it is the negation—i.e., "absence of acid at level x or presence of lime"—then since excess levels of lime can kill the plant as well (let us suppose in the same way by preventing it from metabolizing certain minerals), we could have $P(\text{Death}/(A \text{ and } B)Z) = P(D/(-A \text{ or } -B)Z)$ when $(-A \text{ or } -B)$ was instanced by $-B$, the presence of lime, thus precluding the acidity from counting as a contributing cause. So we need to retain the neutral levels of other factors in assessing the causal nature of the components. To avoid ambiguity, I shall henceforth use the notation A_0 for the neutral state of a factor, rather than $-A$.

§16. How This Affects Relative Frequentists

I have put the problem so far in terms of the contrast between positive and negative relevance. The issue runs deeper than this, for it affects relevance relations in general. A simple adaptation of the drug example given in the last section will show that if administration of another drug Y, equivalent in its effects to a moderate dose of X, is event C_4, we can have $P(E/C_1) - P(E/C_4) = 0$ with the other inequalities remaining the same.[22] Then relative to C_2, C_3, C_4, event C_1 is, respectively, positively relevant, negatively relevant, and probabilistically irrelevant. Thus, even those who are concerned not with the difference between positively and negatively relevant factors but only with relevance simpliciter will suffer from the ambiguity of the contrast case.

This is a matter of importance not only for causation but for probability, because the relative-frequency interpretation of probability rests upon relevance claims of just this simple kind. For relative frequentists (see §18), a probability attribution to a individual event is correct just in case that event has been assigned to a homogeneous reference class, and a class is homogeneous if the specification of the reference class is such that any factors not included in the specification are probabilistically irrelevant. As we have just seen, however, whether a factor is probabilistically irrelevant or relevant to another factor will depend upon the choice of a contrast case. Indeed, the standard approaches to relative frequency interpretations of probability are quite clearly oriented in a way which makes their techniques diverge from causally based approaches. In particular, relative-frequency interpretations which use divergence from the probability of the (inhomogeneous) class or sequence left from previous partitions are flawed in that whether a factor alters the frequency or not depends on the order in which the partitioning is applied.

Suppose that we start with an inhomogeneous reference class for which the relative frequency of A is an average over the values of the homogeneous subclasses. Let us suppose that, as a matter of fact, there are only three conditioning factors, F_1, F_2, and F_3, such that $P(A/F_1) = .25, P(A/F_2) = .5,$

[22] Let $P(C_i) = .25$ and $P(E/C_4) = .4$. Then $P(E) = .475$.

$P(A/F_3) = .75$, and $P(A) = .5$, where $P(A/F_i)$ means the frequency within the subclass defined by F_i alone. We start out in the standard way with the class defined by A and subdivide it by means of the F_i's. Then whether F_2 is considered a probabilistically relevant factor will depend upon the order in which the subdivision is performed. If we subdivide according to F_2 first, it will be classified as probabilistically irrelevant because $P(A/F_2) = P(A) = .5$. However, if we first subdivide by F_1 and then by F_2, F_2 will be seen as probabilistically relevant. It would, I believe, be generally accepted that whether or not a factor is statistically relevant should not depend upon the order of partitioning. A relative frequentist could reply to this objection in the following way: if the factors are applied simultaneously to subdivide the original class, the problem just noted will not arise. So we must test possibly relevant factors in groups as well as individually. This will then classify the combination of F_1F_2 as relevant, even though F_2 alone is not. This poses a serious problem for the original intent of relative-frequency theories, however, because part of their appeal is that they provide us with a method for arriving at the correct probability value. Under this revised proposal we cannot determine that a given factor is irrelevant until all factors have been tested, because the fact that it was irrelevant when taken with $N - 1$ other factors does not entail that it will be irrelevant when taken with N factors.

§17. A Tripartite Distinction

There is an important distinction between a probabilistic theory of causality and a theory of probabilistic causality.[23] In the former, the theory uses the apparatus of standard probability theory, but its use does not entail that the causal relation itself involves an irreducible element of chance. In the latter, by contrast, the probability is placed directly into the relation between the cause and the effect, so that the causal relation contains a properly probabilistic element. As we observed earlier, even this basic distinction leaves the second kind of causation open to further division. It could be maintained that the chance has some genuine causal role, thus making the causality itself genuinely probabilistic, or alternatively, as the present position has it, that although there is probability in the relation between the cause and the effect, the chance itself has no causal role, the causal actions having operated on the structural distribution of chance rather than on the effect directly. In this last case, it is, I think, misleading to speak of probabilistic causality.

---

[23] Deborah Rosen (1982) was the first to point out this important distinction.

This tripartite distinction has not been observed in much of the literature, and repeated reference to 'probabilistic causality' tends to perpetuate the confusion. In order to avoid the unwanted connotations that accompany this term and to emphasize the underlying unity of the deterministic and indeterministic cases, I shall henceforth employ the terminology of 'contributing cause' and 'counteracting cause', with the modifier 'probabilistic' used only when necessary.

§18. Passive Empiricism and the Trivialization Problem

CHILD'S PUZZLE: If you cut through each of the loops in your shoelaces, how many pieces would you have?

ANSWER: Three, but since you worked this out in your head, you still only have one.

We have said that a probabilistic contributing cause of an effect is (with additional constraints) a factor that increases the chance of that effect. What are we to make of the chance that is used here, if causation is to be a feature of the world? The position that we adopt is in part influenced by the inadequacies of a long philosophical tradition that I shall call *passive empiricism*. The essence of passive empiricism is the view that humans are special kinds of receiving devices capable of assessing observed data for empirical properties, that in the case of Humean causation, for example, would be regular temporal succession, spatiotemporal contiguity, and the kind of regular association that constitutes a lawlike regularity.[24] Within Hume's own account of sensory impressions, for example, what produces the impression is irrelevant; what is crucial is that the impressions lead to associated ideas, associated both in the sense that each type of idea is correlated with a distinct type of impression and in the sense that a mental association, or habit, between ideas is generated, this psychological habit (notoriously) accounting for our belief in the necessity of the causal relation itself. This disregard for the origins of the impressions is reasonable within a certain kind of empiricism. If one thing that motivates you to be an empiricist is the desire to remain epistemically conservative, then to avoid moving beyond the security of the immediately given to inferred entities is desirable, because such inferences are fallible; alternatively, if such inferences require a move from an observed effect (the impression) to an unobserved cause (the source), one might object to the circularity of such a move within the context of an empiricist analysis

---

[24] "When both the objects are present to the senses along with the relation we call *this* perception rather than reasoning; nor is there in this case any exercise of the thought, or any action, properly speaking, but a mere passive admission of the impression thru' the organs of sensation" (Hume [(1739–40) 1888], bk. 1, pt. 3, §2).

of causation. But whatever the reasons, the analysis is conducted at the level of the observations, and the source of the empirical data is not a part of the analysis itself.

The distinction we have been emphasizing between single-causal influences and multiple-causal influences is reflected in a methodological division— single-causal influences are the goal of the experimental method, and multiple causation is the realm of nonexperimental methods. (By 'experimentation' we include both controlled laboratory experimentation and randomized experiments in field settings, in which uncontrolled influences are distributed so as to have zero average effect.) It is not surprising that the philosophy of science, which has traditionally seen physics as the central science, should have (1) taken causation in physics as exemplary, (2) used laws of physics in its logical reconstruction of causation, as a result (3) been concerned almost exclusively with laws formulated primarily for application in closed experimental systems, involving single causal influences, and consequently (4) focused largely on causal chains and ignored nets and fans. There has been, in addition, an even more powerful philosophical tradition militating against experimental accounts of causation, namely, the Humean version of empiricism.

When Hume, in his powerful criticism of the existence of necessary connections in nature, suggested that the objective properties of causal relations between events consisted solely of three things—contiguity in time and space, temporal succession, and constant conjunction—he presented an image which, if taken literally, would seriously limit our ability to distinguish causal relations from noncausal correlations. For the image that his criticism conjures up is that of a passive observer, coolly and dispassionately observing the world go by. Phenomena run their course, we observe their regular or irregular successions, and we draw causal conclusions. This kind of spectator sport would be appropriate if we were a conscious version of Mount Rushmore, fixed and immobile, unable to intervene in the ways of the world. Such an observer would, one imagines, conclude that there was a causal relationship between the length of the shadow of his nose and the disappearance of picnic baskets in the parking area below, whether the shadow was a mere accompaniment to the end of the day or the approach of winter, or a genuine cause when it fell across the families, producing a sudden chill.

This passive approach omits one of the principal devices we have for making causal inferences, that of experimental control and manipulation. Such a device ought to be as congenial to an empiricist as is the passivist picture. Mill knew this and so called his famous methods the Methods of Experimental Inquiry.[25]

---

[25] Curiously, having pointed out that an event which raises the probability of another event's occurrence can be causally related to that second event, even though it is neither necessary nor

A similar passive orientation persists in probabilistic causality. As the quotation from Suppes that is cited in the next section shows, a strong Humean influence was present in his own theory. Moreover, much of the basic formal apparatus that underlies the theories of Reichenbach and Suppes had already been constructed by the early twentieth-century empiricist school of statistics, for whom problems about the relationships between causation and various forms of statistical association were a central concern. A summary of such results may be found in Yule ([1911] 1950), a classic textbook that eventually ran through fourteen editions and is still used over seventy years later (the same as Fisher's *Statistical Methods for Research Workers*). Yule had this to say about the nature of his discipline: ''The theory of statistics is the exposition of methods specially adapted to the elucidation of quantitative data affected by a multiplicity of causes.''[26]

Many of the methods introduced by Yule and his contemporaries fall into the category of what is now called 'secondary analysis', within which a set of data generated without regard for the specific analysis at hand is partitioned by means of test factors in order to reveal statistical associations.[27] These methods are generally regarded as inferior to methods based on an explicit statistical model where the generating conditions of that data are known and, ideally, under the control of the statistician. This point is methodological, not philosophical, but it indicates that although partitioning techniques may be forced upon one because of the nature of particular nonexperimental contexts, this approach is neither necessary nor ideal. Such partitioning methods are,

---

sufficient for it, Mill failed to pursue the lead (Mill [(1843) 1874], bk. 3, chap. 17, §2; also chap. 10, § 2). Curiously, because, in a book which contained a sustained evaluation of the methodology of the social sciences and which formulated the famous Methods of Experimental Inquiry, he freely admitted that his methods were inapplicable to those ''moral sciences.'' The presence of multiple causation in the social sciences was his principal reason (ibid., bk. 6, chap. 7, §§2–5). However (as Alan Ryan kindly pointed out), in bk. 6, chap. 9, §1, Mill does reiterate his commitment to the unconditionality of causes, even in the realm of social phenomena: ''The effect produced, in social phenomena, by any complex set of circumstances, amounts precisely to the sum of the effects of the circumstances taken singly.'' Like Hume, Mill rejected the idea that chance was an objective feature of nature.

[26] The distinction between Yule's view of statistics and the more abstract characterization of mathematical statistics that has come to dominate the speciality is enshrined in the Library of Congress classification system (HA versus QC). We should also recall that Karl Pearson, undoubtedly the dominant statistician of that period, held empiricist views that led him, in the *Grammar of Science,* to reject the existence of causal connections, insisting instead that there were only correlations to be calculated by the measures of association invented by him and his contemporaries. Pearson and his followers were involved in a fierce debate over the correct methodology to follow when investigating hereditary characteristics, the Pearsonians rejecting the employment of genetic mechanisms introduced by the Mendelians. The realists were, of course, eventually vindicated. For histories of this period see McKenzie (1981) and Porter (1986).

[27] In particular, computing correlations and regression coefficients from relative frequencies generated in nonexperimental contexts and performing cross-sectional studies on existing sets of data are examples of secondary analysis.

of course, quintessential passive-empiricist devices. There is no purer case of an empiricist association between events than a statistical correlation, and when such associations (as opposed to the theoretical measures of association for which they serve as estimators) concern occurrent events, they are the obvious analogues of classical regularity accounts of causation. These partitioning procedures of secondary analysis are also characteristic of relative-frequency theories of probability, which should not surprise us, for the notion of a probabilistically relevant factor plays a central role in both relative-frequency theories of probability and probabilistic analyses of causation.

It will be philosophically helpful in the rest of this section to draw an explicit parallel between regularity analyses of causation and relative-frequency theories of probability. For both, regularities are primary, instances secondary; for both, inferences are from event types to tokens; and for both, some criterion demarcating laws from nonlaws is necessary to avoid fallacious inferences. But we must keep in mind that whereas the emphasis is on the probability value alone in the relative-frequency case, it is on the relevance difference in the (probabilistic) causal case. Consider how a relative frequentist deals with the probabilistic analogue of the relationship between causal generalizations and singular causal claims when asking, "What is the relation between a general probability claim and a singular one?" The answer to this question requires a solution to the well-known problem of the single case. By their very nature, relative frequencies other than 0 and 1 are not directly properties of a single event, and hence some transfer of relative frequencies from repetition to a single outcome is logically required (unlike the analogous transfer within regularity analyses of sufficient causation, where this transfer is not forced). For most philosophical accounts of relative frequency, the frequency itself is a property of a class or sequence of data within which the relative frequency is calculated. Yet it is clear that a particular event, say the occurrence of a car accident, may be classified as a member of many different sequences—car accidents simpliciter, accidents by drivers aged less than twenty-one, accidents involving cars driven faster than 60 mph, and so on. Hence for relative frequentists, the problem of the single case amounts to: to which class or sequence should a single event be assigned?

With this question the passive empiricist, if mathematically inclined, runs into a difficulty that I shall call the trivialization problem. The difficulty is forcefully brought out for the deterministic case by Russell in his "On the Notion of Cause" (1913). Suppose that one agreed that if a function existed that mapped times onto states of the world, so that each point of time was associated with a unique state, then one had a sufficient condition for functional determinism. This might seem reasonable, since it precludes the existence of more than one state for any given time, ensuring that the universe evolves in a unique way. But then, Russell notes, given the actual development of the world—past, present, and future—however complicated that development might be, such a function always exists. It may be uncomputable, nondifferentiable, highly discontinuous, and quite useless for human predictive purposes, but it nevertheless exists as an abstract entity.[28]

Richard von Mises encountered a parallel difficulty in trying to impose randomness conditions on the infinite sequences of data from which limiting relative frequencies were to be computed. (Although von Mises thought that it was inappropriate to assign probability values to single events, one can use his approach as the basis to an answer to the problem of the single case noted above. A single event should be assigned to the largest random subsequence of the original sequence in both of which the event appears.) Initially he required only that there be no place-selection function that selected a subsequence with a different relative frequency from that in the sequence as a whole. Here, a place-selection function is a choice function that uses data from initial segments of the sequence, including the ordinal of the datum under choice, to select or not select each member of the sequence for inclusion in the subsequence. It was recognized early on, however, that without further constraints on the place-selection functions, a function that picks out a subsequence with a relative frequency of 1 always exists (except in sequences where only a finite number of instances of the datum in question occur in the original sequence). Again, this function exists as an abstract object and may not be predictively useful in the way that a positivist such as von Mises would have liked, but nevertheless, it makes von Mises' original definition of randomness impossible to satisfy (except in the extremal cases). It should be obvious that the point also holds for finite relative frequencies. A large literature has arisen exploring various constraints that can be imposed on Russellian functional determinism or von Mises place-selection approaches to randomness, and this literature has its own mathematical interest.[29]

Two philosophical points emerge from the trivialization problem. The first is that within the logical and mathematical spaces inhabited by the abstract representations of cause and effect, operations are possible that simply cannot be done via real manipulations. The (logical) atomism inherent in these approaches which is, derivatively, present in the treatment of data points as logically independent entities, allows partitioning and conjoining of sets of frequency data that go beyond what is possible with "real" manipulations. There are things that one simply cannot do, or that simply cannot occur, in

---

[28] "What most people have in mind when they speak of the future as determined . . . is a formula by means of which the future can be exhibited, and at least theoretically calculated, as a function of the past. But . . . if formulae of any degree of complexity, however great, are admitted, it would seem that any system, whose state at a given moment is a function of certain measurable quantities, *must* be a deterministic system. . . . But if this be true, no information is conveyed about the universe in stating that it is deterministic" (Russell [1918], pp. 196–97).

[29] For a detailed discussion of such mathematical approaches to randomness, see von Mises (1964), Church (1940), Martin-Lof (1969), Chaitin (1987), and sources therein.

the world because of its causal structure. Yet by dealing with observed relative frequencies and mathematical operations upon them, one is dealing with (abstract representations of) observed effects of the world on us, and these observations are independent (or quasi-independent) in a way that their origins, the actual causes and effects, are not—one can separate the observations in conceptual or mathematical space in a way that is not always possible in the world itself. Indeed, this is exactly what Hume did in insisting that cause and effect are 'distinct existences', and this construal in terms of logical independence, rather than causal independence, especially when accompanied by a primary concern for a non a priori justification for causal *inferences*, moves one in a direction that makes a successful characterization of causal relations, as opposed to noncausal relations, very difficult.[30] This objection is, of course, merely a statement of what many realists, both prephilosophically and postphilosophically, believe has been left out of empiricist analyses of causation, whether probabilistic or nonprobabilistic.

The second point to be made is that employing mathematical analyses on data points without consideration of the generating conditions of those data is to misconstrue the causal aspects of the situation. The data points are not ordinarily causes of one another but joint effects of the generating conditions, and consideration of the data alone will not by itself legitimate the transfer of a relative frequency to a single case. To see the importance of the generating conditions for the single case problem, consider these two situations:

1. An infinite number of repetitions are performed on the same indeterministic system. All causally relevant factors $X_1, X_2, \cdots, X_n$ are held constant. The resulting sequence of outcomes passes all statistical tests for randomness, and the limiting relative frequency is p. Is it permissible to attribute the value p as a single-case probability to each repetition?
2. An infinite number of repetitions are performed on the same deterministic system. The values of all causally relevant variables $X_1, X_2, \cdots, X_n$ are randomized over the repetitions by means of a perfect randomizing device. The resulting sequence of data passes all statistical tests for randomness, and the limiting relative frequency is p. Is it permissible to attribute the value p as a single-case probability to each repetition?

---

[30] These distinctions were clearly drawn by J. L. Mackie in the first chapter of his *Cement of the Universe*. There he argued that three distinct issues need to be separated in discussions of causation. The first is whether it is possible to distinguish causal from noncausal sequences. The second is whether it is possible to justify inferences from cause to effect (or vice versa) on an a priori basis. The third is whether such inferences may be provided with a non a priori justification. (His conclusion is that Hume did not properly separate these issues and that whereas Hume's analysis of causation radically undermines attempts to legitimate a priori causal inferences, it is not effective against the first and third issues.)

Clearly, the correct answer to situation 1 is yes; to 2 it is no. We need, in addition to the frequency value, information about the constancy or lack of constancy of causally relevant factors operating on the source, otherwise the probability value attributed to the single case may not be the true probability that applied in that instance, but rather an epistemic mixture of other values.

This was, I suspect, a reason for von Mises' ignoring selection functions based on physical properties, for, as he insisted, "The subject matter of probability theory is long sequences of experiments or observations repeated very often and under a set of invariable conditions" ([1964], p. 2). This reference to generating conditions of the data is important, because whereas philosophical treatments of relative frequencies in the passive empiricist tradition have, as I mentioned, generally referred only to the sequence of data and ignored the systems or conditions that generated it, probability theorists and statisticians generally have not. Kolmogorov clearly had something similar in mind when he noted of his mathematical theory of probability that "there is assumed a complex of conditions ω which allows of any number of repetitions" ([1956], p. 2).[31] Thus, whatever advantages relative frequencies may have for purposes of confirmation and testing of statistical hypotheses, taken alone they are missing a key component of what is needed for causation.

§19. Antiformalism

You will have heard it said, I expect, that overgeneralization is the occupational disease of philosophers, and in a way one might agree with that.

---

[31] These quotations indicate that Popper's original argument (1957) purportedly showing the superiority of single-case propensities over relative-frequency interpretations cannot be used against von Mises' frequency theory or Kolmogorov's interpretation of his own calculus because Popper's examples involve changing the systems generating the frequencies. Interestingly, von Mises wrote, "The probability of a 6 is a physical probability of a given die and is a property analogous to its mass, specific heat, or electrical resistance. Similarly for a given *pair of dice* (including of course the total setup) the probability of a 'double six' is a characteristic property, a physical constant belonging to the experiment as a whole and comparable with all its other physical properties. The theory of probability is only concerned with relations existing between physical quantities of this kind" ([1957], p. 14). Popper, however, does say that "only sequences which may be described as repetitions of an experiment are admitted and which may be defined by the method of their generation, that is to say, by a generating set of experimental conditions" ([1959b], p. 38). For Hacking ([1965], p. 13), in contrast, anything can be a chance set-up. Even those who, like von Mises, were interested only in the existence of successful gambling systems would be foolish to ignore variations in generating conditions where they occur. Roulette players have been successful in following this strategy (Bass [1986]), and the fundamentalist school of stock-market analysis is predicated on the importance of such variations (as opposed to the technical analysts, who are quintessential von Mises followers).

But for a sneaking suspicion that it's their occupation.
J.L. AUSTIN, "Performative Utterances"

In the early investigations into 'probabilistic causality', there was a tendency
to assume (or hope) that a purely formal theory of probabilistic causality could
be given and that the user of the theory could then interpret the probability
function in whatever way seemed most appropriate to the application at hand.

This formalist technique of providing implicit definitions for primitive terms
is a technique that has been influential in philosophy of science (rather than
mathematics, where it originated) at least since Carnap's *Aufbau*. Within that
tradition, what is primary is the construction of formal theories within some
linguistic framework, with the choice of ontology for the theory's interpretation left as a pragmatic matter.[32] This attitude, within the context of probabilistic causality, is perhaps most explicit in Patrick Suppes' 1970
monograph. Suppes is explicit that his theory must be embedded in some 'conceptual framework': "It is important to emphasize that the determination of
a causal relationship between events or kinds of events is always relative to
some conceptual framework. There are at least three different kinds of conceptual frameworks within which it seems appropriate to make causal claims.
Within each of these, a rather different basic probability measure will be
used" (p. 13).[33] This ontological liberalism is wrong, for it turns out that
deciding on the correct kind of probability that grounds 'probabilistic causality' is crucial to arriving at a correct theory. We are concerned with what
sense can be made of probabilistic causality as a feature of the world, and

---

[32] This position is clearly articulated in Carnap (1928, 1950), where, especially in the earlier
work, the goal is to abstract completely from any ontological content, thus leaving the resulting
formalism ontologically neutral. The themes of empirical underdetermination and ontological
relativity that run through the work of Quine and Goodman were clearly influenced by Carnap's
views, and the recently influential antirealist arguments of Putnam (1980) are in that same
tradition. Excellent discussions of the origins of this 'structuralist' view of theories can be found
in Demopoulos and Friedman (1985).

[33] Also: "Kendall and Stuart, in their well-known treatise on statistics [1961], Vol. 2, p. 317
say 'As with ordinary product-moment correlations, so with partial correlations; the presumption
of causality must always be extra-statistical.' The only sense in which the viewpoint developed
here is consistent with this statement is this. The choice of a conceptual framework or theory is
extra-statistical. In making a claim of genuine causality we must relativize the claim to some
conceptual framework. The quantifier embedded in the definition must be understood to range
just over the events, or in the present case, the random variables or properties of the given
framework. That there are extra-statistical methods of causal inference beyond this fixing of the
framework is denied. I take it that the position being defended here remains close to Hume's"
(Suppes [1970], p. 62). "What has been done here is to generalize [Hume's] concept of constant
conjunction to a probabilistic relationship. What is important to emphasize is exactly what Hume
emphasized. The notion of frequent co-occurrence is at the very heart of causality . . . it is part
of the concept itself to claim relative frequency of co-occurrence of cause and effect" (pp. 44–
45).

our account of probability or chance must reflect that. Thus an individual's or community's opinions about chancy phenomena cannot do the job, nor can evidential relations between logicolinguistic representations of cause and effect. This rules out, respectively, subjective and logical probabilities.[34] As viable candidates we thus have objective chance (or propensity) and relative frequencies. In essence, our position is that standard accounts of relative frequencies are defective for causal purposes because they fail to accord a proper place to the origins of the frequencies, whereas there are reasons to believe that objective chances, associated with a permanent or semipermanent structural basis but freed from appeals to immaterial causal powers, are well suited to the purposes at hand.

§20. Experimental Contexts and Regularities

There is a second line of argument that indicates the need to consider the generating conditions of observed data, and it proceeds in exactly the opposite direction from the trivialization problem. Whereas the trivialization problem arose from the fact that, given enough mathematical apparatus, 'regularities' are too easy to find, this second problem arises from the difficulty of finding enough observed regularities. According to classical regularity accounts of causation, exceptionless universal regularities between observed events are a necessary condition for the existence of a causal law. There is no necessity that such universal regularities have to exist; the world might have been, or may be, so chaotic that not a single universal law holds in it. There are arguments that such could not be the case. Perhaps a world with not a single regularity in it, not even the regularity that there were no regularities, is logically impossible.[35] Perhaps as so-called anthropic principles claim, the assertion that there are no regularities in our world is self-refuting, for it is only in a world where stable regularities exist that sentient beings could evolve or survive to make such an assertion. (Or, to vary this line, no sentence could of itself assert this, even if thrown up by accident in the primordial muck,

---

[34] I use this terminology, rather than 'subjective or logical interpretations of probability theory', because there are reasons to believe that each kind of probability is sui generis, and there is no single theory that captures them all. For more on this, see Humphreys (1984).

[35] Peirce seems to have suggested something like this (*Collected Works*, 5.345). Laws are currently held to be either deterministic or, if not, then probabilistic. By a slight modification of the construction given in the appendix to Humphreys (1981b), essentially consisting of introducing some undetermined events into the sequence given there, it is possible to construct a minimal world in which there is an infinite sequence produced by a common source but which is covered by no deterministic or probabilistic law. This result relies on the assumptions that the deterministic/probabilistic partition is exhaustive and that mere functional connections are insufficient for determinism; on current views, however, these assumptions are widely accepted.

for semantic rules, which are themselves generalizations, would need to exist for it to have content.)

Allowing, then, that there are universal regularities, a serious problem exists for passive empiricists.[36] If one takes the world as it comes, there are very few regularities of this kind—the world as it presents itself to us simply is not regular in the required way. Events rarely come to us in such a pristine fashion that we can just read off the causal relationships, even by habit. So passive Humean empiricists are faced with a real problem. They can either say that because such regular sequences are a necessary condition for the existence of a causal law, there are in fact very few such causal laws in the world (and hence few causes and causally produced phenomena), or they will have to account for why, although the laws are present, the observed regular sequences are not manifest. In addition, those who hold that subsumption under observed regularities (even where not causal) is a prerequisite for scientific explanation will also have serious problems with this absence of regularities.

In contrast, as Bhaskar (see n. 36) has observed, one of the most significant facts about the scientific enterprise is that by imposing experimental controls on phenomena, exactly the kind of exceptionless regularities that are required for a regularity analysis of causation will often emerge. We thus must ask why it is that, if the regularities are real (and the empiricist allows that they are, because under the right conditions they are observed) and the law is identical with the regularity, we require experimental methods to observe them.

There are three possible responses to this question. The first is that if the regularity is the law, as regularity theorists maintain, then the experimenter created the law by creating the experimental context and destroyed it in opening up the closed system. It is undeniably true that one does create regularities when setting up experimental contexts and destroys those regularities when opening it up. But how plausible is it that we have created a law? Not at all, I think. A simple nonscientific example adapted from Mill will illustrate this. Consider two tug-of-war teams—realists and antirealists—pulling on opposite ends of an inelastic rope. Equally balanced, the teams produce no observable movement. I now go to the rope and cut it with a razor. Observable effects occur. Question 1: Did the razor cut produce the law which covered the

[36] As far as I am aware, the problem discussed in the rest of this section was first explicitly noted and discussed in detail in Bhaskar (1975). Although I depart from his conclusions in various ways, the line of argumentation presented here for the existence of unobserved structures is entirely his. As a means of shifting the debate about scientific realism away from referential implications of theories, it represents, in my view, a profound insight. Although Bhaskar acknowledges that some of his theses had earlier been canvassed by Harre, Bhaskar's arguments are, to my mind, much more convincing, and his book is still the best sustained philosophical treatment on the realist implications of experimentation.

subsequent accelerations of the teams? Question 2: Was my razor cut the sole cause of the acceleration? Answers: no and no. (One may agree that the cut triggered the acceleration, but it cannot have produced the acceleration by itself. Ask the team sweating on the other end of the rope.) Hence the law and the other cause must have existed before the acceleration was produced, even though it produced no observed changes prior to the cut. A second reason why this response is unappealing is that it creates an extreme anthropomorphism. Most laws would be dependent for their existence on the existence of human experimenters to create the regularities. No humans, few laws. In consequence, our own existence would have evolved in a world almost free of biological (and other) laws, making it a good deal more surprising than it already is. This position is possible to maintain, but unattractive.

A second option open to an empiricist is to claim that the regularity was indeed already there in the nonexperimental context but was obscured by the presence of other factors. The regularity was, in effect, embedded in statistical noise much as Michaelangelo's sculptures were already present in the Carrara marble, waiting only to be freed by his chisel. We do, on this picture, literally discover causal laws. To discover is to bare, to uncover or expose to view, a meaning largely usurped in the epistemological realm by the wider notion of obtaining knowledge of something previously unknown.

This perspective is, perhaps, one that lies behind the statistical analysis techniques discussed in §18. Within the data set, it is believed, lies a subset with the true regularity or relative frequency; it just happens to be concealed by being embedded within a great mass of other data. Two things need to be pointed out concerning this option. The first is that the various trivialization results that we discussed in §18 apply directly to these kinds of data-partitioning techniques. The second point is that this uncovering option cannot explain why it is that regularities (or probability values) of the required form regularly appear when experimental controls are imposed but not in other circumstances. Of course, passive empiricists who are not concerned with the origin of their data will not be faced with this problem—certain sequences will simply be much easier to analyze than others. But if the question we posed has any force, this unconcern about origins is misguided, and an explanation is called for, which cannot be given at the level of data.

The third option is, I believe, the correct one, and it is one with which Mill flirted, although he never wholeheartedly accepted it.[37] The option is to

---

[37] Mill was caught in a dilemma between remaining faithful to an empiricist regularity account of causation and adopting a position involving tendencies to produce effects. See Mill ([1843] 1874), bk. 3, chap. 5, §§1–3, 6, for the first view; bk. 3, chap. 10, §5, and chap. 5, §5, for the second view. This last section is not in the first edition and contains Mill's somewhat obscure views on dispositions: he says there that 'capacities' are not real but are merely names for inferential habits. Whether this Humean line applies to tendencies, which are active capacities, is not stated. Mill's dilemma has been widely discussed by, among others, Geach (1961), pp.

allow that the observed regularity results from something permanent, something that is distinct from the sequence of data, and that this entity, although permanently present, produces the regularity only via interactions that occur in special experimental conditions. To do this means abandoning passive empiricism, but not thereby rejecting an empiricism of a more scientific kind. This option requires us to recognize that the observed regularities are not all that there is to causal regularities but that they are the result of something unobserved and permanent that, in the right circumstances, generates the observed regularity which the passive empiricist mistakenly identifies with the causal law. The next section contains a detailed argument for the existence of such permanent objects.

§21. An Argument for Unobserved Structures

Consider an experimental situation S in which a regularity R has been isolated, one in which a single observed factor A is uniformly associated with a second observed factor E; i.e., E regularly appears whenever A is present.[38] Then introduce into S a third factor B which, in S, in the absence of A, is uniformly associated with a fourth factor F. Now suppose that we claimed that a straightforward Humean regularity was sufficient, in the simple situation we have described (together with certain additional features such as temporal succession—what these are does not matter here), to identify A as a cause of E and B as a cause of F. Suppose further that neither E nor F is observed when both A and B are present and that the situation is completely deterministic. Now ask what has happened to E. Why is it not present when B appears together with A? Now, as I mentioned earlier, it is possible for someone to deny that an explanation of this fact is called for. In such a view, there are three brute facts: situations with only A also have E present; situations with only B have F present; and situations with both A and B have neither E nor F. I assume, in contrast, that the burden of proof is always on those who deny that an explanation exists for a given fact. And the case we have in mind should be taken to be the most routine, everyday kind of situation, with no exotic quantum effects. The rope example without the razor will do.

If E was initially present but disappeared when B was introduced into S, something must have been responsible. Let us call this 'the feature which prevents A from causing E in S'. We must establish that this feature, although

---

101–4; Ryan (1970), chap. 4; Bhaskar (1975); Cartwright (1980); Creary (1981); Gibson (1983); and Forster (1988). Of the most recent four, only Gibson's discussion appears to be written with an awareness of this prior philosophical work.

[38] Take 'factor' to represent whatever one considers the causal relata to be: event types or tokens; changes in variables, states, or conditions; etc. The specific ontology adopted here was described in §12.

existent, goes beyond what a passive empiricist would allow as real. What is this a feature of? If the feature which prevents A from causing E in S is a permanent feature of B,[39] then B would, when alone in S, simultaneously possess both the feature of causing F in S and the feature of preventing A from causing E in S. This second feature, given that it is permanent, cannot be (observably) instantiated, because it is false to claim that something has the (observably) instantiated feature of preventing A from causing E in S if A, by virtue of being absent from S at that time, does not have the feature of causing E in S. This permanent, but not always observably instantiated feature, gives us the required realist entity.

If, on the other hand, the feature of preventing A from causing E in S is a transient feature of B, then consider the possible cases when both A and B are present. Either A permanently possesses the feature of causing E in S, or it transiently does. If it permanently possesses it, we again have a realist feature, for it is not observably instantiated when B is present in S. It cannot transiently possess it when B transiently possesses the feature of preventing A from causing E, because in that situation A's feature is not observably instantiated and would hence be permanent, because A possesses it when alone in S and when accompanied by B. If A transiently possesses its feature when B's transient feature of preventing A from causing E is absent, then we have no explanation of why A's feature does not result in E. It is impossible for A transiently to lack its feature and for B transiently to possess its feature, for B cannot possess the feature of preventing A from causing E when A does not have the feature of causing E, any more than I can prevent a demagnetized tape from recording a message. Finally, if both A and B transiently lack their properties, then we again have no explanation for why A causes E when B is absent but does not cause it when B is present, because the fact that A lacks the property of causing E is the fact which needs to be explained, and there is nothing in B or S to explain that fact.

Thus we must either allow the existence of permanent features which are sometimes not observably instantiated or claim that there is no explanation for why the factor E is present in closed experimental systems and disappears when the system is opened, even minimally. The first option is, to my mind, preferable to the second.

I want to emphasize that this kind of argument is not antiempiricist in nature. It simply maintains that empiricism is not to be identified with the passive observation of events as they present themselves to us but that we must explain what happens when the activist intervention in the natural course of events which experimentation allows produces a regularity which otherwise

[39] The term 'feature' is used rather than 'property' to avoid unnecessary worries about the status of properties. I have taken the latter as a basic feature of my ontology, but even if one does not want to allow properties as real, there are many features of the world which uncontroversially exist for empiricists.

would not have occurred, and we must explain what happens to those regularities when other causal influences are added. The argument is applicable only in those cases in which the other causal factor(s) do not permanently alter the causal properties of the original cause. For example, by grounding an electrically charged sphere, I remove the causal disposition to move the leaves of a gold-leaf electroscope apart. But we can identify which situations are of this kind by isolating the causal factor before and after its interaction with the other factor(s). If the same regularity reappears, we have a case to which the argument applies. The difference between the two types of situation is commonly acknowledged in ordinary discourse, as when the physician is enjoined to treat the disease rather than the symptoms. In the case where the original cause retains its dispositional properties, its effect or symptoms are counteracted; in the case where the disposition is destroyed, the cause itself, or the disease, is counteracted.

This argument establishes nothing beyond the bare existence of the underlying entity. It says nothing about what that entity is like, other than that, under the right circumstances, it produces a Humean regularity. To move beyond this minimalism, we must consider arguments that take into account the specific scientific and probabilistic features of causal systems.

Cause and Chance

§22. Chance

We have argued that a permanent structure underlies the display of relative frequencies. This much should be unsurprising, as should the claim that the distribution of chances depends upon the specifics of that structure. The mass distribution of a coin, commonly called its bias, if shifted, will alter the parameter value of the binomial distribution associated with coin flipping. Change the potential barrier in a radioactive atom by changing its atomic number, and the parameter of the associated exponential distribution (representing the half-life) will change. Chances are ordinarily relational.[1] If one alters the environmental factors, say by increasing the gravitational force around the coin, the probability distribution will change (for a biased coin) because the effect of the bias becomes more influential. Keep the structure of a gas the same while changing the external temperature, and the Maxwell-Boltzmann law for the distribution of velocities in a gas will be altered. This law has the form, for an ideal gas, of

$$n(\mathcal{V})\mathrm{d}\mathcal{V} \;=\; \frac{2\Pi N}{(\Pi KT)^{3/2}}\,(\mathcal{V})^{1/2}\,e^{-\mathcal{V}/KT}\,\mathrm{d}\mathcal{V}\;.$$

In contrast, when a system is closed, naturally or artificially, these external factors will not affect the distribution. For example, in the case of induced

---

[1] This last again depends upon how we characterize the system—closed systems have only intrinsic chances, whereas open systems are usually relational. Yet many intrinsic chances are grounded in collections of subsystems, each of which is relational. For example, the chance to decay of a radioactive atom is essentially independent of most external influences, but we could equally well view the same chance as the probability for an alpha particle to escape from the potential well inside the nucleus. Except in cases where a particular system is genuinely atomistic, the most general account will allow chances to be relational. An everyday illustration of how it is possible to assign a propensity to either of two subsystems lies in the difference between British and American car insurance practices. In Britain the driver is assigned the risk and carries it from car to car, whereas in the U.S. it is the car which is insured, allowing different drivers to use it.

emission of photons, the probability of emission per unit time is given by

$$
\frac{4\Pi^2 e^2 I(\omega)}{m^2 c \omega^2} \left| \int u_p^* \exp(-i\mathbf{k} \cdot \mathbf{r}) \, \epsilon_{k\lambda} \cdot \nabla u_j \, d^3 r \right|^2 ,
$$

where $I(\omega)$ is the intensity of the incident field, whereas the probability for spontaneous emission per unit time is not dependent upon $I(\omega)$. (See Schiff [1968], p. 531, for the derivation of this formula.) But natural systems for which no relevant external factors exist are rare, and ordinarily it is their relational nature that allows chances to be causally influenced.[2]

We must now face the fundamental issue of what chances are, and here much of what I have to say is negative. Let me temporarily use the term 'propensity' to indicate what others have insisted is a dispositional property, with no implication here that such properties exist.

First, one cannot identify a propensity with its structural basis, because the same structure can serve as the basis for distinct dispositions.[3] Thus, if the bias of a coin was its propensity for heads, because the bias also serves as the basis of a propensity to surprise me when I cut it open after losing $100 gambling on it, by the transitivity of identity, the propensity to surprise me would be the propensity to land heads, which is absurd. Conversely, the same disposition (type) such as flammability can have two different kinds of structural basis, as with magnesium and gasoline vapor, but we should not want to identify the last two.

Second, it is standardly held that one cannot identify a propensity with its manifestations, for in doing so, the propensity would have to be either in-

---

[2] Examples can easily be multiplied to illustrate the relational feature. For a quantum linear harmonic oscillator initially in equilibrium with a heat reservoir at temperature T, the statistical operator has the form

$$
\rho = \frac{e^{-H/KT}}{\text{Tr } e^{-H/KT}},
$$

where T is the temperature and H is the Hamiltonian for the system. In the case of accident-proneness in industry, the model used is a compound Poisson distribution, where the parameter λ of the Poisson distribution is itself a random variable with a distribution

$$
dF = \frac{c^r}{\Gamma(r)} e^{-c\lambda} \lambda^{r-1} d\lambda \qquad 0 \leq \lambda \leq \infty, r > 0, c > 0.
$$

[3] By identifying the propensity with its basis and taking 'propensity' as some numerical estimate of the probability, one would be unable to account for the fact that degrees of propensity are very often dependent upon relational properties of the situation, rather than simply upon the permanent basis.

termittently present, which runs counter to the permanence of dispositions, or continuously displayed, which not only would remove the unactualized potentiality that is characteristic of a disposition but would, supposedly, make indeterministic propensities impossible. A caveat is necessary for the indeterministic case, however. Such probabilistic dispositions, given that the required relational features which give a nondegenerate distribution are in place, do display themselves continuously; for example, a radioactive atom not decaying has a nonzero propensity not to decay as well as the more 'active' propensity to decay. Since an atom can remain undecayed throughout its life, it is thus possible for such a propensity to be continuously displayed. The proclivity for refusing to allow nonoccurrences as displays comes, one suspects, from a preoccupation with deterministic dispositions. Of course, not every outcome that is a possible manifestation of the propensity can be continuously displayed, for that would be logically impossible, but at the very least, this argument shows that great care has to be taken in transferring properities of deterministic dispositions to indeterministic dispositions.

Third, propensities appear to be temporally dependent: an oak tree's propensity to shed its leaves is greater on October tenth than on July fourth. But this temporal dependence is superficial—the increased propensity is due to changes in the internal state of the tree brought about by external climatic changes. I should not deny that chances may evolve spontaneously, although it is a highly uncommon thing. Much of the time I shall thus not bother to specify the time at which a propensity value is determined. In causal contexts, the temporal specification of a propensity will always be at the time of occurrence of the causal factor under consideration (where there is more than one, the last one).

Fourth, the quantitative aspect of propensities makes them different in kind from ordinary dispositions. Coupled with their relational nature, this feature resolves many problematic aspects of dispositions. For example, it is ordinarily said that a crystal vase is fragile even when no stresses are being applied to it. Yet in that situation it has no propensity to break—the probability of its breaking, even in terms of relative frequencies in that type of situation, is zero. Again, a collection of disassembled car parts that, when assembled, made up a 1966 Lotus 7 could, in an extended sense, be said to have a disposition to travel at 120 mph, even if that collection was dispersed around the world. But its propensity to do so is 0. It rises to a positive number when the components are properly structured, and to close to 1 on a day when the temperature is 75°F and the relative humidity 10 percent.

The recognition that propensities are quantitative, relational features of systems brings us close to an actualist treatment of them. A sugar cube that is never placed in water always has a propensity of 0 to dissolve, and a coin that is never flipped has a propensity of 0 to land heads up. If it was flipped, of course, it would have a different value of the propensity, but that is to build in to the property an obviously subjunctive aspect, one that is better disguised in 'The coin, when flipped, has a propensity of one-half to land heads', and hence the unsurprising consequence that that propensity cannot be analyzed in an actualist fashion. We are concerned, remember, with singular causal sequences—those in which the antecedent factors, including the causes, were present, as were subsequent factors, including the effect. We thus do not (yet) face the subjunctive aspects of propensities which do legitimately concern causal generalizations (although there the problems are ones of inductive generalization, rather than merely counterfactual).

To recapitulate: by moving beyond an event ontology to one that incorporates physical structures, we can capture the permanency that is part of propensity talk.[4] The manifestations are the outcomes of interactions between the structural basis and the exogenous factors, except in rare cases where a purely spontaneous outcome manifests itself. That the same basis can result in different manifestations through interactions with different sets of variables is a virtue, for it allows us to detect and identify a basis of a disposition without circularity. Thus, multiple-indicator models in economics measure different manifestations of the same underlying structural features of the economy, and this multiplicity of effects saves the postulation of the basis from vacuity. Were Molière's infamous 'dormitive virtue' detectable only by opium's effect of producing drowsiness, we could still make fun of it, but 'dormitive virtue' was a placeholder for the structure of morphine, first postulated by Gulland and Robinson in 1925, that in interaction with neurotransmitters, produces drowsiness in a way that is still incompletely understood.

Thus we are analyzing dispositions not in terms of a set of conditionals, as is the standard empiricist practice, but in terms of a cluster of material entities, giving us a realist rather than an instrumentalist account.[5] The manifestations of the dispositions are entirely contingent: there are no 'degrees of necessitation' involved. Also, nothing that has been said should be interpreted as entailing that only the structural features are causally important, and not the intrinsic properties of the substances of which the structures are composed. Quine once held a purely structural view of dispositions,[6] but as C. B. Martin has pointed out,[7] there could be two substances each having identical structures

---

[4] It may be no coincidence that the standard examples of dispositions are such impermanent features as fragility and solubility—such tenuous bonds holding the world together! How much better it would be to think in terms of impenetrability, rigidity, and so on.

[5] Armstrong (1968) and Prior (1984) are also realists of this type. However, Armstrong's a priori argument ([1968], pp. 86–87) that every disposition must have a categorical basis is much less persuasive than is Bhaskar's argument discussed in §20.

[6] E.g., Quine (1960), §46. He appears to add nonstructural features in Quine (1969), p. 135.

[7] "A New View of the Mind," unpublished ms.

but with different chemical properties because of their having different kinds of constituent particles. Indeed, this is exactly what occurs with isomorphic chemical substances.

Hence, for the purpose of analyzing singular causal sequences, we can drop the 'propensity' terminology except as a shorthand for the cluster of features discussed above, with one exception. We have not yet said what chance is. Yet here is where Hume was correct. Chance is literally nothing; after the basis and the exogenous factors interact, things either just happen or do not. There is no need to posit any further 'causal powers'. In essence, what is being done in asserting the existence of such a modality is reifying some 'natural necessity' to a status akin to logical necessity. That is, the logical operator for necessity is usually treated as being the same for all propositions, and the task is to find the correct theory for it. Yet in the case of natural necessity, there is, if such a thing exists, reason to think that there is no monolithic 'power' that brings about things but a variegated set of structures and properties of very particular sorts. And why, for the realist, should there be something that pervades all causal connections between objects of radically different types?[8] In short, once we have focussed on the structures or processes, no further move to a more abstract level of generality is necessary in order to avoid the problems encountered by Humeans. And then we have to ask: do not we already have names for these things? Indeed we have—electromagnetic force, sexual attraction, economic influence, capillary action, and so forth. There are no causal powers of a peculiarly indeterministic kind, no dispositional properties, no propensities. We do not need them, and hence we shall not use them.

Causation is thus grounded in the basis of the physical chance and is not in the chance itself, for the changes in propensity are the effects of causal changes on the conditioning factors. This entails that causation is primary and chance secondary for our account, in contrast to the neo-Humean relative-frequency approaches in which probability is primary and causation is analyzed in terms of relative frequencies. This orientation makes the philosophical account different from the frequency versions of causation, for the latter can appeal to logicomathematical representations of relative-frequency relations, with the expressed methodology that, once the data is available, a purely formal analysis will yield the correct causal conclusions, an approach that lies squarely within the formalist tradition discussed in §19. A different approach is required when one relinquishes the pure relative-frequency basis, and to this we now turn.

---

[8] A grammatical note: 'propensity' is a noun (phrase) that always takes substantival or infinitive complements. Thus an object cannot simply have 'a propensity'; it must always be a specific propensity for some type of outcome. This is another reason for not identifying a relational propensity with its basis, for then the propensity will not be determinate.

§23. Common Causes and Structural Stability

I contrast the present approach with an argument which has been widely used in favor of realism—an argument based on the principle of the common cause—in order to indicate how that principle is subject to certain limitations which can be overcome to a certain extent by experimental manipulations or reliance on natural variations. The principle, as stated by Reichenbach ([1956], p. 163),[9] is

If coincidences of two events A and B occur more frequently than would correspond to their independent occurrence, that is, if the events satisfy relation $[P(AB) > P(A) \times P(B)]$ then there exists a common cause C for these events such that the fork ACB is conjunctive, that is, satisfies

(1) $$P(AB/C) = P(A/C)P(B/C)$$
(2) $$P(AB/-C) = P(A/-C)P(B/-C)$$
(3) $$P(A/C) > P(A/-C)$$
(4) $$P(B/C) > P(B/-C)$$

The first thing to note about this principle as stated is that it is either obviously false or, if strictly interpreted, of very limited application. Reichenbach clearly meant the "coincidences" to be strictly interpreted, for immediately after stating the definition he added this rider: "This principle means that a statistical dependence of simultaneous events requires our explanation in terms of a common cause," and in fact Reichenbach is careful in most of his examples to require the simultaneity of the two effects. Yet most actual "coincidences" do not involve simultaneous events. When two individuals fall sick from food poisoning because of a common spoiled meal, the onset of symptoms is rarely simultaneous.[10] In order to employ the principle in most actual cases, therefore, we need to interpret "coincidence" as not entailing simultaneity and to add to the antecedent of the principle "and if there is no direct causal connection between A and B." This in turn means that to use the principle in most situations requires auxiliary causal knowledge to eliminate the possibility of a direct causal connection. Although in select cases this might be possible by means of a very general causal principle, such as the relativistic upper bound on the speed of transmission of causal signals, most situations will need background causal information about what kinds of causal factors might be involved in order to rule out a direct connection. Thus although the principle of the common cause is usually discussed as an abstract

---

[9] This definition is repeated and discussed at length in Salmon (1981); Salmon (1984), chap. 6; and in van Fraassen (1980), p. 28.

[10] This example has been frequently used by Salmon, e.g., in Salmon (1984), p. 158.

principle of inference and can occasionally be used that way, in most applications additional causal knowledge of the kind discussed in §29 will be required.

The second thing to note is that, although conditions (1)–(4) jointly entail $P(AB) > P(A)P(B)$, this latter association will appear only when the common cause, which we shall denote by the variable c, varies between C and $-C$. For if C was always present, then by (1) A and B would be independent in that case. Similarly by (2); if $-C$ was always present, A and B would be independent, and the scientific realist would be unable to use the argument from the principle of the common cause.

To put this in a slightly fanciful way, the slogan "to be is to be the value of a variable" is correct if the variable is a causal variable rather than a logical variable and if the variable is not "bound," as is, mutatis mutandis, required by Quine's criterion, but is *really* a variable. What is directly inferred is the existence of a variable and not an event (type) C, as the principle seems to imply. Thus a necessary condition for its use is that the common cause vary, and this places a second important restriction on its use. For at the level of the most fundamental structures which occur in nature, it is plausible that permanency will be the case. Let me illustrate this with reference to two situations, one from the area of social science models, the other from the area of celestial mechanics. We shall see that the situation in which the instrumentalist is safest is also the situation where the principle of the common cause is unavailable to the realist. Consider a simple set of linear equations of the kind that occur in causal models in the social sciences (q.v., §13), in particular, in economics. It is well known that at equilibrium, the theoretical constants for such systems are underdetermined by the empirical data. In short, there is an infinite number of surfaces which could be drawn through the vector of equilibrium, each corresponding to a different theoretical process which had produced that equilibrium.

A more interesting point was noted by Marschak and Hurwicz, however.[11] As they pointed out, as long as the structural parameters remain constant, knowledge of the "real" values (as opposed to "fictitious" values obtained by linear transformations) is unnecessary for prediction of the values of Y, given x. Suppose, however, that the underlying structure of the system changes. Then we need two things to predict values of Y inductively from values of x in the future. We need a dynamic theory of the unobservable parameters, and we need to have values of those parameters before the change, so as to predict their values, via the dynamic theory, afterward. They emphasized the second part of this requirement, which is the issue of identifiability, i.e., whether the structural parameters are uniquely determined by the data. Equally important from the point of view of the realism issue are the

---

[11] See Hurwicz (1950), pp. 266–72.

reasons such considerations give us for having a theory of the unobservables. Contrast the situation in the social sciences, where instability of structural parameters is a constant threat, with the situation in many natural sciences, where either experimental control or a natural constancy enables these potential variations in the underlying structure to be disregarded.

An example from astronomy will illustrate the point. For a particle moving under the influence of an attractive inverse square force, the orbit is constrained by the two relations:

(5)
$$(d^2/d\theta^2)\frac{1}{r} + \frac{1}{r} = GM/C^2$$

(6)
$$r^2\dot{\theta} = C = r_0v_0 \sin \omega_0 \, ,$$

where G is the universal gravitation constant, M is the mass of the central body, and C is the angular momentum per unit mass. The solution to these equations, as is well known, is a conic section, and its exact form is determined by the condition:

$$r_0v_0^2 < 2GM \quad \text{orbit is an ellipse,}$$
$$r_0v_0^2 = 2GM \quad \text{orbit is a parabola,}$$
$$r_0v_0^2 > 2GM \quad \text{orbit is an hyperbola,}$$

where r_0 is the initial distance from the central force, and v_0 is the initial velocity. Ordinarily, each of the terms in the conditions is considered to be a constant, with r_0 and v_0 being initial conditions and G and M being structural parameters. What is the point of introducing such parameters as G and M when we could predict the orbit by means of a purely descriptive curve-fitting technique, much as Kepler did? There is in fact no predictive justification, because despite astronomy's position as the nonexperimental science par excellence, the stability of G and of M renders the orbit itself stable and knowledge of them predictively irrelevant. But suppose that the mass of the sun was not constant and subject to periodic changes in value. Then knowledge of the parameters in (5) and (6) would become crucially important for predicting the form of the new orbit as the structural parameters changed. Similarly, in the case of the exponential-decay law for alpha particles, the parameter λ in the distribution $P(T > t) = e^{-\lambda t}$ comes to be of predictive importance only when the structure of the atom changes by alteration of the atomic number, and in this case an explicit theoretical characterization of how λ is related to changes in the underlying structure is essential for predictive purposes.

These arguments concerning the limits of a purely observational approach to science are predictivist in form—unlike our earlier argument in §20 they do not require that explanation be part of the scientific process. As with the older discussions of the theoretician's dilemma, they suggest the indispensibility of terms referring to unobservables and the use of theories detailing the characteristics of those unobservables. But unlike those earlier arguments, they are not concerned with definability or the logical structure of scientific theories; they are instead methodological in tone. If we label as an instrumentalist position any attitude toward science which includes the assertion that the only legitimate function of science is to form predictive relationships among observables, with reference to unobservables to be avoided (at least in principle) whenever possible, then we can formulate this general principle: an instrumentalist account of theoretical parameters can be successfully implemented only when those parameters are not subject to change. The greater the degree of experimental control or lack of natural variation there is in the terms occurring in a scientific theory, the more amenable those terms are to an instrumentalist treatment. Conversely, the less the degree of experimental control and the greater the degree of natural variation there is within a system, the more realistically we have to construe the terms referring to unobservables. We thus have as a (contingent) consequence that the structures occurring in the social sciences are not as amenable to an instrumentalist interpretation as are structures in the natural sciences.

This relationship between stability and instrumentalism is, perhaps, one of the reasons why instrumentalism seems to be more plausible in the case of fundamental theories. Fundamental quantities for isolated systems do not usually change in value, and one of the appealing things about universal constants is that they make further theoretical investigation unnecessary for predictive purposes. And realist arguments from the principle of the common cause will fail exactly where predictivist accounts succeed most easily. I want to emphasize that the principle of the common cause is not quite such a restricted principle as this might make it appear to be. For although unobservable common causes clearly occur below the currently accessible level of observation, because observability and manipulability are logically independent, lack of observability does not entail that we cannot change the unobservables in the required way. Indeed, we should recall that intervening variables form an important class of unobservables as well and that many such intervening variables are also common causes. Thus in many causal models involving multiple indicators and latent-structure analysis, the latent variables will be observable by means of the indicator variables of which they are the common cause, and with many psychological traits of this kind they can be affected by changes in environmental factors.

The third thing to note about the principle is that, as with our argument for the existence of an unobserved structure, it allows us no inferential conclusion other than the purely existential one that c exists. Additional information about c must come from some other source, and again that will ordinarily be existing causal knowledge. Indeed, as Suppes and Zanotti (1981) showed, a necessary and sufficient condition for there to exist such a common cause is the existence of a joint-probability distribution that is compatible with the given statistical association.[12] This result is one aspect of the trivialization problem we discussed in §18 and indicates the need for further constraints to be put on the principle, because it is so easy to construct cases of correlations between simultaneous events where no common cause could plausibly be thought to exist, as introductory texts in statistics always point out so gleefully.

§24. The Probabilistic Case

We can now draw some parallels between the relative frequentist's solution to the problem of the single case and the issues raised in §18. First, recalling the quotations cited from von Mises and Kolmogorov, we note that the post hoc partitioning of reference classes by physical factors would, in most cases, be unnecessary if the data had been generated under a complete fixed set of experimental conditions, as they suggested. Thus, if it were possible to generate frequency data on auto accidents by repeatedly sending cars into curves with worn tires, driven by youths at high speeds, the passive empiricist's partitioning would be unnecessary for infinite sequences of data (except in certain sequences that fall into the measure-zero sets for which convergence theorems fail). There are, of course, obvious practical, ethical, and epistemic reasons why the frequentist often has to rely on nonexperimental data, but the point is simply that the frequentist is retroactively trying to achieve what would, under "ideal" conditions, be achieved by experimental controls.

Second, we can now see that relative frequentists realized at an early stage of development of their theories the exact analogue of what Humean accounts of deterministic laws originally missed: that mere observation and recording of data is not enough—the data from nonexperimental contexts will rarely give us directly the correct probability or law. One might respond: I can easily think of counterexamples—a sequence of discrete decay times from an ensemble of radioactive atoms will provide us with a naturally occurring sequence of data that is already maximally specific and hence contains the correct relative frequency for a particular elapsed time before decay. But this is only true if one has atoms which are all of the same kind, and hence the relevant generating conditions have been kept constant. Pure substances of this type rarely, if ever, occur in nature. Now let us ask the analogue of our question

---

[12] Further results along these lines are in the appendix of Suppes (1984) and Suppes and Zanotti (1984). The principle of the common cause is of particular interest for discussions of the Bell results and hidden-variable theories. There is now an enormous literature on this topic and to go into it would be inappropriate here.

in §20: Why do we ordinarily need to impose experimental controls (or their statistical surrogates) in order for the correct probability law to manifest itself?

Consider in this regard a very "clean" example, that of radioactive alpha decay. Suppose that we first isolate (separately) two radioactive species, 1 and 2 (say on the basis of their masses), and empirically find the emission of alpha particles falls under the empirical regularities $A_t^1 = A_0^1 e^{-\lambda_1 t}$ and $A_t^2 = A_0^2 e^{-\lambda_2 t} =$, where A_t^i is the activity of species i at time t. Suppose also that the decay rates for the two species are different, say $\lambda_1 = 5\lambda_2$. Plotting A_t against t on semilogarithmic axes will thus give us linear relationships between time and activity for each species. Then we go out into the world and discover that type-1 and type-2 species are always found naturally mixed together. The observed activity outside the laboratory is:

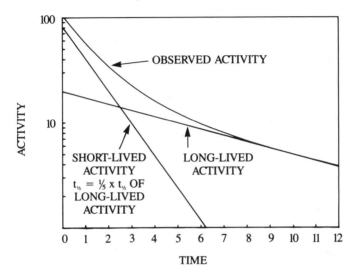

A Two-Component Decay Curve

Reproduced with permission from J. G. Cuninghame, *Introduction to the Atomic Nucleus* (Amsterdam: Elsevier Science Publishers, Physical Sciences and Engineering Division), p. 65.

Question: what has happened to the law for type-1s alone? Does it apply when the material is embedded in a mixture of type-1s and type-2s? The Humean will have to say that it has been replaced by a new law, for the type-1 regularity is not observed in the mixture. Yet this is a peculiar claim to make, for if the new law applies universally to all decay events occurring within the mixture, then the mere imposition of a simple experimental control consisting of removing the type-2 atoms will result in not only a change in the law covering type-1 atoms but (consequently) a change in the probability for decay of these very type-1 atoms. Thus, even though alpha decay is notoriously impervious to attempts to alter it (resisting enormous changes in pressure, temperature, chemical potential, and so on), the mere removal of type-2 atoms can achieve it—a remarkable feat, given that even relative frequentists will agree that atoms decay independently of one another.

Under the realist's construal, in constrast, because the experimental law is not identified with the observed regularity itself and because the observed regularity is the product of structural features manifesting themselves under controlled conditions, we can claim that the ability to produce the law is still there. Indeed, because this is an unusual situation, we can claim more—that the law is in fact manifesting itself, even though it is not identical with the Humean regularity in the uncontrolled case. The reason for this is the afore-mentioned remarkable invariance of alpha decay under changes of external conditions and the additional assumption that the two species decay indepen-dently of one another (i.e., neither is a decay product of the other, and emission of particles from one species does not induce decay by irradiation in the other). Thus the type-1 species actually *is* following its own activity law outside the artificial conditions, even though, if we observe only the presence or absence of alpha particles (and not, say, their energies), there will be no way to decompose the observed convex relation into two linear relationships on the basis of observational data alone.

It must immediately be acknowledged that the appearance of a new regu-larity by virtue of controlling some physical factor entails neither that the regularity is a law nor that the factor used is causally responsible for the emergence of the regularity, for we might have used a factor, such as the characteristic spectrum of the atom, to select out the type-1 atoms, rather than using a centrifuge. The causal factor operative in the latter technique happens to be closely related to a key feature of the structural basis of the chance (the atomic weight of the atoms), whereas in the former it is not. In order to establish that we do have a genuine cause, we need to impose a condition that is a stronger version of our Assumption 2 of §13.

§25. Mill's Unconditionality Requirement

In *A System of Logic,* Mill argued that the distinguishing characteristic of a causal sequence was its unconditionality, this characteristic being exactly what is meant by a cause necessitating its effect: "That which is necessary, that which *must* be, means that which will be, whatever supposition we may make in regard to all other things" ([(1843) 1874], bk. 3, chap. 5, §6).

With some clarification about what the scope of the 'unconditionality' re-striction requires, this principle is indeed a necessary condition for something to be a cause. In order to do this, one does not need to construe it, as Mill did, as a criterion of causal necessitation. For the legacy of Hume's problem is to provide some way of distinguishing between genuinely causal sequences and mere associations, and although the pretender to that role for Hume and his descendants was some form of necessity, we should not be bound to necessity as the only kind of possible distinguishing feature. For, using our terminology, we can see that the kind of contribution required of a cause by Hume and Mill was the strongest possible one, that a cause necessitates its effect. This linkage between causation and necessitation still has a strong grip on the philosophical mind, but if one has any sympathy at all for causes that contribute in other ways to their effects, it is foolish to require that necessitation be a requirement for causation.

We may adapt Mill's insight to our own requirements in the following way. Take any singular sequence BA for which it is claimed that B increased the chance of A, yet there are other circumstances X within which a B-type event is not followed by an increase in the chance of an A-type event. Then in those circumstances in which a B-type event does raise the chance of an A-type event, including, by hypothesis, our sequence BA, it was not B simpliciter that increased the chance of A but B together with the absence of X or the absence of certain elements of X. Thus the original assertion that it was B that raised the chance of A is wrong at worst, misleading at best, and it should be sharpened to include the nonoccurrence of X or some part of X. Hence in order to correctly claim that B increased the chance of A and by virtue of this was a contributing cause of A, B must be such that it produces the increase invariantly, or 'unconditionally', as Mill put it. This is an argument directed not at how we speak of causes or how we should represent them but at the very way in which factors bring about their effects.

It might appear that this argument, by emphasizing the sufficiency of B in increasing the chance of A, is at odds with the indeterminism that motivates probabilistic causality. Yet as I emphasized in §14, chance itself has no causal role, and if B indeterministically increases the chance of A, then the two components of chance that compose that sequence can be combined into a single component.[13] This argument is also at odds with ordinary modes of speech, within which components of the total cause are often singled out as 'a cause' or even 'the cause' of an effect (not *the* effect—causes generally have multiple effects too). There is no objection, in principle, to calling one member of the collection that makes up an invariant cause a 'causal factor', or even, more loosely, 'a cause' of the effect, as long as it is understood that these are not genuine contributing (or counteracting) causes. For we are concerned, as I mentioned in §2, not with ordinary modes of speech but with what causes what, and such selective talk belongs in the realm of pragmatics, not ontology. (Elements of pragmatics are discussed in §41.)

---

[13] Probability distributions in which the parameters themselves have chance distributions yield probability distributions, as, for example, in the compound Poisson distribution. (See n. 2, this chapter.)

Raising the chance does not entail increasing the relative frequency because statistical fluctuations in the short run may decrease the frequency, and much less likely, in fact with zero probability measure, this may happen in the infinite long run. Relative frequencies need to be linked to chance by statistical testing techniques rather than being taken as constitutive of the probabilities themselves. Separating the two, and remembering the comparison built into the characterization of a contributing cause, enables us to dispose of an obvious objection. If a contributing and counteracting cause are operating simultaneously on a system, the relative frequency may well, if the counteracting cause is strong enough to outweigh the contributing cause, actually be lower than when neither is present. In such a case, how can the contributing cause invariantly increase the chance? Because the comparison is between the case with both present and the case where the contributing cause is reduced to zero, all else, including the counteracting cause, remains as it is.

Thus we have, in the case of singular causation, the following definition:

> B is a *direct contributing cause* of A just in case
>   (i) A occurs;
>   (ii) B occurs;
>   (iii) B increases the chance of A in all circumstances Z that are
>   physically compatible with A and B, and with A and B_0,
>   where B_0 is the neutral state of $\mathcal{B}$, i.e., $P(A/BZ) > P(A/B_0Z)$ for all such Z; and
>   (iv) BZ and A are logically independent.[14]
> Similarly, B is a *direct counteracting cause* of A just in case (i),
> (ii), (iii), and (iv) hold, with 'increases' replaced by 'decreases' and
> with the inequality reversed.

This definition, although applicable to singular causal sequences, appears to go much beyond the actual singular circumstances by virtue of the unconditionality requirement. But on any occasion in which B is a genuine contributing cause of A, all the elements required to contribute to A are present in B, even though many of these elements are the absence of confounding factors. Indeed, singular sequences must be causally self-contained, for it is entirely contingent whether that sequence is embedded in a regularity. To allow that a given sequence is causal because there exist multiple replicas, many far removed in space and time, none having any causal effect on the original, and most of them nonactual, whereas that very same sequence, were it to have occurred in isolation, would then have been deemed noncausal, seems absurd. For a singular sequence to be causal entails that there be an unconditional, hence universal, regularity. Our account is thus quite different from

---

[14] This last condition is designed to rule out the kinds of dependence detailed in Kim (1973b). It also precludes B from being A itself.

those that provide a definition of causes 'in the circumstances'. The need to impose this modifier is closely tied to the pragmatic aspects of ceteris paribus conditions and counterfactual claims, which are discussed in §41. Causal generalizations are thus universalizations of singular causal sequences (these generalizations themselves inheriting the unconditionality of their constituents). The quantification is over event types, where event types are the possession of properties by systems and where it is irrelevant at what time these possessions take place. Thus, event types are not abstract entities but substructures of spatially located events (which play causal roles). For example, each batch of gas that I put in the tank is subtly different, but if the contaminants are causally inert, the benzene structure is the event type which is the causal factor in this case.

It must be emphasized that the causal generalization is an inductively inferred entity, and the direction of justification is from the singular to the general. The singular sequence does not acquire its causal nature by conforming to a regularity. Nor must it be assumed that every singular causal sequence is part of a regularity. There may be genuinely singular phenomena in the world that are beyond the reach of scientific investigation.[15] Nor is it assumed that everything has a cause; some event(s) may be genuinely capricious in that nothing affects the chance of their occurring. If this is so, such an event has no causal explanation. It may have some other kind of explanation, but such lie outside the scope of this book.

The definition is not intended to be used as a criterion—at best the definiens may serve as a set of falsification conditions for a causal claim, with whatever statistical methods are appropriate being used to link the single-case chances with relative frequencies. Nor can we stipulate a priori what is physically compatible with a given factor. The invariance requirement goes well beyond the universalization of the singular claim and includes many nonactual situations. But it is the world and the way it is that determines what is compatible with a factor, not a formal semantics of possible worlds or a mental construction. The testability of the invariance condition by experiment is crucial— that aspect of scientific empiricism we respect—but our realism about the physical basis of chances need not extend to a realism about dispositional properties or unactualized possibilities.

§26. Consequences

We have said that a direct contributing cause unconditionally increases the chance of the effect. No restrictions were placed on the temporal relations

---

[15] Not all unique phenomena are of this kind—accidental confluences of otherwise well-understood phenomena can be scientifically explained, and the early stages of the evolution of the universe are unique on noncyclic models of cosmogony.

between B, A, and Z. Suppose some element C of Z occurs temporally between B and A and renders B probabilistically irrelevant, as would be the case if C were part of a causal chain between B and A. Then B would not be a *direct* cause of A in that chain (although there might be some other chain in which it is a direct cause) because of the defeating C. But are there not always such intervening events when we insist on a detailed specification of the system? No, because to assert that there are is to require the existence of a continuous (causal) process between any cause and effect, and this appears not to be true of many indeterministic systems, since indeterministic state transitions can be temporally discontinuous. If B is a probabilistic contributing cause of A, B affects the chance basis of the system. A, then, when it occurs, *just happens*, which has the consequence that once B affects the chance, there is nothing more causally to be said regarding A, given that the chance of A remains static, at $P(A/BZ)$. There are, of course, dynamically evolving chance distributions, and their evolution may be continuously affected by causal factors. Yet even this does not by itself preclude B from being a direct cause of A, because if B makes its contribution to the chance of A and the other factors contribute independently of B, in the sense that B's contribution is invariant, then even if the chance distribution continues to evolve by virtue of those other factors, B has directly contributed to the chance of A. Thus if there is an increase in the money supply in October, which is then held constant, and if there is an increase in inflation in December after a fall in the international value of the currency in November, that fall being produced by factors other than the October money-supply increase, then the October event contributed, probabilistically, to the December event.[16]

By comparison, the fact that a completed process connects cause with effect does not mean that inevitably the probability of the effect steadily increases until, right before it occurs, it has the value 1. This does indeed hold for some processes, but to believe it true in general is to fall prey to a "chicken counter's fallacy" in which an incorrect image of the causal process heading toward the effect's fixed point of occurrence plays a large role. The (conditional) probability of the effect can easily decrease, as can be seen by considering a process in which E becomes progressively more probable, yet $-E$ eventually occurs. The (conditional) probability of the effect can also stay constant across time. Thus an indeterministic effect can be uncertain right up to the point at which it actually occurs and so is not overdetermined, even when multiple causal influences are present. This shows that chances will change discontinuously, as we noted above, because right up to the time an event occurs it can have a probability of less than 1, yet at the moment it

---

[16] This example is simplified, of course, at least to the extent of shortening the lag between cause and effect, and it is likely, I suppose, that there are more direct effects of the factors cited than an increase in inflation. If so, use those.

does occur, the chance changes to unity. Indeed, this discontinuity is a necessary feature of indeterminism. Take any nonzero, nonunity value of chance $P(A/B) = p$. It must be possible for A to occur when $p < 1$, otherwise A would be impossible and $P(A/B) = 0$. Hence at any point where $p < 1$, A can occur, and when it does, $p = 1$.

One reason why we do tend to believe the truth of the chicken counter's fallacy in actual systems is the fact that they are not isolated. The contingent sufficiency of the cause for the effect means that as time goes by, the chances of a counteracting intervention from outside the system preventing the effect from occurring becomes progressively less, and so the probability of the effect increases.

One might want to cast all this in terms of lack of intervening factors relative to our current state of causal knowledge. If so, all the better, in the sense of widening the number of causes considered direct. Then one will have to alter the terminology accordingly, to make factors direct contributing causes relative to epistemic state K. There is no objection to that, but that it can be done illustrates the point that epistemic versions of ontic theories are easy to construct, but not vice versa, which is why, when possible, the ontic forms are to be preferred.

This discussion presupposes that causal processes are Markov—i.e., later states in a process, when they exist, render earlier states probabilistically irrelevant. Non-Markov processes can arise in two ways: when there is action at a temporal distance, or when there is another causal path between the indirect cause and the effect that bypasses the direct cause. If the former exists, then direct causes are more common than standardly allowed. If it does exist, there is not much evidence for it.[17] With the latter, one can

---

[17] As opposed, perhaps, to action at a spatial distance, which some hold is exhibited in the experimental arrangements designed to test Bell's inequality. A caution: temporal action at a distance is not what was discussed earlier, for in each of our examples, the system S preserves the chance at the value it was raised to by B. In Collingwood (1940), it is argued that imposing Mill's condition of unconditional causation logically entails that action at a distance is impossible. This is wrong and results from the same confusion of physical possibility with logical possibility that led Russell (1913) to claim that the contiguity requirement in causation was incoherent. We can include *all* the "conditiones sine quibus non" upon which Collingwood insists, but this does *not* mean that we must describe the whole process up to and including the effect. Whatever action at a distance is, it may well be that between times t_1 and t_2, or space points x_1 and x_2, it is physically impossible, given the way the world is, for anything to intervene to prevent C at $t_1(x_1)$ from causing E at a distance at $t_2(x_2)$. We need to keep separate, of course, singular causal claims and causal generalizations. In the first case, it may be that as a matter of (physically contingent) fact, there are no counteracting causes "near enough" to prevent C from causing E. In the case of generalizations, we cannot use that specific contingent fact—it has to be a matter of general law that in all circumstances, when C is at $t_1(x_1)$, then nothing can (physically) intervene to prevent E at $t_2(x_2)$. This is not all that difficult to achieve. Suppose that it is a nomic fact that gravity cannot be shielded. Then whatever happened between x_1 and x_2, a gravitating body at x_1 would have its effect on x_2.

reduce each path to a chain having the Markov property and can proceed as above.

Next consider factors that occur after the effect A. Ordinarily, by the time such factors have occurred, A has occurred and has its chance fixed at unity, precluding anything from contributing further. Hence the chance of A will remain invariant across all later events. If, however, one is inclined to conjecture that time-reversed causation might occur, so that it makes some difference to A whether a later event E occurs or not, then those later events must be treated, mutatis mutandis, as are earlier events.

What of factors that occur at any time but are causally irrelevant to A? Z can include all these, for they make no difference. Vary any of those factors F, and the chance of A remains as it was. Hence one may as well condition on noncausal factors as well. One might find correlations between F and A, but that is a quite separate matter, and one for experimental and statistical methodologies to deal with, rather than a philosophical analysis.

What if B is both a direct and an indirect cause of A?[18] To see that our definition correctly classifies B as a direct cause in these cases, consider the most problematical situation, one where B also causes C, which is a counteracting cause of A.

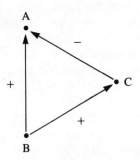

To make this case concrete, we can think in terms of the administration of a drug (B) that has a moderate success rate in promoting survival (A) in all individuals, by virtue of destroying an infectious agent. In some individuals, however, B also produces a high toxicity level (C) that counteracts survival in the individual so affected. Dexter is such an individual, is given the drug, and survives. Was B a direct contributing cause in this case? Yes, because $P(A/BC) > P(A/B_0C)$ and $P(A/BC_0) > P(A/B_0C_0)$, where we have assumed B and C are the only causally relevant factors, and we have here relaxed the detailed specification of A to classify it merely as a survival, rather than a survival with toxic side effects (which would rule C a contributing cause of *that* A'). The second inequality is of particular importance: it says that the

---

[18] This kind of situation is discussed in Otte (1985), pp. 121–22, as a counterexample to Cartwright's theory.

drug increased the chance of survival over not administering the drug, when the high toxicity levels are absent in both cases. The requirement that BZ be nomologically possible means that when B is sufficient for C, the second inequality does not apply (see §27C for further discussion). When B is insufficient for C, the test case of BC_0 can arise naturally or by some other means of preventing C. And this affirmative answer is correct, for the drug did directly contribute to survival, even though its side effects also counteracted that very survival. It is true that, as a policy decision, we may want to avoid giving B to Dexter, for in toto, the sum of the direct and indirect effects of B may decrease Dexter's chances of survival, but given that he did survive, the drug contributed to it.

What if he had died? Then B would have been a direct counteracting cause of death, as well as an indirect contributing cause (this last presupposes a position on transitivity of causes that is proved in appendix 3).

A number of further consequences immediately follow from adopting the invariance condition. First, as already mentioned, causal generalizations are simply universal generalizations of the type versions of singular causal claims. For every instance of an A-type event **A** and a B-type event **B**, the propensity of **A** conditional on **B** exceeds the propensity of **A** conditional on **B**$_0$.

Second, the invariance condition requires us to adopt a fallibilistic attitude toward causal claims. It is hard to confirm causal assertions and relatively easy to falsify them.[19]

Third, when the invariance condition is satisfied, the Z in $P(A/BZ) > P(A/B_0Z)$ will contain factors that, at most, affect the value of the propensity and not the direction of the inequality. Thus, we may drop Z in the specification of P itself, allowing that P need not be the true propensity associated with A. Thus we need not conditionalize on *all* causal factors to arrive at a claim of probabilistic causality, but merely on the causal defeaters.

Fourth, the invariance condition ranges not just over all other factors that are "held fixed,"[20] but over all other factors, fixed or varying, subject only

---

[19] Suppes notes that with this kind of invariance condition, "there is no end to the analysis of data in a practical sense" ([1984], §1). True enough, if 'practical' were replaced by 'mathematical', but it is exactly the kind of highly refined knowledge about what can and cannot sensibly be considered a causal influence that is possessed by scientists immersed in the practical aspects of a causal theory. Suppes himself, of course, has frequently insisted that one should pay attention to this kind of detailed knowledge of the working scientist, and it is surely entirely appropriate to appeal to it here. It is worth noting that a failure of Mill's condition is a failure of what Campbell and Stanley (1963) call 'external validity'.

[20] E.g., Cartwright (1979) and Skyrms (1980). What is meant by "held fixed" is unclear in both those accounts. Cartwright, for example, says, "A cause must increase the probability of its effects—but only in situations where such correlations [with other causal factors] are absent. The most general situations in which a particular factor is not correlated with any other causal factors are situations in which all other causal factors are held fixed" ([1979], p. 423). According to Skyrms, $\Pr(E/C \& B_i) \geq \Pr(E/-C \& B_i)$, for all "maximal conjunctions of [causally] relevant

to the constraints already mentioned. This follows from our use of chances rather than relative frequencies.

Fifth, if there exists a sufficient condition S for A that was absent on the occasion in question, then its absence must be included in the specification of the cause on that occasion, for in the situation(s) in which S is present, B cannot contribute to the chance of A. (I note here that Skyrms's condition is not subject to this, since he allows a weak inequality in the invariance condition, but Cartwright's is.) Similarly, if a necessary condition D exists for A and if D was present on that occasion, then its presence will have to be part of the cause, for otherwise, on an occasion where it is absent, there can be no contributing *or* counteracting causes.

Sixth, the conditioning factors Z cannot be a Carnapian state description, nor can it be a mere logical conjunction of causal factors, because some causal factors may preclude the presence of others. The conjunction is over what is physically possible.

§27. Further Discussion

The kinds of invariance conditions we have discussed have been widely used in probability and probabilistic causality, with such features as maximal specificity conditions,[21] objective homogeneity requirements,[22] and randomness criteria[23] all employing versions of probabilistic invariance. Skyrms (1977) used a 'resiliency' condition applied to subjective probabilities in order to analyze the relations between propensities and subjective probabilities and then extended this resiliency idea to causal relations in Skyrms (1980).[24] For reasons I have tried to give in some detail, the difficulties that are associated with the trivialization problem (difficulties which led Skyrms to adopt pragmatic criteria within his subjective theory of probability) do not arise once one has insisted on the physical nature of chances and abandoned the formal mode of treatment. For somewhat different reasons, Cartwright (1979) employs a frequency-based principle of relevance invariance to arrive at a theory of probabilistic causal generalizations. But again, valuable as that theory is, by remaining at the level of frequencies, it misplaces the level at which the invariance condition must be applied for causal purposes. In order to see how

---

background factors" B_i, where for at least one B_i, the strict inequality holds ([1980], pp. 107–8). Thus it is left unclear whether the B_i represent causally relevant factors that are experimentally controlled so as to remove their influence or causally relevant factors that are present in an open system.

[21] See, e.g., Hempel (1968) and Fetzer (1981) for examples of these.

[22] E.g., Salmon (1984), chap. 3.

[23] See citations given in §18.

[24] Skyrms gives full credit there to Mill, although his own theory is, of course, a significant and original development of the basic idea.

the present theory deals with problems that persist in the area of probabilistic causality, we must show that it can provide an adequate solution for each such problem. The following list covers an assortment of problems not dealt with elsewhere in the book, with an emphasis on how the probabilistic theory can avoid difficulties at the limit of 0 and 1 chances. The emphasis is deliberate, for probabilistic theories of causation frequently break down at the very point of connection with classical deterministic theories, and as I have mentioned earlier, one of the themes of this book is to emphasize the continuities between the two theories. The list is by no means exhaustive, but I hope that it is representative.

A. SPURIOUS CAUSATION

Here the problem is the existence of correlations between joint effects of a common cause, these correlations being induced by variations in that common cause. (Recall the discussion of §23 of common causes.) The standard solution is to show that the two effects become statistically independent when the probabilities are conditioned on the common cause (see §23 conditions (1)–(4) for the simplest case of this). This technique, however, is simply a representation of an experiment in which the common cause is controlled, variations occur in the two effects (since the situation is probabilistic), and variations in one effect do not alter the probability of the other (e.g., (1) of §23 is equivalently $P(A/BC) = P(A/-BC)$, so that changes from B to $-B$ do not alter the chance of A when c is fixed at C, and similarly for c fixed at $-C$ in (2)).[25] Thus the experiment demonstrates that our invariance condition for probabilistic causality is violated because there is a set of circumstances Z, which here consists of fixing C, within which B does not contribute to the chance of A, and hence B cannot be a cause of A.

There is one extremal case of spurious causation that our theory is unable to deal with. It is the situation

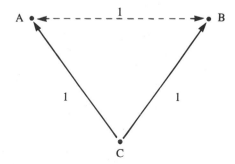

---

[25] I use $-B$ here rather than B_0, merely as a notational convenience.

where C is nomologically necessary and sufficient for both A and B. Then the conditioning factors B_0C and BC_0 are nomologically impossible, and the comparisons $P(A/BC)$ with $P(A/BC_0)$ and $P(A/B_0C)$ with $P(A/B_0C_0)$, at least one of which is needed to classify C as a cause of A, are not possible. (We assume that all other factors Z in $P(A/BCZ)$ etc. are irrelevant.) Thus although the theory gives $P(A/(BC)Z) > P(A/(BC)_0\ Z)$ and thus allows BC as a contributing cause, this is incorrect, for it is C that causes A, and B is causally irrelevant.

It seems that we must introduce other criteria into these cases where events are not just perfectly correlated but nomologically inseparable. Although one could resolve the difficulty by restricting the scope to properly probabilistic situations in which no conditional probabilities have value unity, this would be unwise, for it would indicate an essential difference between the probabilistic and deterministic cases that arises from a deficiency in the theory, rather than an objective difference in nature. It would be natural to appeal to the existence of a connecting process between C and A, and the absence of such a process between B and A, as a criterion that provides the correct answer in this case. However, for reasons that are spelled out in §32, I do not think that a process-based approach to causality is itself entirely satisfactory. I would also note that such nomologically inseparable triads of events are rarely found in practice. It is almost always possible to break the correlation between A and B while leaving C as a cause of A. Nevertheless, this is a problem case for the present approach.

B. The Apparent Negative Relevance
of Contributing Causes

A problem initially raised by Hesslow (1976) seemed to indicate that factors we should ordinarily consider to be contributing causes of an effect could, in certain cases, bear negative frequency relations to that effect. The example used by Hesslow was a population of women, some of whom were taking birth control pills. Although estrogen birth control pills do increase the chance of thrombosis, they reduce the frequency of pregnancy, which itself increases the chance of thrombosis to a much stronger degree. Hence, if one looks at relative frequency data, the frequency of thrombosis among women taking birth control pills may be lower than the frequency of thrombosis among those who do not. The solution to this prima facie problem is now widely agreed upon, and results from not controlling for the other relevant factor (the pregnancy or lack thereof). When such a controlled (or stratified) experiment is performed, we have

Prob (Thromb/b.c. pills, pregnancy) >
Prob (Thromb/b.c. pills$_0$, pregnancy),

Prob (Thromb/pregnancy, b.c. pills) >
  Prob (Thromb/pregnancy$_0$, b.c. pills),
Prob (Thromb/b.c. pills, pregnancy$_0$) >
  Prob (Thromb/b.c. pills$_0$, pregnancy$_0$),
Prob (Thromb/pregnancy, b.c. pills$_0$) >
  Prob (Thromb/pregnancy$_0$, b.c. pills$_0$),

which, given that in our simplified example pregnancy and birth control pills are the only two relevant factors, means that both factors satisfy our invariance requirement. Moreover, given the invariance condition, it is true that taking birth control pills is a contributing cause of thrombosis for each individual that does take them (but not taking them is not a counteracting cause of thrombosis—it is not a cause of any kind because it is the neutral state of estrogen levels) and in the population as a whole.

C. SUFFICIENT CAUSES

Consider a sequence $C \to B \to A$, where C is sufficient for B and B is positively relevant to A. Then, as Otte (1981) notes, $P(A/BC) = P(A/C)$, and Otte takes this to show that B is a spurious cause of A. Recall, however, that in our theory we need to compare $P(A/BC)$ with $P(A/B_0C)$, not with $P(A/C)$, and since B_0C is nomologically impossible because C is nomologically sufficient for B, B_0C will not be part of the invariance conditions. So B is not ruled out as a cause by the presence of a sufficient antecedent. This also avoids the problem that if every prior cause in the chain leading to B is sufficient for its effect and there is no first member, then there would be no cause of A if B were not it. (For this objection see Rosen [1980], p. 78, although there she considers only the case where B is also sufficient for A.)

Because we have motivations for adopting the specific contrast case B_0 that are independent of the present issue, this is not an ad hoc device to avoid a potential problem. But perhaps something more needs to be said on this score. Recall that probabilistic causality is a comparative relation and that the experimental method that is the ideal test criterion for a causal relation requires that B must contribute to A, in that a change in $\mathcal{B}$ from B_0 to B must result invariably in an increase in the chance of A. Now, assuming C is genuinely sufficient for B, in order to assess the chance of A in the absence of B, we must remove C as well. If C is not also necessary for B, and $P(B) < 1$, then one can, in principle, construct a test case with B present and C absent and with B absent and C absent. If in that test case B raises the chance of A, that is prima facie evidence that B is a contributing cause of A. We require, of course, by the invariance condition, that there be no case in which B does not raise the chance of A. But cases in which C is present are not of that kind because to change B in those cases also requires changing $\mathcal{C}$ from C to C_0.

So nomologically we cannot have evidence that a change from B_0 to B fails to raise the chance of A with C present, and it is thus inadmissible as a counterexample. If C is necessary as well as sufficient for B, then even the test case that would lead to B's being a prima facie candidate as a cause cannot separate B's role from C's role, and we have a case of nomologically perfectly correlated factors, which was discussed in a somewhat different context in part A above.

In a second example, Otte ([1981], p. 173) considers two sufficient causes operating in independent causal chains:

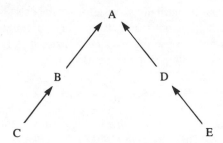

where the specific example is throwing a rock (C) that hits a window (B) and the window shatters (A), where a little later than C's occurrence, a shot is fired (E) that hits the window (D) simultaneously with the rock. Then,

$$P(A/CE) = P(A/C_0E) = 1,$$
$$P(A/CE) = P(A/CE_0) = 1,$$
$$P(A/BD) = P(A/B_0D) = 1,$$
$$P(A/BD) = P(A/BD_0) = 1,$$

and hence according to the probabilistic criterion, none of the displayed events are causes of A.[26] But that is exactly as it should be. This is a classic case of overdetermination of the effect A (see §7, but modulo the underdescribed effect, see §37), and so any theory that singles out any of these antecedents should be suspect. (Perhaps calling them 'spurious' is misleading, but we have not employed that terminology.)

If, as Otte does (ibid., p. 174), one changes the example so that D occurs slightly before B, then we no longer have overdetermination, but a clear case of D's causing A. Recall our ontology (§12), within which there is a system upon which the causal factors act. Without that system, there is no effect event. If the window has been shattered by the bullet's momentum by the

---

[26] Since Otte's example is directed at Suppes' definition of spurious₁, he concludes that that definition allows C, the earliest event, as the only nonspurious cause.

time of arrival of the rock's momentum, there is nothing for that second momentum to act on. So B cannot be a cause of A, properly interpreted.[27]

Similar considerations apply when B is insufficient for A but D is sufficient for A.[28] Then there is no reason to count B as a cause of A, since D already determines A, and B is thus irrelevant.

D. INEVITABLE EVENTS

Davis (1988), p. 142, raises the point that inevitable events, having a probability of 1, cannot be caused under probabilistic theories. That is correct, but they should not be caused under any theory, if what is meant by 'inevitable' is that nothing makes or can make a difference to whether they occur. This is surely the case with logically inevitable events.[29] Hence our principle gives the correct answer here. Moreover, crudely characterized physically inevitable events such as 'dying' are not the subject matter of the theory. When we want to explain why a man died, we are asking for an explanation of why he died in the specific way he did, and the method of detailed specification of events (§37) ensures that x's dying of Y is not unconditionally inevitable. Even the vague question, "Why do people die?" is properly construed as asking why all people die eventually, and if not a request for all possible fatal conditions, is asking the deep question of why human physiology has a finite, determinate, upper bound on its functioning.

A related problem affects inevitable events as potential causes, because when $P(C) = 1$, $P(E/C) = P(E)$. Here we should ask how C acquires the probability of 1. If it is made inevitable by an earlier event that is sufficient for C, so that $P(C)$ is actually a conditional probability $P(C/D) = 1$, then this reduces to the cases discussed in the previous section. Are there any cases of (not yet occurrent) singular events having a unit chance of occurring that do not fall into the categories of the last paragraph above? We might say that a gas coming into thermal equilibrium with its surroundings is one such case, yet this is conditional on the absence of an adiabatic wall. By inserting one, it would be possible to test the contribution of the thermal equilibrium to

[27] Otte ([1981], p. 175) also notes the method of detailed description of events (see §37) as a response to this example. I add that, given that Otte's events are time subscripted, the rock has no propensity to break the window at t, the time it is broken by the shot, even though it would have a propensity of 1 to break it at $t + e$, were the window still intact. Although Otte's examples do not serve as counterexamples to my theory, I do not in the least dispute his conclusion that probabilistic relations alone cannot provide for an adequate theory of causation.

[28] See, e.g., Cartwright (1979), p. 428; Otte (1985), p. 113. Note that, although they are concerned with generalizations rather than singular causal sequences, the remarks made here still apply.

[29] To have such, we should need logical compounds and must attach the predicate 'occurs'. Thus the 'event' of its either raining in Charlottesville on June 6, 1988, or its not raining there and then is, in terms of occurrence, logically inevitable.

whatever event it was claimed to cause, say the particular reading of a thermometer. What then of the internal thermal equilibrium of a gas enclosed within such an adiabatic container? Is that not such a sure-fire event? Practically, yes.[30] But what could it be a cause of, given that it is a thermally isolated system? Erasure of skepticism about the laws of thermodynamics in a student perhaps, but it can contribute to that conditional only on other circumstances being appropriate, and C by itself will not be a cause. And then it begins to seem that C by itself can lead only to an event internal to the isolated system, rather as the heat death of the universe could not cause anything outside itself. These considerations lead me to believe that *unconditional* chances of 1 are not of causal importance and that it is only the case of sufficient antecedents, with which we have already dealt, that is of concern.

E. POTENTIALLY OVERDETERMINING EVENTS

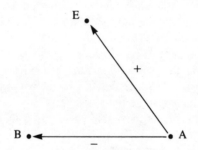

Suppose that the factor A is sufficient for E and is also sufficient to preclude B (and/or any process leading from B to E). If A is absent, then B occurs and is itself sufficient for E. Cases cited here are a back-up perfect assassin (B) who goes into action if and only if the primary perfect assassin (A) does not show up. All agree that A causes E and that B does not, when, as in the above figure, A occurs. A and B are the only causal candidates. Note that AB and A_0B_0 are impossible, given the causal structure of the situation as stated, and hence $P(E/AZ) = 1 > P(E/A_0Z) = 0$, since neither B nor B_0 will be included in Z. Hence A is a cause of E. Furthermore, B is not a cause of E because it failed to occur and hence violates clause (ii) of the definition in §25. What if A does not *preclude B*, but on this occasion A occurs and B happens not to, but might have. Then A is not the cause of E, as it occurred, but AB_0 is, for if AB had occurred, E would have been overdetermined and hence would have been different, or if the same, causal attribution is not possible. We have, in the case of AB_0, $P(E/AB_0Z) = 1 > P(E/(AB_0)_0Z = 0$

---

[30] Leaving aside the 1 in $10^{10^{19}}$ chance of its spontaneously performing the work of Maxwell's demon.

for all Z compatible with AB_0, $(AB_0)_0$. (Note: see §15 on neutral states of compound events for an explanation of why $(AB_0)_0 = A_0B_0$.)

F. Noncausal Necessary Factors

The example of an individual's birth being necessary for his death, yet not causing it, can be avoided within our theory because our event ontology requires the existence of a permanent carrier of properties. Thus the neutral state of being born, which presumably is not being born, is, given the kind of individual we are, physically incompatible with one's existence. Thus, since the existence of the system is always part of Z in our definition of a direct cause, the comparison of the chance of death conditional on being born cannot be compared with the chance of death conditional on not being born, and hence clause (iii) is not satisfied in our definition. If there were two kinds of individuals—one that had existed always up to now and then died, and ordinary humans who are born and then die—but were otherwise identical and so the presupposition of being born is not part of an individual's existence, we should have to argue that the birth in the second kind of individual contributed nothing to the probability of death in a given year, compared with the contrast case of the infinitely old but mortal individuals. Were they not structurally identical, one could still assert that for a given individual, qua second kind of individual, the birth was a precondition of the system's existence. Other examples involving such necessary conditions of existence can be dealt with in a parallel fashion.

G. The Frequency-Dependent Causation Problem

Elliott Sober (1982) raised the following problem for Giere's (1980) theory of causation. To alter one of his examples slightly, consider a population of butterflies that includes many true members and a few mimics. The true members have an offensive taste (which is lacking in the mimics) that results in birds' refraining from eating them. Mimicking the wing patterns of the true species enables the mimics also to avoid being eaten. Giere had claimed that C is a cause of E in a population P if the probability of E would be greater if all members of P had C than if none of them did. Clearly, in a population composed entirely of mimics, mimicry would not increase the chance of survival over the case where none of the population was a mimic (in fact, it would lower it).

It might appear that a similar kind of counterexample could be raised with respect to our unconditionality criterion, for a mimic will not have its chance of survival increased under all conditions: in particular, it will not under the condition of living in a population entirely composed of other mimics. This, of course, is correct, but it serves to emphasize how the unconditionality requirement forces us to recognize that causal factors are often compound in form and to underscore the relational nature of single-case chances. Mimicry per se is not a cause of survival—it is mimicry and the environment within which the butterfly lives containing a majority that are true members. This fact has been emphasized by Fetzer (1986) in a thorough assessment of this frequency-dependent problem, and his analysis is, I think, the definitive answer to this problem.

The apparent 'population dependence' of causation is taken care of in a similar way by the relational nature of causation. If a factor F is a cause in one population but not another, that means that F is incompletely specified and that what goes into the relation includes the type, or number of members, of the specific population.

§28. The Scope of the Theory

There is one special case of "multiple causation" which deserves attention because it affects even isolated causal chains, and that is the case where an event can occur spontaneously. Spontaneity is a particularly puzzling form of aleatory activity because there appears to be nothing which we can ultimately identify as a cause of the spontaneously produced event other than a nonzero chance of its occurrence. Actual examples of this type of situation, where an event can occur either spontaneously or after being induced by some physical stimulus, are a liquid that is placed in a freezer, where it also has an infinitesimally small chance of freezing spontaneously; and a laser beam, where there is a practically negligible probability of coherent light being emitted spontaneously rather than by stimulated emission. We can, of course, provide detailed descriptions of the physical structures underlying such phenomena, but that simply pushes the spontaneity to a deeper level. Such spontaneous occurrences can be ruled out as caused under our theory of causality. The reason is simply that there is no contrast situation available with which to compare the effect of the ever-present spontaneity. Even modern treatments of 'spontaneous' occurrences which tend to attribute what was formerly spontaneous to an ineradicable residual field (as, for example, the treatment of spontaneous emission of radiation in Sakurai [1973]) appear to suffer from the same lack of a contrast case in that it is physically impossible to eliminate the zero-point field. Thus our theory does not hold to a principle of universal causation, for there is reason to believe that some events are uncaused, even in a probabilistic sense.

Does the theory of *probabilistic* contributing causes apply only to indeterministic systems, those for which the conditional chance is strictly between 0 and 1? The answer is yes. Does this severely limit the application of the theory? Not if the polemic of §10 has any force to it: the thesis that most systems are not indeterministic bears the burden of proof, and until demonstrated otherwise, the reasonable assumption is that the scope of that part of our theory is very wide indeed. Straightforward cases of sufficient causes, those that are neither overdetermining nor involved in the complex examples discussed in §27C above, also can satisfy our definition of a direct contributing cause, and so our theory is not restricted to probabilistic causes either. Further discussion of the sufficiency case is contained in §36.

§29. Causation as Inductively Defined

It is common to try to define the relation 'causes', usually by means of an explicit definition involving noncausal terminology. If this were successful (and other causal terminology could be defined in terms of this basic relation), then the logical equivalence of definiens and definiendum that an explicit definition provides would allow the elimination of causal terminology from scientific (and other) languages. Given the suspicion with which passive empiricists have traditionally viewed causation,[31] this elimination would, to them, be a significant achievement. Hence, definitions in terms of genus and differentia are common, as when extra conditions are imposed on correlations to capture the genuine (nonspurious) causal correlations, or when additional constraints are suggested to narrow counterfactual dependence to causal dependence.

This drive toward eliminability of causal terminology is interesting for philosophy of science only when motivated by epistemic or ontic concerns. Logical simplicity of a language or conceptual economy of a theory may have its aesthetic appeal, but the desire for logical aridity is not itself a compelling reason to eschew causal talk. What passive empiricists want, of course, is to reduce causal claims to an epistemic basis that provides an acceptable criteriological foundation. One can entirely sympathize with that motivation, but we ought to ask whether an explicit definition is the appropriate route for attacking the epistemological problems associated with causation and whether the criteriological basis of passive empiricism is the only one acceptable to empiricists.[32]

It is thus worth considering an alternative to providing an explicit definition of the causal relation. Suppose that we could give an inductive characterization of causation in which certain primitive cases of causation are taken as basis cases, and these primitive cases are used cumulatively to capture more complex instances of causal relations by means of clearly specified principles of

[31] For example, Carnap (1928), §165; Russell (1913); Putnam (1983).

[32] We saw in §19 that an implicit definition of probabilistic causality has its own deficiencies.

combination. By 'inductive characterization' here I mean this: certain base cases of causation are taken as primitive, uncontroversial examples of causation. Then principles of combination are given which employ cases of causation that are already accepted at a given stage of construction in order to justify the causal nature of relations at the next stage of construction. 'Inductive characterization' here is not to be taken in the sense in which it is often considered as synonymous with 'recursive definition' in logic and mathematics. In the case of recursive definitions, the constructive apparatus is finitely and completely specifiable in advance. Thus, in recursively defining the sentences of a given language, the logical operations of disjunction, negation, existential quantification, and so on are such that closure of the language under those operations is fully specified in the definition. As a criterion, these logical definitions are ideal, for they allow a completely mechanical, error-free check of whether or not a syntactic string is a sentence of a given language, as long as the set of primitive symbols is itself recursively specifiable. The inductive characterization of causation which I have in mind differs from these recursive definitions in two ways. First, there is no reason to suppose that the set of primitive causal relations can be completely or finitely specified. Second, the combination procedures are even less completely specifiable. Roughly, they will consist in our specifying that causal factors known to be relevant to the designated relation must be controlled for, and that others, known to affect causally the putative cause but not directly the putative effect, must be used to vary the putative cause between the neutral state and the causally efficacious state.

This inductive approach is closely tied to the experimental orientation toward causation that lay behind the arguments of §§20 and 21. Let us review what is needed for an experimental analysis of causation to succeed. First, we need prior causal knowledge of which variables are relevant; second, we need causal knowledge of how to vitiate the influence of all but one of them on the phenomenon under investigation; third, we need causal knowledge of how to manipulate the independent variable; fourth, we (usually) need causal knowledge of indicators to measure the influence on the dependent variable; and fifth, we need knowledge of what constitutes the neutral state of the independent variable. Some of this knowledge is quite primitive, as in knowing that high humidity causes pinewood to expand; some is moderately sophisticated, as in knowing that for light the width of diffraction fringes is inversely proportional to the width of the slit; and some is esoteric, as in knowing that heating methylsuccinic acid with chromic acid in aqueous sulfuric acid produces acetic acid. Much of this causal knowledge is theory independent, although it can readily be applied for theoretical purposes. For example, the last piece of knowledge allows the number of carbon-linked methyl groups per molecule of methylsuccinic acid (the C-methyl number) to be calculated, but the process can be characterized atheoretically (the tests for identifying the chemicals involved can all be described without referring to any sophisticated theory).

In order to use this causal knowledge, we must agree to two epistemic facts. First, that we possess elementary causal knowledge that is at least as secure as observational knowledge. I know that knocking the cup of coffee that is on my desk will cause it to fall and spill. There are, of course, circumstances in which that would not happen—it might be glued to the table, for example, but I already know the kinds of counteracting causes that would prevent it from falling, and I can check to ensure they are absent. All this elementary causal knowledge is fallible, of course, but no more so than elementary observation reports, and we must live with that. Consider how one assesses philosophical theories of causation. Is it not initially by testing them against cases where one *knows* that the relation involved is causal or not causal? And this not by virtue of what we should ordinarily say about the case, for we need to be assured that what we should ordinarily say is correct. How could the problem of distinguishing between correlations due to the effects of a common cause and correlations due to a direct causal relation ever be a problem if we did not already know, securely, cases of each? So on grounds of certainty, causal empiricism is on no less secure a basis than is classical empiricism. Second, there is nothing "occult" about this elementary causal knowledge, because we are not asserting natural necessity for the connections, only that we know some connections to be causal and others not to be, in rather a similar way that we know some experiences to be visual and others (olfactory) not to be. That is, classical empiricism's problem was that it required natural necessity to distinguish causal sequences from noncausal, and if that can distinction can be made in some way other than by postulating natural necessity, then we need not concern ourselves with such necessities.

A charge that is frequently leveled against manipulability definitions or criteria of causality is that they are circular. For example, it is pointed out that in order to manipulate the independent variable in an experiment, one needs to know that the manipulation will indeed cause the changes in that variable, rather than vice versa.[33] But this circularity is a problem only if one is using the manipulability account as the basis of an explicit definition of

---

[33] This kind of circularity charge can be found in Hausman (1986), p. 145, for example. Circularity criticisms have also been raised against Salmon's use of the mark method to distinguish genuine causal processes from pseudoprocesses (e.g., Kitcher [1985], pp. 637–38; Sober [1987], p. 254). Since marking a process ordinarily involves an (experimental) intervention in the process, a charge of *epistemic* circularity could be avoided by appeal to the arguments of this section. It would not, however, avoid a charge of *ontic* circularity, if the motivation of the mark method was to reduce causal processes to a noncausal category of markability. I am not sure whether that reductionist motivation is what Salmon intends.

the universal term 'causes' or as a criteriological definition of the universal. Because our concern is with distinguishing causal from noncausal sequences, there is no circularity of the first kind involved here, and there is no epistemic circularity within the cumulative account I have suggested. There is no circularity involved if one causal relation is used as a ground for asserting the existence of, or knowledge of, another, different causal relation, and that is exactly what is involved in the manipulability approach. To assess whether a dimmer switch going to the left is a cause of the light bulb's dimming, I may need to know that it is my hand's rotation that is causing the dimmer switch to go to the left, but that is exactly the kind of secure causal knowledge that I do have, and it is not at all dependent upon whether the dimmer switch is causally linked with the light.

Indeed, this employment of prior causal knowledge plays a key role not only in classical experimentation but in the more recent method of quasi-experimentation (see Cook and Campbell [1979, 1986]) which is employed in field settings where it is possible to control from whom and when measurements are taken, but neither to control to whom and when treatments are administered nor to randomize exposures. What is needed to establish the validity of causal inferences in quasi-experimentation is explicit attention to various kinds of confounding influence (which, if randomized trials were possible, would in most cases be automatically taken care of), and to do this requires knowledge of other specific causal influences on the systems.

One final point needs to be made in this regard. Most modern analyses of causation have been logically oriented, with their principal concern being to give precise criteria for '(causally) sufficient' or '(causally) necessary'. Into this category fall both contemporary versions of regularity analyses, within which the causal relation is transformed into a logical relation between sentences representing laws and singular causal antecedents on the one hand, and singular-effect consequences on the other; and various counterfactual analyses with their concern for providing semantics or assertability conditions for various causal conditionals. But by virtue of working in the formal mode, rather than the material mode, all these analyses have laid themselves open to often very artificial logical counterarguments (see, e.g., Davidson [1967], Kim [1973a], and, in the case of explanation, Eberle, Kaplan, and Montague [1961]). These counterexamples and arguments can be constructed because manipulations are possible in logical and conceptual space that have no counterparts in the actual causal nature of things. By tying empiricism too closely to passive empiricism and by allying it with logic, logical empiricism and its successors set up a program that is inappropriate for causation. By downplaying the formal analyses of causation and upgrading the role given to real manipulations along the inductive lines suggested, we can get back to the essence of causal connections.

§30. Contributing Causes and Necessary Conditions

We noted in §14 that a sine qua non cause is a special case of a probabilistic contributing cause. This follows immediately from the fact that if B is necessary for A, $P(A/-BZ) = 0$, and hence, assuming that B does lead to A on each occasion Z, $P(A/BZ) > P(A/-BZ)$. Note that any other factors that are necessary for A must also be included in B, for if not, then their absence will be included in some values of Z, violating the inequality. This may seem rather strict, but it conforms to our conception of what constitutes a cause, for if it is true that, if C was absent, A would not occur even in the presence of B, then it is CB that contributes to A, not B alone.[34] However, it may seem that there is a difference between two types of necessary condition and that the theory of probabilistic causality is applicable to only one of these. There are factors, of which catalysts are the quintessential example, which do not by themselves lead to the effect, even though they are necessary for the effect to be produced. In contrast, others, such as tertiary syphilis, are necessary for their effect (paresis) and are intrinsically capable of (indeterministically) bringing about the effect. This distinction is similar to the traditional one of predisposing versus triggering causes or passive versus active causes.

Now, since we are dealing with objective chances, rather than relative frequencies in a population, and because a contributing cause has to increase the propensity for the effect to come about, and because we have emphasized the role played by experimental isolation of causal influences in closed systems in causal discoveries, it might seem that a passive, predisposing factor can never raise the propensity for an effect by itself because, by itself, the effect never occurs, and hence that only factors of the second kind can be probabilistic contributing causes. This contrast is only apparent. There is no essential difference between the situation where all but the catalyst are present, the catalyst is added, and by chance, the effect occurs; and the situation where all but the syphilis is present, the syphilis is added, and by chance, the paresis occurs. Recalling that a contributing cause is one that invariably raises the probability, the contributing cause in these cases is the complete set of factors that produces an increase in the chance of the reaction, or of the syphilis. It may be that, given a particular system, a single factor rather than a cluster can be a contributing cause, but this is an accidental feature of the situation and of no philosophical consequence. As we have said before, pragmatic criteria may be used to single out one component of a cluster, but this has no ontic significance.

---

[34] The need to address this point is brought out in Otte (1985), pp. 113–14.

§31. Counteracting Causes

Most of what has already been said about contributing causes can, with obvious modifications, be applied to counteracting causes. There are some special features of counteracting causes that are worth noting, however. Two types of counteracting causes exist—those that act against a contributing cause to overcome its effect (partially or totally), and those which can act alone to lower the neutral-state probability. Although both are genuine counteracting causes, in that they lower the value of the probability, they are separate kinds, because the action of the first kind affects only the sort of mechanisms peculiar to a particular type of contributing cause. In some cases it will be true that without the contributing cause the base level of the probability would be 0, and hence the counteracting cause by itself could not lower it, but even in some cases where the contributing cause is not necessary for the effect, counteracting causes may have selective actions.[35]

In addition, there is a significant difference between the probabilistic and nonprobabilistic cases. In the nonprobabilistic cases, the effect variables can often take on negative values, and hence it will be easy for the system to have causal variables that are counteracting, simply because they have a negative influence on the effect variable. But since probabilities are intrinsically nonnegative, this cannot happen. However, this difference between the probabilistic and nonprobabilistic cases does not entail that counteracting causes are rare in probabilistic systems. To take a simple binary example: if B is a necessary condition for A, then B is a counteracting cause of $-A$; i.e., since $P(A/B) > P(A/-B) = 0$, then $P(-A/B) < P(-A/-B) = 1$. If B is invariantly necessary, say in being a frequency of radiation above the threshold frequency incident on a metal, and A is the event of a particular electron's being ejected from the metal, then B is a counteracting cause of $-A$ in our sense.

Unlike contributing causes (see appendix 3), counteracting causes are not transitive. If A counteracts B and B counteracts C, then, in general, A does not counteract C. Placing a weight of 2.5 kg on a scale counteracts the effect of a weight of 2 kg that was tipping the balance in one direction. By coun-

---

[35] For the sufficiency case, von Wright (1974) has noted that, for example, a hand against the door is only a counteracting cause of its opening when there is a force that is tending to open the door. We might want to consider potential counteracting causes, but on occasion these can turn into contributing causes, as I discovered to my cost. Having once traveled from Crete to Santorini by boat in heavy weather and having suffered the consequences, I decided before the next leg of the journey to counteract the seasickness with transdermatological scopolamine. The early departure of the boat coupled with the need for prior application required my applying the patch before retiring. Awakening to catch the boat, I found the hotel room was pitching and rolling, and I could scarcely remain upright. The subsequent sea journey was, needless to say, as smooth as glass, and I felt sick as a dog.

teracting the effect of the 2.5 kg with a 1-kg weight, we thereby contribute to the original effect.

As a final point, it may well be the case that at certain values, a factor is a contributing cause, and at others it is a counteracting cause. Because our analysis takes the actual value and assesses the causal influence relative to the actual circumstances, it allows for this kind of variation. Even if double doses of a drug are less efficacious than single doses, as long as they are still better than nothing, they are a contributing cause to recovery, although not as strong a cause as would be a single dose. Only if the double dose inhibited recovery would it have turned into a counteracting cause of recovery. An amusing example of this need to specify the value, or range of values, for a given factor concerns the recent discovery that temperature is a causal factor of sexual determination in many species of reptile. When alligator eggs are kept at or below 30°C, all develop into females. At 34°C and above, all develop into males. At 32°C, the chance of an egg's developing into a female is .867. (Similar findings have been made for some lizards and turtles.)[36] Thus it will often be misleading to talk of causal relationships between variables, rather than between specific values of the variables, unless the causal relationships or kinds of causal relationships hold for all values of these variables.

§32. Are Processes or Mechanisms Necessary?

Our theory thus far has employed only properties and changes in properties together with permanent structures that carry the chances. Can we get away with that, or do we also have to employ processes connecting cause and effect, as some have argued?[37] It would be a slight advantage if our theory did not proscribe causal action at a spatial distance and left it to the world to decide whether such exists. It is certainly true that, epistemically, we make causal attributions in cases where a mechanism connecting cause and effect has not been discovered, although there is also little doubt that we feel more secure in those attributions when the link is found. These epistemic concerns, which we have largely avoided until now, are of interest for causal explanations, for we should like as part of our desire to capture partial explanations, to say that we have discovered a part of the causal explanation in those cases where knowledge of the mechanism is absent.

Consider an adaptation of an example introduced in Mackie (1974), pp. 40–43. A chocolate machine N has these properties: A chocolate bar can be produced in two ways, either by putting a coin in the slot or by kicking the

---

[36] See Ferguson and Joanen (1982). This is a peculiar instance where a cause that is structural in some species (chromosomes in mammals) is an exogenous variable in others (temperature in some reptiles).

[37] Principally Mackie (1974) and Salmon (1984).

machine. Neither of these processes is deterministic: there is a chance of .8 that an individual coin will produce a bar and a chance of .8 that an isolated kick will produce a bar. No coin ever produces more than one bar; nor does any kick. When we insert a coin and kick the machine simultaneously, however, we sometimes get two bars, sometimes one, and sometimes none. By means of a long sequence of experiments, we establish that the coin process and the kicking process are statistically independent and that no bar ever emerges unless either a coin or a kick precedes it. Furthermore, there is no identifiable continuous process that leads from a coin to a bar (when a bar does emerge) or from a kick to a bar. A coin is, simply, followed by a bar, on average, 80 percent of the time, and similarly for a kick. Now suppose that in ten repetitions of the action of simultaneously kicking the machine and inserting a coin, the improbable occurs, and we get twenty chocolate bars out. We can surely assert that ten of those bars must have been due to the coins, and ten to the kicks, even though we cannot say which of each pair was a "coin" bar and which was a "kick" bar. Note that nothing in the situation has violated the underlying indeterminism of the situation; it is just that an improbable sequence has occurred. So for each pair $(B_1, B_2)_j$, exactly one of these counterfactuals is true for each value of $i = 1, 2$:

(1) If coin j had not been inserted, bar B_{ij}, would not have emerged.
(2) If kick j had not occurred, bar B_{ij} would not have emerged.

(The argument can be made with a *single* repetition, but it is clearer with the multiple repetitions.)

We can also, I believe, go further than the counterfactual and properly claim that exactly one of the propositions 'coin C_j caused the emission of bar B_{ij}', 'kick K_j caused the emission of bar B_{ij}' is true. That we can do this is a consequence of the simple structure of the set-up, where all confounding influences have been excluded that would undermine the credibility of the simple regularity, "No coin or kick, no bar."

Consider now a similar experiment, but one where a more likely outcome is observed. Only thirteen bars emerge in the ten repetitions of the experiment. We can certainly know here that *at least* three bars were due to the coins and at least three due to the kicks, but again not whether each such specific bar was due to a coin or a kick. Thus for at least three j's (and we can isolate which j's they are), exactly one of the counterfactuals above is true, and with it the causal claim. Yet if we are willing to assert that *as a matter of fact* at least three bars were caused by coins and at least three were caused by kicks, there is no reason to withhold from asserting the same about the other seven, for they differ only in that they were not accompanied by another bar. To put the matter another way: I have assumed that six of the bars came out in three pairs, the rest singly. But since the processes are independent, it should make no difference in fact whether, given that a bar was caused by a coin, say, it happened to be accompanied by another bar or not. (The case would have been even more persuasive had the thirteen bars came out in, say six pairs and a single.) Hence we should allow that each bar that came out singly was, in fact, caused by a coin or caused by a kick, though we do not know, and cannot know, which was responsible. Lastly, consider the case where only eight bars were produced from a total of ten repetitions. Here, if no pairs were produced, we have no logical certainty about the causing of some individual bars, but once one has agreed to the second case above, there is no reason to refuse to allow the counterfactuals to be true in this case as well, and hence the corresponding causal claim.

This informal argument seems plausible. What happens if we use a specific semantics for counterfactuals rather than the informal judgement? Using Mackie's own account (which is not a semantics per se, but a reconstruction), we take a situation where both a coin and a kick were used and only one bar emerged, and we conjecture that the bar was, as a matter of fact, caused by the coin's insertion. Now take the situation up to the start of the trial, remove the coin but not the kick, and let the world run on with the laws that it has. Can we say that in those circumstances the bar—that very same bar—would not have come out? The situation is indeterministic, and so on the rerun the kick might result in a bar. But *that* bar? I think we cannot say with certainty.

There is a problem of bar identity here, and it is important because we want to say that if the coin caused the appearance of the bar and the kick did not, it was *that* bar whose appearance was caused and not some other non-existent but possible bar that might have been, but was not, caused by the kick. If one holds that the causal origins of an object are crucial to its identity, that a kick-produced bar cannot be the same as a coin-produced bar, and if one holds a particular sort of position on counterfactual definiteness, to the end that whether or not we know it, the kick bar either would be or would not be the same as the coin bar, then one has an answer. But the second position is false in these indeterministic situations—it might or it might not be, not that it would or would not be—and the first position is sufficiently question begging here that it had best be avoided. And so it seems that connecting processes do play a role in causation, not in making A a cause, but in making A a cause of B, where B is the singular specific effect under consideration. The requirement is not universal, for where multiple causes or spontaneous production are absent, or where the method of detailed specification of events (§37) can be brought into play, the identification problem may be resolved. As we have emphasized the prevalence of multiple causal influences on the same structural basis of chance, we must, however, concede that these other conditions will often not be met. Hence we cannot avoid the inclusion of processes entirely.

Scientific Explanations

§33. Introduction

In §3, we considered an example showing how a scientific explanation of a given phenemenon is progressively discovered. This activity of searching for and discovering an explanation of a given effect is something which, although not exclusive to scientific research,[1] is a sufficiently important feature of scientific activity that special methods have been developed to isolate such discoveries. These methods may be experimental, they may use statistical surrogates for experimental controls, or they may use theoretical idealizations to mimic such controls. Which method is used will depend upon a complex of conditions, involving the nature of the subject matter, the state of scientific and technological knowledge, ethical constraints, and so on. In each case, however, the emphasis is on isolating causal factors, structures, and mechanisms whose operation may be taken to constitute partially the explanation of the phenomenon at hand.

There is also no denying that linguistic explanations are required for conveying this information beyond the point of discovery. So what is the relation between these two quite different uses of the term 'explanation'? It is clear that the first sense, the objective sense in which one can discover explanations, is intimately linked with causation, so closely linked in fact that some writers have wanted to deny that our first sense is in fact a genuine kind of explanation—sometimes because explanations are supposed to generate intensional contexts, whereas causes plausibly do not; sometimes because explanations might have inescapably pragmatic aspects, whereas causes do not; sometimes because the logicolinguistic forms of natural-language representations of explanation seem to be different from those of causal claims. Such views tend, I think, to evolve from the ordinary-language strategy that was criticized in §2. This strategy takes explanatory discourse as a given, a storehouse of factual information about explanations which, after philosophical analysis, will yield

---

[1] Etymological note: the original meaning of 'research' is a search for something; it has as its source the French *recherche*. The modern, much looser meaning would correspond to *rechercher*, 're-search'.

the correct form for explanations.[2] Within this approach the logical structure of linguistic explanations is taken as primary, and causal explanations, where applicable, have to conform as a special case to the general logical structure.

I believe that it is worth employing a different kind of strategy. It is significant that most of the counterexamples to Hempel's deductive-nomological (D-N) and inductive-statistical (I-S) models of explanation hinge on those models' inability to capture causal relationships correctly. In addition, a significant body of work on the nature of causal relata has exposed difficulties inherent in descriptive representations of events, which suggests that an adequate account of causal relations must involve some direct representation of the causal relata.[3] Increased understanding of probabilistic causality has made it clearer how causal explanations for undetermined effects might be given. And a revival of interest in the role played by experimentation in science tends to make one aware of the limitations imposed by purely logical analyses of causal structure. These considerations lead me to take our project as a synthetic one: it is to see how the analytic methods of science discover the structural form of causal explanations of phenomena, and then to construct an appropriate linguistic representation which faithfully preserves that structure.

Our task is thus a restricted one. It is to provide an account of the nature of singular causal explanations.[4] In various places I shall emphasize the role

[2] Strawson, for example, writes, "We also speak of one thing explaining, or being the explanation of, another thing, as if explaining was a relation between the things. And so it is. But it is not a natural relation in the sense in which we perhaps think of causality as a natural relation. . . . It does not hold between things in the natural world, things to which we can assign places and times in nature. It holds between facts or truths. The two levels of relationship are often and easily confused or conflated in philosophical thought" ([1985], p. 115). The remarks in section 4 of Davidson (1967) also exemplify this position, which is widely held. One aim of this chapter is to argue that this position ought to be reconsidered. The almost exclusive emphasis on linguistic explanation characterizes such otherwise diverse accounts as Aristotle's *Posterior Analytics,* bk. 1, chap. 13; Popper (1959a), §12; Nagel (1961); Hempel (1965); Bromberger (1966); Friedman (1974); Railton (1978); Fetzer (1981), chaps. 5–6; Kitcher (1981); Niinuluoto (1981); Brody (1973); van Fraassen (1980), chap. 5; and Achinstein (1983). The emphasis on linguistic carriers of explanations is particularly striking in the case of those who have noted the central role of causation in explanation yet have retained a sentential structure for their analyses. For example, Brody (1973), pp. 23, 25, explicitly retains the deductive-nomological explanatory framework, even while supplementing it with causal and essential properties.

[3] See, in particular, Kim (1973a) for a convincing set of arguments on this point.

[4] I acknowledge here that there are other kinds of explanation than those which cite causes of the explained phenomenon. Achinstein (1983), p. 93, notes three: an explanation of what is occurring, an explanation of the significance of something, and an explanation of the purpose of something. There are many more uses of the term 'explanation' in English—we ask miscreants for an explanation of their behavior (give reasons for their actions) and an engineer for an explanation of how a pump works (this is often close to a causal explanation but emphasizes mechanisms). The fact that the English language contains such a variegated set of uses for the

played by probabilistic causality in explanations, but the framework is designed to apply to nonprobabilistic cases as well.

§34. The Canonical Form for Linguistic Explanations

We have seen in chapters 2 and 3 that a number of features are characteristic of causal systems. First, they are subject to multiple causal influences. Second, those influences, to be causal, must satisfy an invariance condition. Third, experimentation can separate the causal influences of each factor. Fourth, probabilistic causes come in two kinds, contributing and counteracting, and we shall see that this division extends into the realm of sufficient causes as well. Fifth, it is rare that we know of all the causal influences on a given phenomenon—our causal knowledge is ordinarily incomplete—yet that incompleteness does not preclude causal claims from being true.

An adequate linguistic explanation should preserve these characteristic features of causal explanations. To see what is needed, consider an example. The bubonic plague bacillus (*Yersinia pestis*) will, if left to develop unchecked in a human, produce death in between 50 percent to 90 percent of cases. It is treatable with antibiotics such as tetracycline, which reduce the chance of mortality to between 5 percent and 10 percent.[5] The causal mechanisms involved, the mode of transmission, and the action of the treatment on the infected human are sufficiently well established that there is no doubt that infection with *Yersinia pestis* is a contributing cause of death in a human, and administration of appropriate antibiotic treatment is a counteracting cause of death. It is also true that the contributing cause is not sufficient for death and that the counteracting cause does not guarantee recovery, as the cited probabilities show. Now suppose that Albert has died, and we ask for an explanation of this event. As always, it is imperative to separate the different causal influences on the effect to be explained. In order to do that we shall need to use a new explanatory format. Historically, the standard format for explanations has always been the simple '*Y* because *X*' mode, but one of the striking features of explanations involving contributing and counteracting causes is that this historical format is quite inappropriate. It is absurd to claim, "Albert's death occurred because of infection by the plague bacillus and the administration of tetracycline." Instead, an appropriate response at the elementary level would be, "Albert's death occurred because of his infection with the plague bacillus, despite the administration of tetracycline to him."

term 'explanation' is one reason why it seems preferable to work from causes to causal explanations rather than from a general sense of explanation down to a subcase.

[5] The plague is estimated to have killed almost one-third of the population of Europe during the Black Death of the fourteenth century. One wonders how much a single vial of tetracycline would have fetched at auction then, had it been available!

Here, then, is a linguistic mode for providing explanatory information in the case of specific events, which explicitly provides for each of the features discussed above. (The role of the second will become clear in a moment.) If one wishes to request an explanation, the canonical form will be, "What is the explanation of Y in S at t?"[6] An appropriate explanation will be, "Y in S at t (occurred, was present) because of ϕ, despite ψ," where 'Y', 'S', and 't' are terms referring to, respectively, a property or change in property, a system, and a trial; 'ϕ' is a (nonempty) list of terms referring to contributing causes of Y; and 'ψ' is a (possibly empty) list of terms referring to counteracting causes of Y.[7]

The explanation itself consists in the causes to which the elements of ϕ jointly refer. ψ is not a part of the explanation of Y proper. The role it plays is to give us a clearer notion of how the members of ϕ actually brought about Y—whether they did it unopposed, or whether they had to overcome causal opposition in doing so. Thus ψ may be empty, in which case we have an explanation involving only causes contributing to Y's occurrence, but if ϕ is empty (while ψ is not) then we have no explanation of Y's occurrence, merely a list of factors which lessened the chance of Y's occurring.[8]

We have already seen an elementary application of this format to the plague case. A somewhat more sophisticated example involves the case of enzyme-catalyzed reactions mentioned in §4. Thus, if the phenomenon to be explained is an increase in the reaction velocity of a metabolic process, we can assert (omitting references to the system and time), "The increase in reaction velocity occurred because of the increases in enzyme and substrate concentration to optimality, despite the increasing oxidation of the dehydrogenases and irradiation by ultraviolet light." (I note here in anticipation of a later claim that although each of the explanations discussed so far involves phenomena which are plausibly not determined by the cited factors, there is no mention of probability values in their explanations.)

---

[6] This is to be compared with Hempel's "Why is it the case that *p*?" ([1965], p. 334), where *p* is a propositional entity, and Salmon's "Why is it that *x*, which is an *A*, is also a *B*?" ([1984] p. 34), where *x* is an individual, and *A* and *B* are properties. I emphasize here, however, that linguistic explanations are not to be necessarily construed as answers to questions. They stand as entities in their own right.

[7] Achinstein ([1983], pp. 159–62) imposes a requirement on explanations that no singular sentence in the explanans or conjunction of such can entail the explanandum (he terms this the 'NES requirement'). As far as I can tell, the present model satisfies that condition. Also, Ryle's (1954) test for topic-neutrality was that a nonnative speaker who understood only those expressions and no others could gain no understanding of the subject matter of a passage in which those terms appeared. Among those he suggested passed this test were 'because' and 'although'. This seems to me to be correct, and it means that our canonical format for explanation (*X* because of *Y*, despite *Z*) is indeed topic neutral.

[8] This may illustrate one difference between explanation and understanding, for although only the contributing causes explain the outcome, a specification of the counteracting causes is necessary in addition for a full understanding of how the phenomenon came about.

Although I have stressed the way in which probabilistic causality makes us aware of the need for a new explanatory mode, such explanations are also possible for phenomena which we have every reason to suppose are deterministic in character. For instance, in theoretical representations of the value of the angular momentum of the earth, the simplest model treats the sun as fixed. Then, to a good approximation, the angular momentum of the earth is constant, and its value is given by the relevant conservation law. But this idealized picture is too simple, and a number of small but important causal influences have to be considered to explain the actual motion of the earth. First, the earth is an oblate spheroid rather than a sphere, and this produces a precession in the orbital plane of the moon, which in turn produces a precession in the earth's angular momentum. Second, tidal friction gradually slows the earth's rotation due to a couple acting on the equatorial tidal bulges. Third, there are thermodynamic "tides" in the earth's atmosphere due to periodic heating by the sun, with a consequent gravitational couple from the sun which acts to speed up the earth's rotation. Fourth, the nonuniformity of the sun's gravitational field results in an additional precession of the earth's angular momentum.[9]

Consider how we should respond to a request for an explanation of the increase in angular momentum of the earth over the conserved value. The response would be, "The increase is because of the precession of the moon's orbital plane, the nonuniformity of the sun's gravitational field, and the action of thermodynamic tides, despite the slowing effects of tidal friction." It is important to note that these explanations can be given, even though they are incomplete. There is no pretense that all causal factors affecting the angular momentum of the earth have been cited. The omissions are not due to the scientist's selecting those factors which interest the listener, or to being constrained by the form of the request for an explanation. It is because there are many influences on the earth's rotation beyond those cited, most of which are as yet unknown. The geophysicist knows that there exist these unknown causal factors, yet the factors cited do provide an explanation, however incomplete, of the explanandum. Furthermore, the explanation given is true. Every factor cited is a cause of the earth's angular momentum, and the explanation correctly classifies them into contributing and counteracting causes. (The reason why we can extend this terminology of contributing and counteracting causes beyond the probabilistic realm is given in the next section.)

This example is characteristic of many scientific investigations, both theoretical and experimental. In the theoretical realm, corrections to the ideal gas laws due to intermolecular forces (by means of virial coefficients),[10] the elabo-

---

[9] For a treatment of some of these factors, see Kibble (1966), pp. 151–54.
[10] See Hill (1960), pp. 261–66.

ration of three-variable causal models in sociology to four-variable models,[11] and time-independent perturbation theory for representing the coulomb repulsion between electrons in multielectron atoms[12] all use this cumulative approach to explanation.[13] Sometimes this cumulative filling-in is made via the intermediate device of theoretical models, when influences which have been known about and deliberately omitted for the sake of simplicity are added to refine the model or to introduce a student to a higher level of sophisticaton in the explanatory account, but in these theoretical treatments, it is crucial that the substitutes they pick out from the real system must actually exist. It is no explanation to provide a distorted representation of the world, and the 'understanding' induced by such incorrect models is illusory at best.

§35. Explanatory Ontology

Scientific analysis separates causal influences, and our representations must preserve this separation. So events cannot be identified with spatiotemporal regions[14] because any given spatiotemporal region ordinarily contains many properties and changes, some of them causally relevant to a given effect, many of them not, and those that are relevant may be of different types. For example, the spatiotemporal region containing an increase in temperature from 20°C to 800°C of a sample of magnesium also may contain a change in color and length of the Bunsen flame, a change in the sound emitted by the Bunsen, a change in the volume of the magnesium sample, the presence of oxygen, the lack of an oxidized layer on the magnesium, and so on, each of these factors except the first and last two being causally irrelevant to the effect, which here is the ignition of the magnesium. A similar remark may be made

---

[11] In, for example, Blalock (1962).

[12] See Mandl (1957), pp. 131–33.

[13] It must be acknowledged here that the method of analyzing complex phenomena into their component causes may well not be a universally successful methodology, for it depends upon a suitably liberal notion of additivity of effects. As we have seen in §13, a sufficient condition for additivity is that the cause have its effect at whatever level the other factors are held constant. It is not the business of philosophy to legislate that this must be the case, but that causal perturbations can be often thus combined is indisputable, for by the key test for the reality of a causal factor, if the perturbations are removed individually, then the resulting phenomenon changes in a way exactly corresponding to the contribution of that factor. This would be completely inexplicable were such causal perturbations not real. Because this issue is one of scope, one should also avoid inferring from the existence of nonlinear phenomena in areas of fundamental physical research that additive models of causality and explanation have no application in other areas of science. The most mathematically sophisticated science is not necessarily the best representative of science as a whole.

[14] As, for example, is done in Quine (1970), p. 30. In Quine (1985) this is reiterated, with some reservations (p. 167).

about the spatiotemporal region containing the effect, which also contains numerous irrelevant features, including the spatiotemporal location of the effect, the manufacturer's brand name stamped on the sample, the property of being held by Paul Humphreys, and so on.

In our formulation of quantitative causation, I employed this ontology: An event is *the possession of, or change in, a property of a system on a given occasion* (trial).[15] That ontology is preserved here with the continued understanding that events are taken as concrete, specific entities, actual instantiations of or changes in worldly properties of a system, these properties being possessed by specific structures, themselves a part of the world, with these structures persisting through the change in properties which constitute an event. (For simplicity I restrict myself to monadic properties. Events involving relational properties may be dealt with analogously.)

§36. The Deterministic Case

Recall that the characteristic feature of a probabilistic contributing cause was that it raises the chance of the effect, i.e., *it produces an increase in the value of the chance of the effect.* So, assuming the existence of physical chances, the *direct* effect of a contributing cause is an increase in the chance (of some property). But this is no different from any familiar and uncontroversial case of sufficient quantitative causation. Increase the voltage in a wire of a fixed resistance, and the effect is an increase in the value of the amperage. Increase the intensity of a classical radiation field on a particle, and the effect is an increase in the chance of the induced emission of a quantum of electromagnetic radiation. This enables us to see why it is possible to apply the contributing-cause terminology naturally both to deterministic cases such as the angular momentum of the earth and to probabilistic cases such as the bubonic plague. In both cases a contributing cause increases the value of a quantitative variable—it just happens that in the probabilistic case the variable is the value of the chance.

The application of this approach is, I believe, quite straightforward, but cases where quantitative variables are specified exactly do need some discussion. I shall deal with the deterministic case here, because the examples are clearer. Consider an individual who acquires an extreme fondness for

---

[15] The structure of events that I have used is essentially that which Jaegwon Kim has employed and argued for in a number of subtle and interesting papers (1971, 1973a, 1976). I refer the reader to those articles for a detailed exposition of Kim's views. The arguments which led me to adopt this account are rather different than those used by Kim, which emphasize the logical structure of events.

chocolate and tries to lose weight by taking diuretic pills. The chocolate intake produces an increase of ten pounds of fat over the level the individual had without the chocolate input. The diuretic pills produce a decrease of five pounds of water, compared with the weight level the individual had before taking the pills. The net *observed* increase in weight is five pounds, but in this case both the contributing and counteracting causes had their full effect. One could actually collect the increased fat and the lost water if one so desired. Thus, not only are the causes operating separately, they produce clearly separable effects which together produce the effect to be explained. Thus it seems appropriate to assert in the qualitative case, "The increase in John's weight occurred because of the chocolate's caloric content, despite the diuretic action of the pills."

Now consider a case where the contributing and counteracting causes produce their effects through mechanisms that are not so easily separable, for example, when fat is burned off by exercising. Is there any essential difference between this case and the previous one? Suppose that the fat was first put on and then part of it burned off by running. Then there would be no difference between the first situation and this one, and our explanatory form could still be used. How about the case where the chocolate input and the running occur together? Recalling our characterization of an invariant cause, if one reduces the exercise level to 0, the individual will not lose five pounds, and if one reduces the chocolate intake to 0, the individual will not gain ten pounds, in each case compared with the situation where the putative cause is present and all other factors remain as they are. Hence each influence was operating on the system during the trial, and each played its role in the way the effect came about. And so, "The increase in John's weight occurred because of the chocolate's caloric input, despite the burning off of fat by running" is also correct.

These are all cases where the causes and the effects are taken to have only qualitative properties, and there is little doubt that the approach works well there. The quantitative case, it turns out, is not so transparent, in that ordinary use appears to allow two different representations: the traditional 'because' account and the mode suggested here. To decide between them we again need to look at the causal mechanisms underlying the observed phenomenon. Consider a room which is both heated and air conditioned, and suppose that the temperature rises by 5°C (compared with the situation where neither is operating). Alone, the heater would raise the temperature by 10°C; alone, the air conditioning would lower it by 5°C. Again, the qualitative case appears to work: "The temperature of the room rose because of the input from the heater, despite the cooling of the air conditioner." Now consider these two claims: (1) The increase of 5°C in the temperature of the room occurred because of the input of 10,000 Btu from the heater, despite the extraction of

5,000 Btu by the air conditioning; (2) the increase of 5°C in the temperature of the room occurred because of the input of 10,000 Btu from the heater and the extraction of 5,000 Btu by the air conditioning.

Prima facie, (2) seems more plausible than does (1). Why is this? There are, in fact, two aspects of the explanandum event that need to be explained: the increase in the temperature and the exact value of that increase. Emphasize the former, and (1) will have some appeal;[16] emphasize the latter, and the superiority of (2) is evident. That (2) was preferable on first inspection is accounted for, I believe, by an entirely justifiable tendency to prefer precise, quantitative explananda to imprecise, qualitative explananda within scientific contexts. This example shows us two things about our canonical form for causal explanations. The first point, which I have already discussed and have more to say about in §42, is that it must always be clearly specified which aspect of a spatiotemporal event is the object of an explanation, in order that ambiguities may be avoided. The second point is more important. In any deterministic explanation in which the explanandum is the value of a quantitative variable, all causally relevant factors will contribute to the system's having that exact value, and hence the traditional 'because' format will be the appropriate one. In contrast, where the causal factors are only probabilistically related to the explanandum, what is crucial are increases and decreases in the chance of that explanandum rather than the precise value of that chance, even in cases where the explanandum is itself quantitative in form. Consequently, the canonical format for explanations described earlier will frequently need to be used because of the presence of counteracting factors.

This difference between the deterministic and the indeterministic cases explains why the inadequacy of the traditional 'because' format is not revealed within a very broad class of deterministic cases. (The reader will have noted that my earlier example involving the earth's angular momentum involved an increase in its value rather than the value itself.) The deficiencies appear only within the domain of qualitative deterministic explanations and qualitative or quantitative indeterministic explanation. This is not to say that the canonical format is the wrong one for quantitative deterministic explanations. It is simply that the 'despite' clause is not used because of the absence of counteracting causes.

This argument rests on the claim that the precise value of the probability is not something that is involved in explanations of stochastic phenomena. Section 38 is devoted to establishing that claim.[17]

---

[16] Note that it satisfies the invariance condition—under all circumstances an extraction of 5,000 BTU results in a decrease in temperature, compared with the same situation without the extraction.

[17] The position suggested in this section seems to be consistent with some brief comments made by Hume about quantitative causes: ''The absence or presence of one part of the cause is

§37. Detailed Specification of Events

We noted in §7 that many supposed cases of overdetermination are not genuine but gain their plausibility from a lack of detail in the specification of the effect. David Lewis ([1986b], postscript E) considers using a detailed construal of events (what he calls "fragility" of events) in order to rule out, as I did, most cases of overdetermination. He rejects it, in part, because its use would apparently conflict with many of our, particularly negative, causal judgments. One of his suggested counterexamples may be dealt with by using the deterministic quantitative form of counteracting causes which we discussed in the last section. In his example, a man eats a large dinner and then consumes poisoned chocolates. The poison passes more slowly into his bloodstream because of the dinner than it would have without it, and hence the event of the death by poisoning occurs rather later, and more slowly, then it would otherwise. Thus, since that particular death would not have occurred without the dinner's being eaten, under the sine qua non analysis eating the dinner was a cause of the death—which seems absurd.

Consider, however, the event quantitatively. The dying took a certain amount of time to occur, and in consequence, the death occurred when it did, a certain amount of time after the ingestion of the chocolates. Without the dinner, the dying would have proceeded more quickly; without the poison, as it did, not at all (note: this is a death with the characteristic properties of poisoning). Noting that we require a conceptual decision about which direction of the quantitative variables constitutes a contribution, and which a counteraction, let us assume that any factor shortening the time to death is a contributing cause and that any factor that delays the time of death counteracts it.[18] Caution: what characterizes an event (type) is not the time at which it occurs—if we allowed that, there would be no repeatability and no possibility of satisfying the invariance condition. Although there is a figure of speech that allows us to say "He caused it to happen when it did," that can be reconstrued to mean that he caused it to have different relationships to other events than it would have had without the cause.

Given this conceptual point, the dinner was indeed a cause, but a counteracting cause. It is false to say, simpliciter, that the dinner caused the death and, concomitantly, to say that the man died because he ate the dinner. He died because of the poison, despite eating the dinner. This locution would be clearly correct if, for example, he had deliberately eaten the dinner to slow the poison in order to get to the hospital to have his stomach pumped, but as things turned out, this ploy failed.

---

here suppos'd to be always attended with the absence or presence of a proportionable part of the effect" ([(1739–40) 1888], bk. 1, pt. 3, §15).

[18] This is a position defended in Bennett (1987). For a different view, see Lombard (1986).

Lewis's other example is somewhat harder to handle (although he himself thinks that the poisoning case is the more solid counterexample to using fragility). In this case, we have a firing squad consisting of nine soldiers, one of whom refrains from firing for moral reasons.

A death by eight bullets is different from a death by nine bullets, hence the death, as it was, would not have occurred had the ninth soldier not refrained from firing. Hence, Lewis concludes, the soldier's not firing caused the executed man's death, and this, for him, is a reductio of the method of detailed specification of events. Note that a death by eight bullets rather than nine is not defined as one that is caused by eight bullets but as a type that, contingently, is only caused by eight bullets—we should not necessitate causal connections by defining effects in terms of their causes.

Now take a detailed specification of the events involved in the death. Here, the absence of the ninth bullet is, in fact, the zero level of kinetic energy of that bullet system—it is not the bullet that ordinarily causes the death, it is its kinetic energy and the resulting trauma that does it. An individual could have a bullet surgically implanted in the heart without death resulting (recall the car example of §12). Because that zero level is the neutral state for the system of the ninth bullet, the absent bullet cannot be a contributing or a counteracting cause of death.

The methodology in each of these cases is thus to fix first the conceptual input that determines which direction of a quantitative variable is to count as an increase, and which a decrease. The change itself is an objective feature, but not whether it is called an increase or a decrease.[19] Then, what counts as a contributing rather than a counteracting cause is an objective feature, given that stipulation on directionality.

The moral to draw from this analysis is that Lewis's examples are indeed prima facie puzzling and have to be answered. Yet the answer ought not to be forced to conform to what we should *ordinarily* say about the case. It is to be expected that a more detailed specification of the situation— i.e., one that more accurately portrays the true structure of the situation— should result in deviations from what a casual, everyday account would give.[20]

---

[19] A point that affects order structures in general because of the isomorphism of relations such as 'greater than' and 'less than'.

[20] Lewis writes, "When common sense delivers a firm and uncontroversial answer about a not-too-far-fetched case, theory had better agree. If an analysis of causation does not deliver the common-sense answer, that is bad trouble" ([1986a], p. 194). What counts as common sense is, of course, notoriously vague in philosophy. Berkeley, for example, cites himself as following precepts of common sense, whereas Hume's analysis of causation, undermining as it does ordinary conceptions of causal relations, can hardly be rejected on that score.

§38. Why Probability Values Are Not Explanatory

We have seen the role played in explanations by the multiplicity, diversity, and epistemic incompleteness of causes. We are now in a position to argue for a fourth thesis—that probabilities have no explanatory role. Let us begin by noting that every other contemporary account of probabilistic or statistical explanation requires that a probability value be cited as an essential part of the explanation of phenomena whose occurrence is, or is taken to be, properly stochastic in nature.[21] The most common reason for this is that they are all versions of a covering-law model of explanation, and the covering law is a probability law (i.e., a law which assigns a probability value to the explanandum, either absolutely or conditionally or relationally). Because it is standardly required that all the elements of the explanans must be true, the probability law, being part of the explanans, must satisfy this requirement, and hence the true probability must be assigned to the explanandum by virtue of falling under this true covering law.[22]

As an exegetical aside, I believe that there was an equivocal attitude toward the role of probabilities in Salmon's early work on statistical-relevance (S-R) explanation, and this attitude has perhaps not been resolved even in his more recent work. One of the striking advantages of Salmon's original S-R model of explanation was its use of arguments and examples to demonstrate

---

[21] These include the accounts given in Hempel (1965, 1968), Salmon (1984), Fetzer (1981), and Railton (1978). For Hempel, the probability is a logical probability, which gives the degree of inductive support afforded to the explanandum sentence on the basis of the explanans. In Railton's deductive-nomological-probabilistic (D-N-P) model of explanation, the probability value of the explanandum event's occurrence appears explicitly both in the probabilistic laws occurring in the explanans and in the statement of the probability of the explanandum fact ([1978], p. 218). In Fetzer's causal-relevance model, the strength of the propensity value occurring in the probabilistic conditional is an essential feature of the explanation. Salmon (1984), I think, has come very close to giving up the probability requirement (p. 266), but not completely. For a more detailed dicussion of this point, see Humphreys (1986b) and the next two paragraphs in the text.

[22] This claim relies on interpreting a standard solution to the problem of the single case in a particular way, namely, a probability attribution $P(A/B) = r$ is *true* if and only if there is no further factor C such that $P(A/BC) \neq r$. Discussions of the single-case issue tend to talk in terms not of truth but of appropriate or correct reference classes or sequences. In fact, when discussing the problem of ambiguity, Hempel (e.g., [1968], p. 117) claims that two incompatible relative-frequency statements can both be true. In the sense that the relative frequencies $P(A/B) = r$ and $P(A/B') = r'$ are the frequencies relative to some reference class, this position is correct. However, because we are concerned with the explanandum event itself, not a representation of it in a class, the appropriate probability is that of the single case, not of the type within a class. One also cannot preserve the ambiguity of probability values by claiming that applications of relative frequencies to single cases are relative to the explanandum sentence which describes the explanandum phenomenon because then the two different probabilities would not be applied to the same object.

that factors which are explanatory must be statistically relevant to the explanandum. Thus in the introduction to Salmon (1971), we have, "S-R model (Jeffrey, Salmon, Greeno): an explanation is an assembly of facts statistically relevant to the explanandum, regardless of the degree of probability that results" (p. 11). In the article that constitutes the principal contribution to that book, however, we have that "As the discussion develops, we shall see that the homogeneity of the reference class is the key to the explanation" (p. 46) and "On my view, an explanation is a set of probability statements, qualified by certain provisos, plus a statement specifying the compartment to which the explanandum event belongs" (p. 77). It thus became clear in the development of that article that the relevant factors are explanatory only in an indirect sense in the S-R model. They are actually means to an end, that end being the attribution of the correct probability to the event in question.

In Salmon's later work on causal relevance (especially Salmon [1984]), the use of causal interactions as the basis of causal production, in contrast to the causal propagation that processes provide, would seem to have restored the correct emphasis on relevance as the key to causation. Yet the stress that Salmon places on markable processes as a means of transmitting probability distributions seems to indicate that the other view still plays an important role. "If positive statistical relevance is not the essential ingredient in a theory of probabilistic causality, then what is the fundamental notion? The answer, it seems to me, lies in the transmission of probabilistic causal influence. . . . The basic causal mechanism, in my opinion, is a causal process that carries with it probability distributions for various types of interaction" (pp. 202–3). Because my own view retains the focus on increases and decreases in chance as the key feature of causality, this attitude makes, I think, for a fundamental disparity of views between myself and Salmon.

Although the S-R model was perhaps the most explicit about this, the other models mentioned above (n. 21) all contain this feature of requiring the attribution of the correct probability to the explanation. I now want to show why this requirement is both unnecessary for an adequate explanation and unduly restrictive. Let us call any such model that requires a statement of the probability of the explanandum as part of the truth conditions for an explanation a *probabilistic* model of explanation.

THESIS. Probabilistic models of explanation cannot distinguish between complete explanations and true explanations.

Once the requirement that the correct probability value must be cited has been imposed, the standard requirement that the explanatory material must be true entails that a maximal specificity condition has to be added to the model. Let us call a maximal specificity condition any condition which requires that all probabilistically relevant factors must be cited in an explanation.[23] Such conditions may be imposed either for epistemological reasons or as truth conditions, depending upon the kind of probability used. In the first case, they are often used as a kind of epistemological insurance policy, guaranteeing that our explanation will not be overthrown by the discovery of previously unknown but relevant factors which would alter the value of the probability in an undesirable way. This seems to have been Hempel's original reason for imposing it, because within the I-S model, we must be sure that there will be no discovery of factors which change the inductive probability from a high to a low value. (There seems to be no reason why the discovery of new factors which raise a high probability value even further cannot be allowed, however, and so a partial maximal specificity condition seems compatible with the I-S model.)

A more important reason for such conditions, however, is to avoid the attribution of false probability values. The omission of even a single statistically relevant factor will (except for fortuitous cancelings) result in an incorrect probability value being assigned to the explanandum and a false statement occurring among the explanans sentences, usually in a probabilistic law. This completeness condition of relevant factors results in a hopelessly unrealistic ideal being imposed upon explanations which will rarely, if ever, be satisfied. For example, if a man dies from lung cancer, having been a heavy smoker, omitting from a probabilistic explanation any of the following minor relevant factors will result in a false probability claim: cosmic radiation from Alpha Centauri, particles from a chimney in Salem, Oregon, and a smoke-filled room he entered briefly at the Democratic convention eight years ago. It is good to be strict in matters of completeness, but not to the point of absurdity.

Because this completeness condition for probabilistically relevant factors, which surfaces in different ways in maximal specificity conditions, objective homogeneity conditions, and randomness requirements, cannot be separated from the truth conditions for the probability covering law when it is applied to single-case explanations, explanations which require the true probability value to be cited cannot omit even absurdly small probabilistically relevant factors and remain true.[24]

[23] Such conditions may be found in Hempel (1965, 1968), Salmon (1971), and Fetzer (1981), for example.

[24] It must be said that relative-frequency theories often cast the issue in terms not of the truth of probability laws but rather of the correctness or appropriateness of the probability attribution. This attitude is, no doubt, a consequence of the instrumentalist approach to probability that is congenial to its empiricist advocates. Thus, if the term 'true' is disturbing, simply substitute 'correct' in the above argument. Hempel (1968) does construe relative-frequency laws as true, in the sense that it is true to say that the relative frequency of Bs in reference class A is r. But relative frequentists would not ordinarily agree with this, in that A cannot be just *any* reference class but must be the correct one—e.g., the broadest homogeneous reference class. Indeed,

Furthermore, since it is now generally agreed that it is irrelevant to the goodness of an explanation whether the explanandum has a high, a low, or an intermediate probability value, given the explanans, what can be the explanatory power of the probability value itself? Would it make any difference to the explanation if the probability of paresis was, say, .00003 among syphilitics rather than .28? Clearly not. Would it even matter if the distribution covering radioactive decay waiting times was normal rather than exponential? Again, clearly not. It is enough that the event in question can be explained as the result of a set of causal influences.

In contrast, if one holds that it is causally relevant factors which are explanatory, where a factor is causally relevant if it invariantly changes the propensity for an outcome (i.e., a change in the factor results in a differential change in the propensity, irrespective of what other changes or conditions are also present), then specification of one or some of the causally relevant factors will allow a partial yet true explanation, even in cases where the other factors are not known and the true probability value cannot be calculated. The fact that a causal explanandum is incomplete does not thereby render it false. If all of the causal factors identified in the explanation are genuine causes of the explanation phenomenon, then that explanation is true. Whereas it is necessary to insist on the truth of an explanation, it is unwise to insist upon its completeness, for to do so would rule out almost every explanation ever put forward of a natural phenomenon. This distinction between true and complete accounts is similar to the distinction which has been common in English law for centuries between the truth and the whole truth. Of course, there everything is epistemically relativized, whereas the contrast here is between the truth and the complete truth. So we might say that for linguistic explanations we require the truth, nothing but the truth, yet not the whole truth, where for causal explanations this means citing the causes, nothing but the causes, yet not all the causes.[25] This approach has the advantage that when a complete explanation is available—i.e., when all causally relevant factors have been specified—then a specification of the true value of chance or correct

---

Hempel denies that we can speak of true I-S explanations, because of their essential epistemic relativization ([1965], p. 403). See also n. 22 above.

   [25] Jeffrey (1971), pp. 21–22, cites the following example as an explanation because "it proves that the fact is a fact by citing causes and not mere symptoms."

The glass is falling.
Whenever the glass is falling, the atmospheric pressure is falling.
Whenever the atmospheric pressure is falling, the weather turns bad.

The weather will turn bad.

This argument is not a proper causal explanation because it cites as a factor "The glass is falling," which is causally irrelevant to the explanation event. (That this is an explanation of a future event can be disregarded.)

reference class is automatically given by the constituents of the ϕ and ψ elements of the explanation (although the probability value may not be calculable from this information, because there is no guarantee that all such values are theoretically computable). This fact that probability values are epiphenomena of complete causal explanations indicates that those values have themselves no explanatory power, because after all the causal factors have been cited, all that is left is a value of sheer chance, and chance alone explains nothing.[26]

This position has a number of immediate consquences. First, it follows that there can be more than one true explanation of a given event (i.e., of an aspect of a spatiotemporal 'event'), when different sets of contributing and counteracting causes are cited. This feature of explanations involving multiple factors, while tactily recognized by many, is equally often ignored in the sometimes acrimonious disputes in social and historical explanations. Very often, a plausible case can be made that a number of supposedly competing explanations of, for example, why the Confederate States lost the Civil War, are all true. The dispute is actually about which of the factors cited was causally most influential, given that all were present, and not about which of them alone is correct. Conversely, different aspects of the same spatiotemporal event may be explained. Thus a given psychological phenomenon, such as depression, may have a number of different manifestations, and the explanation of lassitude may be different from the explanation of compensatory eating, although both are common components of depression.

Second, our account enables us to distinguish between cases where a phenomenon is covered by a probability distribution which is *pure,* i.e., within which no parameters appear which are causally relevant to that distribution (more properly, to the structure to which the distribution applies), and cases where the distribution is affected by such parameters.[27] There is good reason to believe that the traditional resistance to allowing explanations of indeterminate phenomena arose from a naive belief that all such phenomena were the result of purely spontaneous processes which were covered by pure distributions. While sympathizing with the intent behind this resistance (because, as we have argued, pure chance explains nothing), we have also seen an

---

[26] Hempel characterizes a partial or incomplete D-N explanation as one in which the explanadum event is assigned by the explanation to a wider class than is characterized by the explanadum sentence ([1965], p. 416). An incomplete I-S explanation (p. 418) is one which confers the specified probability on an analogously weaker explanandum sentence.

[27] I myself doubt whether there are many genuine cases of pure probability distributions. This fact is disguised by the common use of uninterpreted parameters in representations of probability distributions, whereas even in cases such as the binominal distribution for coin tossing, the parameter p is a function of the center of gravity of the coin, and in the exponential distribution for radioactive decay, the parameter λ is a function of the atomic number of the atom. These factors are, it is true, usually structural aspects of the systems, but that does not necessarily rule them out as contributing factors. For more on this matter, see Humphreys (1986a).

important difference between situations in which the pure chance remains at the end of a comprehensive causal explanation and situations in which pure chance is all that there is. This illustrates an important difference between covering-law approaches to explanation and the present approach. Covering-law accounts can explain events that have no causes—we cannot.

Third, the traditional maximal specificity requirements which are imposed on explanations in order to arrive at a unique probability value must be replaced by the requirement of causal invariance described earlier. This invariance requirement is strictly weaker than a maximal specificity condition because the presence of a second factor can change the propensity for a given factor to produce an effect, without thereby changing that given factor from a contributing cause to a counteracting cause, or vice versa, whereas if the second factor confounds a putative contributing cause and changes it to a counter-acting cause, a change in the value of the chance must accompany this. Of course, epistemically, we can never know for certain that such confounding factors do not exist, but that is an entirely separate matter, although regrettably relative frequentists have often failed to separate epistemic aspects of proba-bilistic causality from ontic aspects. The values of chance that define the relevance difference need not, therefore, be the true values in order to char-acterize a factor as contributing or counteracting. The invariance condition is on the sign of the relevance difference, not on its value. Of course, if we want to attribute the degree of causal influence due to a given factor, then the true value of the relevance difference will be needed. This rejection of the explanatory value of probabilities is the reason that I originally called my causal account one of "aleatory explanations" (Humphreys [1981a, 1983]). This was to avoid any reference to "probabilistic explanations" or "statistical explanations," while still wanting to convey the view that causal explanations are applicable within the realm of chancy, or aleatory, phenomena. It is, perhaps, not ideal terminology, but it served its intended purpose.

Fourth, aleatory explanations still require laws to ground explanations, but reference to these laws does not appear directly in the explanations themselves, and they are not *covering* laws. The role that the causal laws play here is as part of the truth conditions for the explanatory statement. In order for some-thing to be a cause, it must invariantly produce its effect, and hence there is always a universal law connecting cause and effect. The existence of such a law is therefore required for something truly to be a cause, but the law need be referred to only if it is questioned whether the explanatory material is true. I want to avoid the terminology of 'covering laws', however, because the term 'covering' carries implications of completeness, which is quite at odds with the approach taken here.

Fifth, there is no symmetry between predictions and explanations. As is well known, the identity of logical form between explanations and predictions within Hempel's inferential account of explanation initially led him to assert that every adequate explanation should be able to serve as a prediction, and vice versa. What we have characterized as causal counterexamples led him to drop the requirement that all predictions must be able to serve as explanations. Arguments due primarily to Wesley Salmon were influential in persuading many philosophers that we can explain without being able to predict. That independence of prediction and explanation is preserved here. We have seen that probability values play no role in the truth of explanation; a fortiori neither do high probability values. They do play some role in the goodness of an explanation, for as I previously noted, factors can contribute more or less to a phenomenon's occurrence, and we need changes in propensity values to assess degrees of contribution. But even a large contributing cause need not result in a high relative frequency of the effect, for it may often be counteracted by an effective counteracting cause. Thus, as noted earlier, the plague bacillus contributes greatly to an individual's propensity to die, yet the counteracting influence of tetracycline reduces the relative frequency of death to less than 10 percent. It is also worth noting that predictions differ from explanations in that when we have perfect predictive power (a set of sufficient conditions), there is no sense in asking for a better prediction, but better explanations may exist. Furthermore, we can predict but not explain the merely possible in the stochastic case.

Sixth, aleatory explanations are conjunctive. By imposing the causal invariance condition, we ensure that there are no defeating conditions which turn a contributing cause into a counteracting cause, or vice versa, or which neutralize a cause of either kind. Thus, two partial explanations of E can be conjoined, and the joint explanation will be an explanation also—indeed, a better explanation by the following criteria: If $\phi \subset \phi'$ and $\psi = \psi'$, then the explanation of Y by ϕ' is superior to that given by ϕ. If $\phi = \phi'$ and $\psi \subset \psi'$, then again ϕ' gives a superior explanation, in the sense that the account is more complete.[28]

[28] I believe that this kind of causal approach also captures rather better than do traditional accounts how we approach closer to the whole truth. Many accounts of Carnapian verisimilitude use a counting measure on the degree of correspondence between correct state descriptions and proffered state descriptions. That can be replaced by a similar counting measure on $\phi \cup \psi$. One can make this more precise and include a measure of the relative contributions of the causal factors to Y, by using such concepts as explained variance, but I shall not pursue that here. In response to Achinstein's criticism ([1983], pp. 103–6, 116–17) that we must distinguish between criteria for a good explanation and for a correct explanation, the present model can easily do that. Any explanation that cites only genuine causes of an explanadum is a correct explanation. The difference between a correct, a good, and a complete explanation is a matter of degree— the more factors cited and the more they contribute to the explanandum, the better and more complete the explanation. We may rank explanatory factors according to the degree to which they contribute to the effect. Given two explanations E_1, E_2, if they each have explanatory factors of degrees $d_1, \cdots, d_n$, but E_1 has at least as many of each degree as E_2 and at least one degree with more, then E_1 is a better explanation than E_2. One can of course construct measures of explanatory goodness when faced with situations in which smaller numbers of more important

One thing should be made clear here. By abandoning probability values as explanatory, we do not revert to an explanation merely in terms of factors that made the outcome possible—the traditional "how possibly" explanations discussed by Hempel ([1965]), pp. 428–31) and more recently by Nozick (1981). To use the radiation example again: the emission of a photon is already made possible by spontaneous emission, but spontaneous occurrences as we have explained are not caused. Thus showing that something is possible does not entail that we have given a causal explanation, although the converse entailment does, of course, hold.

Seventh, it may be responded that we should be after ideal explanations, not actual explanations. Well, so am I, and this response results from construing 'ideal' in a particular way. It comes from focusing on the Peircean limit of ideal science, the state achievable when all the facts and theories are in, when we can hold a discussion on an equal footing with Laplace's omniscient predictor. This limit view is widespread in discussions of scientific realism, and I find it limiting in a different sense. If we, as philosophers of science, can say something true about science as it is practiced now, rather than about Keynes's deadly long run, we ought to do it. Thus by 'ideal', writers usually mean 'complete', and we have given ample reason why, in the case of probabilistic phenomena that are the result of multiple causal influences, completeness is an ideal to be aimed for but not necessarily achieved. Each aleatory explanation is 'ideal' in the sense of being true, and to be so will sometimes require taking the explanation sketches that, for pragmatic reasons, serve as conversational substitutes for genuine explanations and supplementing them in order to satisfy the invariance condition. These aleatory explanations then will be 'ideal' in the further sense of a refinement of commonplace talk.

Nor should it be assumed that an ideal, complete explanation must attribute certainty, or a chance of unity, to the explanadum. Section 10 should have undermined any prejudice in favor of determinism, and to want more when all causally relevant factors have been cited in a complete aleatory explanation is to want what does not exist in nature.

A common argument that has been leveled against the possibility of causal explanations in the social sciences is that the laws involved are so complex that there often will be only a single instantiation of them, this concerning the fact to be explained, and such unrepeatability renders the explanation open to charges of ad hocness. The use of causal invariants in the present sense goes a long way to avoiding this objection. If the complete set of causal factors influencing Y is $(X_i)_{i=1}^n$, where n is some very large number, the

---

factors are compared with larger numbers of less important factors, but this project is not one which has any real philosophical interest. Given that the conjunctive condition is satisfied, we should simply combine them.

complete specification of that set may be practically impossible, but that does not prevent us from citing X_m as a partial explanation of Y when X_m is present, as long as none of the other causal factors are defeating conditons for X_m. We may also have good evidence that a given factor is indeed invariant, and this can be established independently of the instance at hand.

§39. On the Very Possibility of Explaining Chancy Events

Stegmuller (1973), reported and discussed in van Fraassen (1978) and Kruger (1976), presented an argument designed to establish that explanations of indeterministic events were not possible. As expounded by van Fraassen, the argument was formulated in terms of explanations that give us a reason to expect the explanandum (or that justify the belief that it occurs). Because our account has denied that explanations must have this justificatory role, I want to reformulate the argument so that it applies to our account. Suppose we ask why E occurred rather than F, where F is some event incompatible with E. For simplicity's sake, we can consider the case where $F = -E$. Now require of an explanation that it provide a reason why E occurred rather than $-E$. Take any indeterministic case in which A, which is cited as the explanation, is followed by E, and we may assume that A is a complete explanation. Then consider a second situation in which A is present and $-E$ occurs. A trivially gives us no reason why E occurred rather than $-E$ in the second case, because $-E$ occurred. But A is complete, and if it cannot provide a reason in the second case, it cannot do so in the first, because there is nothing explanatorily relevant that differs in the two cases. Since this argument depends only on the indeterminism of the situation, so that A can be followed by either E or $-E$, one concludes that explanation of such events cannot be given.

This argument, I think, captures in a wonderfully succinct way exactly what is to most people disturbing about indeterminism. Yet it is precisely because it fails to appreciate what is characteristic of indeterministic contexts that it does not have the bite which it initially appears to possess. One may differ with the way the argument is set up: as we shall see (§42), the comparative request for an explanation, "Why E rather than $-E$?" is not forced upon us. But the argument does not essentially depend upon that comparative form, and hence we shall not press that point. Now, we have already seen (§§14, 38) that once a complete causal explanation has been given, all that remains is chance, and chance explains nothing. So, given A, there is no *further* explanation of why E rather than $-E$, but that does not entail that there is no explanation of E, when it occurs, and indeed an explanation that gives grounds (usually many) for why E occurred. Although it is not itself part of the explanation, that E occurred, since it is not entailed by a statement of A, is an essential auxiliary aspect of indeterministic explanations: we have to wait to see how things turn out. Take an extreme case in which A contains no counteracting causes of E. Then, if it turns out that then $-E$ occurs, there is indeed no explanation of either E (because it failed to occur) or of $-E$ (because nothing led to it but chance). But had E occurred, preceded by the same A, there would be many factors contributing to E, and these do provide a reason why E occurred.

§40. Testing the Account

Philosophical theories, if adequate, in addition to not being subject to the problem cases that have been raised against alternative theories, should also explain why those theories are prone to those types of counterexample. So here, in no particular order, is a survey of most of the principal problem cases that have proven troublesome for previous accounts of explanation, together with an explanation of how aleatory explanations avoid them. Examples that have been given in previous sections will not be repeated here.

A. THE ASYMMETRY PROBLEM

EXAMPLE: A flagpole of height h casts a shadow of length l. With knowledge of the length of the shadow, of the angle of elevation of the sun, and of elementary laws of geometry and physics, such as the (almost) rectilinear propagation of light, we can deduce the value of h. But citing the value of l does not explain the value of h, although the deduction is a good D-N explanation.

SOLUTION: The problem is clearly due to the fact that the shadow's length does not contribute to the flagpole's height, whereas the converse is true (in particular, because changing the flagpole's height while keeping other factors such as the sun's elevation constant results in a change in the length of the flagpole's shadow,[29] but not vice-versa).

A similar analysis takes care of the problem of the *galactic red shift*, in which the motion of galaxies away from ours causes a shift in their spectrum toward the red, but the converse is false. Here, of course, direct experimental intervention to halt the expansion and eliminate the red shift is not possible, and hence analogical reasoning must be used from laboratory cases of red shift.

---

[29] Except for singularities at 0 and $\pi/2$ angles of elevation.

Such examples are classic cases of the failure of regularity analysis to capture the asymmetry of causal relations.[30]

B. THE JOINT EFFECTS PROBLEM

EXAMPLE: One can deduce (or infer with high probability) from the regularity that falling barometer readings are (almost) always followed by storms, together with the statement that the barometer reading dropped, that a storm occurred.[31] Yet this is no explanation of the storm's occurrence, however good a predictor it might be.

SOLUTION: The problem this time is the inablility of regularity analysis to distinguish between joint effects of a common cause and a genuine causal relation. Here the common cause is a drop in the atmospheric pressure, and the two effects are the drop in the barometer reading and the occurrence of the storm. The explanation has failed to cite the cause of the storm, as is evidenced by the fact that altering the barometer reading, perhaps by heating and cooling the instrument, has no effect on the occurrence or nonoccurrence of the storm. Our treatment of spurious causation was given in §27A to show how the problem is overcome in cases where the joint effects are not nomologically inseparable. As just indicated, the joint effects in the barometer example obviously are suitably separable. How-

---

[30] Patrick Gardiner called a forerunner of the D-N model "the regularity interpretation of explanation" ([1952], p. 65). This was supplanted by William Dray's 'covering law' terminology, which Hempel later applied to both D-N and I-S accounts. Hempel's account of causal explanation of single events is, of course, based on a logical version of a regularity account of causality. The requirement of nomic expectability that forms the core of Hempel's approach is clearly an attempt to substitute an objective analogue to Hume's psychological expectation of the effect, on the basis of the occurrence of the cause. "Causal explanation is a special type of deductive-nomological explanation; for a certain event or set of events can be said to have caused a specified 'effect' only if there are general laws connecting the former with the latter is such a way that, given a description of the antecedent events, the occurrence of the effect can be deduced with the help of the laws" (Hempel [1965], pp. 300–301). A clearer statement of a logically based regularity analysis of causation could not be had. For events to be causally connected they must be an instance of a lawlike regularity, such that the associated law statement, together with linguistic descriptions of the earlier events, allows an inference to be made to a description of the effect event. Hempel was quite clear ([1965], p. 352), however, that not all D-N explanations of single events are causal.

[31] It is not evident to me that this regularity is lawlike, for the subjunctive conditional "were that barometer reading to fall, a storm would occur" requires special constraints on the worlds in which the antecedent is true in order to preclude, among other things, human intervention from producing an artificial drop in the needle reading. Indeed, because this possibility is often present in these cases of causally spurious associations due to common causes, many such regularities will fail the condition of being lawlike.

ever, I remind the reader that our theory is, unfortunately, unable to deal with cases of the joint effects problem when the effects are nomologically perfectly correlated.

C. THE IRRELEVANT FACTOR PROBLEM

EXAMPLE: A sample of table salt is dissolved in warm water. The 'explanation' offered is that it was a sample of hexed salt, and samples of hexed salt always dissolve in warm water. Once again, this counts as a legitimate explanation under the D-N account, a clearly wrong conclusion.

SOLUTION: As well as citing the cause of the salt's dissolving, which is its immersion in warm water, a factor which is not a cause (its hexing) has been cited. (The hexing is not a cause because a change in the property 'is hexed' from presence to absence does not result in a change in the chance of the salt's dissolving.) On an aleatory account of explanation, citing the hexing makes the explanation false, because something which is not a contributing cause has been included in the explanation when it is not a causal factor. Yet everything included in the explanans of the D-N 'explanation' is true, including the regularity that hexed salt always dissolves in water. Thus, the answer to the question raised by Salmon, "Why are irrelevancies harmless to arguments but fatal to explanations?" ([1984], p. 92), is that causal irrelevancies destroy the truth of a causal explanation, whereas arguments, which are concerned only with propositional truth and validity and not causality, have these features preserved under dilution by noncausal truths in the premises.[32]

An exactly parallel diagnosis holds for the related examples cited in Salmon (1971) of vitamin C and birth control pills. To cite the administration of vitamin C as an explanation of an individual's cold clearing up within two weeks is to cite a causally irrelevant factor, as studies of control groups whose members have colds but who are not administered the vitamin C have shown. To cite his taking birth control pills as an explantion of why a man failed to become pregnant is again to cite a causally irrelevant factor because birth control pills do not change the zero probability of a man's becoming pregnant.

[32] This answer is essentially that given by Salmon. Even though he phrases his answer in terms of statistical relevance rather than causal relevance ([1984], p. 96), it is clear from the causal apparatus employed later in the book that causal relevance is meant.

D. The Negatively Relevant Factor Problem

EXAMPLE: A plant is sprayed with a defoliant that has a .9 chance of acting effectively, but on this occasion the plant retains its leaves. Assume that the probability of a plant's self-defoliating is, say .05.[33] According to Salmon's original S-R model of explanation, the spraying is positively relevant to defoliation. Since an event that is positively relevant to a second event is automatically negatively relevant to the negation of that second event, spraying is negatively relevant to nondefoliation. Because in the S-R model all statistically relevant events must be cited in the explanation, whether they are positively or negatively relevant, one would have to assert that the plant did not defoliate because it was sprayed, a claim that is obviously false, as we saw in the similar case of the plague infection discussed in §34.

DIAGNOSIS: The problem arises through misclassification of a counteracting cause as a contributing cause.

SOLUTION: By employing the 'X because of Y, despite Z' format, there is no explanation of the persistence of leaves: "The retention of the leaves occurred despite the spraying of defoliant."

EXAMPLE: A somewhat different problem involving negative factors was raised by Salmon by means of an example that used uranium-238 and polonium-214 atoms. The half-life of the former is 4.5×10^9 years, and for the latter is 1.6×10^{-4} seconds. A U^{238} atom disintegrates. Why? Salmon claimed that by partitioning the mixture into homogeneous classes of U^{238} and Po^{214} atoms, we explain that disintegration by mentioning that it was a U^{238} atom and that there was a small probability of its disintegrating ([1971], p. 64). This is surely not an explanation of why it disintegrated. It is an answer to a how-possibly question, for all the answer does is to demonstrate how it was possible for an atom to disintegrate. Furthermore, the lowering of the probability from the mixture to the homogeneous class of U^{238} atoms is not explanatory.

DIAGNOSIS: The use of relative frequencies rather than propensities to address single-case explanations, the failure noted above to distinguish between explanatory requests and how-possibly requests, and the comparison of the probability with an ensemble average rather than the neutral state conditional probability account for the problem here.

---

[33] This example is a refinement of one given in Cartwright (1979).

SOLUTION: The specific U^{238} atom is the system, and there are no causally relevant factors that alter the half-life of such an atom.[34] Hence there is no explanation of this atom's decay, although there is an explanation of how it is possible for U^{238} atoms in general to decay.

A similar analysis can be given for a rather more detailed version of the counterexample to Salmon's S-R account that was offered by Hugh Lehman (1972).[35] In the population at large (or for a specific individual) there is a probability of .7 that an individual with a blood alcohol level of .15 will fail a behavioral test for lack of motor control, and an identical probability of .7 that an individual who has ingested 5 mg of L-Δ^9-tetrahydrocannabinol (the active component of marijuana) will fail the same task. Now suppose that an individual, Smith, has actually only been drinking, with a resultant elevation of blood alcohol level to .15, and then subsequently fails the motor test. According to the S-R model, one should assign an individual to the *broadest* homogeneous reference class available, and this will be the class of these ingesting *either* alcohol *or* Δ^9-THC. But in Smith's case it was the alcohol not the Δ^9-THC that explains his failing the test.

Here the response is to appeal to the detailed specification of events (see §37). The event of motor dysfunction as a result of alcohol impairment is a different kind of event than a superficially similar event resulting from THC absorption, both subjectively and objectively. In his response to Lehman, Salmon (1973) appealed, as part of his answer, to the fact that different causal processes are involved in alcohol and marijuana intoxication. While that is undoubtedly true, the mechanism of action of Δ^9-THC is, to the best of my knowledge, unknown at the present time. Yet this does not preclude our correctly citing it, rather than alcohol, as the causal factor in certain cases, and the fact that we can do this by virtue of characteristic features of the distinct effects leads me to conclude that, while often helpful, process and mechanisms are not indispensable criteria for causal attribution (modulo the discussion in §32).

E. THE LOW PROBABILITY PROBLEM

EXAMPLE: This problem involves accounts of explanation that require a high degree of probability to be conferred on the explanandum by the explanans. Paresis can be acquired only through prior infection with untreated tertiary syphilis, yet even then, there is only a .28 chance of the victim's contracting paresis. Despite this low

---

[34] At least within an extremely wide range of values of temperature, pressure, electromagnetic fields, and so on that we assume this atom falls between.

[35] A structurally similar but fictional example is given in van Fraassen (1980), p. 108. I conjecture, hypothetically, that it could be treated in the same way.

probability, it seems appropriate to cite the untreated syphilis as an explanation of the paresis.

DIAGNOSIS: We have here the inability of noncomparative proba-bility values to capture probabilistic causal relations (in addition to the failure of these models to allow any place at all for probabilistic causation).

SOLUTION: Untreated tertiary syphilis is a contributing probabilistic cause (perhaps even the only contributing cause) to paresis. This, and the irrelevant factor problem, arises in Hempel's inductive-statistical model because it is essentially incapable of incorporating probabilistic causality, relying as it does on probability values and not on changes in those values. As we showed in §11, the probability value alone cannot be a measure of the degree of causal connection.

F. LAWS OF COEXISTENCE

It has often been claimed that so-called laws of coexistence are not suitable as the basis of a causal explanation and hence that since one can use these laws in explanations, not all explanations are causal. Indeed, in denying that all explanations were causal, Hempel ([1965], p. 352) cites the oft-repeated example of being able to explain the period of a pendulum by reference to its length, but not conversely, and makes the claim that laws of coexistence cannot provide causal explanations in terms of antecedent events. Curiously, Hempel briefly discusses and then dismisses the essence of the correct response to this example, which is that the causal influence of the length on the period, and the absence of a converse influence for a pendulum with a rigid rod, is grounded not in a mathematical law statement but in a physical procedure. Consider a rigid pendulum, but one whose center of mass can be altered by adjusting a bob. If l is the distance between the fulcrum and the center of mass, then the period is given by $t = 2\pi(l/g)^{1/2}$. In this case, by physically changing l by means of raising and lowering the bob, the period t will change. However, because the pendulum is rigid, changing the period by forced os-cillations will not result in a change in the distance of the center of mass from the fulcrum. Thus it is correct to say that the length of the pendulum is a cause of its period, whereas the period is not a cause of its length.

Suppose, in contrast, that the pendulum was elastic and had forced oscil-lations. Then, in this case, we should correctly be able to say that the period of oscillation explains why the pendulum has the length that it does (strictly, the increase in length over its value in the neutral state of no oscillations) because changing the period changes the length of the pendulum, but in this case where the oscillations are forced from outside the system, the converse does not hold. Note, however, that the mathematical relationship is different in the two cases, for with the elastic pendulum, the shorter the period, the longer the length, whereas with a rigid pendulum the longer the length, the larger the period.

Other examples that have been used to make a similar point are Boyle's law, Charles's law, Ohm's law, Newton's law of gravitation, and Pauli's exclusion principle.[36] Not only does the use of these examples seem to suggest that simultaneous causation has been excluded as a possibility,[37] but there is in fact an explanatory asymmetry involved with some of these laws. As Brody ([1973], p. 21) noted, one can explain the value of the internal pressure of a gas by citing its present volume, its previous volume, and its previous pressure, yet explaining its volume by citing the internal pressure and the previous volume and pressure is often not satisfactory, for example, when the volume decreases. I would elaborate on Brody's point and mention that a satisfactory explanation will often require a causal account of how the present state was arrived at, or produced, and in the case of gases, that will often involve the external pressure, the structural properties of the container, and so on, and I believe that Ohm's law and Charles's law possess similar explanatory asymmetries based on causal asymmetries. Pauli's exclusion principle is perhaps the most interesting of the counterexamples,[38] and it may well be that this does provide the basis of noncausal explanation, especially if it is, as is often suggested, a fundamental law of nature that itself has no explanation, in the same way that various conservation laws do not.

G. REJECTION OF EXPLANATORY REQUESTS

In the course of developing his pragmatic theory of explanation, van Fraassen (1980) suggested that any adequate theory of explanation must satisfy two criteria: account for rejections of explanatory requests, and account for asymmetries of explanation. The second of these has been dealt with in subsection A above and accommodated by the asymmetry of singular causal sequences. As for the first, I shall argue (§42) that viewing explanations as responses to why-questions (as van Fraassen does) is the wrong way to construe explanations of the kind described here. Nevertheless there will be cases in which a request of the form ''What is the explanation of Y?'' can correctly have the response, ''nothing.'' These cases will be exactly those in which no contributing causes are present on the occasion in question. (N.B. They must not be present but unknown, for then the null response is simply false.) This includes the cases where (1) there are only counteracting causes, (2) chance

---

[36] See Hempel (1965), p. 352; van Fraassen (1980), p. 122.

[37] Something that I should be willing to go along with, as long as the laws cited are adjusted to the level of sophistication of special and general relativity. This would then rule out Newton's law and would force microdescription versions of Boyle's, Charles's, and Ohm's laws.

[38] There has recently been some theoretical speculation that the principle might not be strictly true. See Greenberg and Mohapatra (1987).

alone is responsible for the outcome, (3) Y did not occur, and (4) the system is in the neutral state of all the causal variables.

The examples cited by van Fraassen to illustrate the rejection of explanatory requests may be handled in just this way. We can explain why John contracted paresis, because his syphilis caused it, and to produce the comparative case that van Fraassen favors but I reject as the basic explanatory format, we can explain why John's brothers failed to contract paresis, because they were lacking an essential contributing factor—the untreated tertiary syphilis. Yet the question, "What is the explanation of John, the syphilitic's, paresis?" has no further explanation than the cause cited in the explanatory remark, for it is sheer chance that, given his syphilis, John went down with paresis. In this case, the questioner may still be given a nontrivial answer to the question by a specification of the intervening causes between the syphilis and the paresis—i.e., a description of the causal process leading from the first to the second. But there are, of course, elaborated examples where no further causes can be cited. Similarly, there is no explanation, because there are no contributing causes, of the disintegration of a uranium atom. In each of these cases, what is not explainable is determinable only a posteriori, as van Fraassen requires.

Relativization of the rejection problem to a whole conceptual framework might appear to raise trickier problems. Perhaps these problems do arise in some cases, although not, I think, in the cases cited by van Fraassen. If an Aristotelian asks a Newtonian, "What is the explanation of the retention of its velocity by a body free of impressed forces?" the Newtonian response is, "Nothing—there are no causes acting on the system—a fortiori, no causes contributing to its velocity." Note, by the way, that even if one is inclined to the view that both Newtonian and Aristotelian theories are false, in 1687 the Aristotelian position was empirically wrong, whereas the Newtonian was not. The Aristotelian question is motivated by a hypothesis that is demonstrably unsupported by evidence: that bodies free of impressed (i.e., unnatural) forces remain stationary or halt. Demonstrably, because experimental demonstration shows it not to happen. Thus, without having to defend the Newtonian explanation as true, we can justify the Newtonian's rejection of the Aristotelian explanatory request.

H. The Nondiscrimination Problem

Explanations can be criticized on the ground that if the very same explanation could be used whatever the outcome, then there must be something wrong with that explanation.[39] This is, of course, not the same as an explanation

---

[39] For example, Ellis (1970) and Mellor (1976).

that can explain everything (that occurs)—for the latter could be a universal theory and, if true, give a unified explanation of all actual phenomena.[40]

Our model passes this adequacy test for an explanation because if X is a contributing cause of A, it would have been a counteracting cause of $-A$ and vice versa, and hence an explanation of $-A$ would be the dual of an explanation of A, with contributing and counteracting causes interchanged. Hence: "He died because of the plague bacillus, despite the administration of tetracycline" and "He continued to live because of the administration of tetracycline, despite the plague bacillus." (Note: the negation of "x died" is "x continued to live," not "x survived," which already contains connotations of sickness.)

I. Explaining Future Events

Is it possible to explain future events? In the case of future events that have already been determined to occur, I see no harm in saying that we have an explanation of, say, an eclipse of the sun that will occur two years hence. But with stochastic phenomena, it would not be enough to add the rider "if the event occurs" because of the problem of negative links (see appendix 3). That is, because it is possible for the intervening causes to be either contributing or counteracting in the stochastic case, we have to wait and see exactly how the specifics of the causal process turn out before we can say what form the causal explanation has or, indeed, whether a causal explanation can be given at all.

§41. The Pragmatics of Causal Explanations

Are pragmatics a secondary and peripheral part of causal explanations, or are they primary and ineliminable? It is impossible to answer this question without a clear definition of what counts as a pragmatic element of a causal explanation and a detailed understanding of where such elements might enter, perhaps through the causal apparatus, perhaps through the explanatory apparatus. The term 'pragmatics' (and even more so 'pragmatism'), having such an appealing sound to the American ear, has been appropriated for so many uses that I doubt there any longer exists a core meaning for it. We shall thus confine ourselves to the special use that it has for elements of language and define a term as having an essentially pragmatic content if its semantics contain ineliminable context-dependent elements, where the context-dependency is a

---

[40] Laplace seems to have had this belief about Newtonian mechanics.

dependency upon a particular user or consumer of that term.[41] That a term (say a predicate) is relational does not make it context dependent in the sense appropriate for pragmatics, of course. What is required is the kind of context-dependency that leads one to say that something is a cause or an explanation for one individual X but not for another individual Y. With some terms, such as indexicals (e.g., 'I', 'now'), this kind of context-dependency plays an inescapable part in the semantics for the term. Where the context-dependency involves the goals, interests, and purposes of the user or consumer, however, the inevitability of a pragmatic element is by no means as obvious. As Hempel ([1965], §5) notes, there is an innocent sense of the pragmatics of explanation, within which one first determines what counts as an explanation simpliciter and then, given an array of explanations, tries them out on an individual in order to discover whether they will aid the understanding of that individual, i.e., be an explanation for that person in this subsidiary sense.

Yet arguments have been given that suggest pragmatics enter the heart of explanations and that the first objective step in Hempel's procedure cannot be made. We must keep firmly in mind that the sense of 'pragmatics' that is relevant here is one that is essentially tied to language and its uses. Because most analyses of explanation are linguistically oriented,[42] and we have tried to avoid that orientation, the present account may not be subject to all varieties of pragmatic content. However, let us proceed with our examination.

There are a number of ways by which pragmatic elements might enter into causal explanations. What we must examine is whether any of these ways affects the kind of ontic explanation with which we are primarily concerned, rather than the linguistic devices that may variously be used to convey information about the causes to specific individuals. An emphasis on pragmatic aspects of explanations often arises when one views explanations as devices intended to convey understanding. Rather than focusing on the objective features of the world that constitute, for us, an explanation of a given phenomenon, or on the logical structure of an explanatory device, as Hempel did with arguments, pragmatists tend to be concerned with the epistemic state of an inquirer. Because one individual's state of knowledge may be different from another's, as may be one's epistemic interests and goals, this approach immediately leads to a relativization of explanations to an individual, thus making them essentially pragmatic in the sense defined earlier. Again, I should like to set aside that whole issue of what constitutes or promotes understanding

---

[41] This definition is consistent with the sense in which it is used in Montague (1974), chaps. 3–4 (wherein the author largely confines himself to indexical expressions); van Fraassen (1980), p. 89, chap. 5, passim; and Hempel (1965), pp. 425–26.

[42] An exception here is van Fraassen (1980), especially chap. 5. His semantic analysis of theories relies on set-theoretic devices rather than (first-order) languages, and his account of why-questions is in terms of propositional entities, rather than sentential tokens (pp. 137–38).

and focus only on what is required of an explanatory candidate that may or may not, for an individual, lead to such understanding.

A. THE DIVISION BETWEEN CAUSES AND 'MERE CONDITIONS'

The first source of possible pragmatic features in causal explanations comes through a division that is often made in the causal factors. There is a widely held view that some distinction must be made between causes and "mere conditions." C. J. Ducasse, for example, claimed that the cause of an event was a change in circumstances before that event, mere conditions being the factors which remained constant.[43] J. S. Mill, on the other hand, insisted that, properly speaking, the cause of an effect was the whole assemblage of prior conditions and events which, taken together, were jointly sufficient for the effect. Within his activity framework, Collingwood suggested that not only is the identification of the cause a result of context-dependent criteria but that there is and can be no interpersonal agreement about what constitutes the cause because what is the cause for an individual a is what a can produce or prevent at will, and because of differing powers and abilities, this may not be the same factor as for an individual b with different powers and abilities.[44] If the distinction between causes and conditions must be made but is essentially dependent upon pragmatic criteria, then the objectivity of causal claims is threatened. Indeed, it has been suggested that this relativity of causal judgments leads to an essential subjectivity in the social sciences because no clearly objective causal laws can be formulated in those areas.[45]

In order to assess the impact of such claims on our theory, we must sharply distinguish between different kinds of pragmatic relativism. First, much of the cause-versus-conditions dispute arises from insisting on the use of the definite article. Once it has been realized that multiple causation is characteristic of situations in which probabilistic causation is applicable, to ask what

[43] Ducasse's position is less appealing than it could be for present purposes because he insists that the cause must be identified with the whole change occurring before the effect, including even what would ordinarily be considered to be minor perturbations to what we should call the principal cause. One must, for example, add the sound waves from a twittering canary to the impact of a rock when considering the cause of a shattered window, if such melodies were in fact present. Our position on the additive nature of causal contributions allows us to avoid this extreme and enables a correct but partial specification of causal factors to be given.

[44] It must be recalled, however, that Collingwood's activity account of causation was not intended to be applied to causal claims in advanced theoretical science. See Collingwood (1940), §§29–32.

[45] See, for example, White (1965) for arguments of this kind. White also argues for a pragmatic element arising from the choice of contrast case: "If we think of the behavior of a country as abnormal when compared with its own behavior just before the puzzling event, we may explain the puzzling event in one way; but if we think of that country as behaving abnormally by comparison with *other countries*, we may seize upon something else as the cause of its abnormal behavior" (ibid., p. 8).

was *the* cause of a phenomenon will be to ask an unanswerable question, in general.[46] There will rarely be a unique cause, and hence the question must be construed as asking either, "Which of the causal factors was the most important?" or, "Which of the factors was a cause, as opposed to a mere background condition?" The first question cannot be answered without some causal ordering. This has rarely been attempted under any analysis of causality, and it is difficult to achieve without some quantitative approach to causation. (See also n. 28, this chapter.)

Within our ontic view, the distinction between causes and background conditions has no explanatory relevance: 'background conditions' such as the presence of oxygen contribute to a fire just as much as does an electrical short circuit, regardless of whether it involves an ordinary house fire or a flash fire in an Apollo training capsule. Of course, we often select from the list of causal factors, for we are human and become easily bored or want to be told how corrective action can be taken in the future, but without the availability of the objective list, these human concerns would have no application. It might appear that the difference between pragmatists and objectivists is itself merely a reflection of one's interests; aficionados of detail will insist on even minor causal aspects being mentioned, whereas those oriented toward the big picture will brush these aside. But if, as I have continually emphasized, science progresses through attention to detail and if pragmatic concerns are motivated by appeal to what we should ordinarily say, then we may legitimately ignore these appeals to ordinary usage when concerned with scientific explanations.[47]

B. Ceteris Paribus Conditions and the Choice of a Contrast Case

A second way in which pragmatic elements have been claimed to affect causal explanations is through the choice of a contrast case. Our discussion of causation has emphasized the fact that causal claims are comparative in form: they tell us the contribution the cause made compared with its absence. The first thing to note in this regard is that our theory of causation is couched in terms of conditional chances and not in terms of statements having the logical form of a conditional. Now, it is well known that contemporary theories of counterfactual conditionals have an essentially pragmatic semantics, and in

---

[46] The corresponding issue concerning what "the" effect of a given cause is has not raised as much interest. It is important, however, in areas such as utilitarianism, where consequences of an act are of central importance. Hart and Honore ([1959], p. 11) discuss this issue in the context of legal situations.

[47] It is, perhaps, significant that although van Fraassen ([1980], chap. 5) advances all of the reasons we cite for the inclusion of pragmatic features in explanations, the recurring theme throughout that chapter is the role played by the (as he puts it) salient causes as opposed to background conditions (see especially pp. 123–26).

consequence, causal theories that employ semantics for counterfactuals (and subjunctive conditionals) in their analyses have in turn an essential pragmatic element. We must thus ask whether the reasons that have led many to adopt a pragmatic theory of counterfactual conditionals should also be reasons that persuade us of a similar need for pragmatics in the present theory.

The first reason given involves examples such as this: "If that match had been struck, it would have lit." This statement will be true enough if a ceteris paribus condition is added to the antecedent of the conditional, for there are things not mentioned in the conditional that could make the conditional false, such as an absence of oxygen or a wet match. This issue has been so widely discussed in the philosophy of science literature that it is surprising how hard it is to find a precise definition of the term 'ceteris paribus'. Here, then, in lieu of a standard interpretation, are four suggestions for what the term means: Literally, of course, it means 'other things being equal', but its use in philosophy of science encompasses at least these applications:

1. Any factor which has not been explicitly included in the causal claim, law, or model is assumed to be irrelevant.
2. All relevant or unknown factors not explicitly included in the causal claim, law, or model are assumed to be constant.
3. All relevant or unknown factors not explicitly included in the causal claim, law, or model are assumed, on average, to have no effect.
4. All relevant factors not explicitly included in the causal claim, law, or model, whether known or unknown, are assumed to be absent (have value zero).

With each of these interpretations, the use of the 'ceteris paribus' rider carries the connotation that the assumption may well turn out to be untrue. The primary use is, I think, the first, and in what follows I shall take that as our interpretation.

Reverting to the role played by such conditions in counterfactuals, one can see that the problem is connected with the issue of whether there are any causal invariants of the kind we require for our theory. If there are, then by specifying them as the antecedent of the conditional, the use of a ceteris paribus clause could be avoided. In denying that such invariants exist, Russell put it this way: "In order to be sure of the expected effect, we must know that there is nothing in the environment to interfere with it. But this means that the supposed cause is not, by itself, adequate to insure the effect. And as soon as we include the environment, the probability of repetition is diminished, until at last, when the whole environment is included, the probability of repetition becomes almost *nil*" ([1917], p.181). "As soon as the antecedents have been given sufficiently fully to enable the consequent to be calculated with some exactitude, the antecedents have become so complicated that it is very unlikely they will ever recur" (p. 182).

In assessing such claims, we must beware of conflating problems that arise from attempting to provide truth conditions for natural-language conditionals with issues that are properly in the province of strict scientific assertions. There is no doubt that most ordinary-language conditionals, for brevity's sake, have antecedents that are seriously underdescriptive of the intended contrast case. But the issue is not whether such informal conditionals are ambiguous for that reason, but whether it is possible to fix uniquely a suitable contrast case. Russell's way of putting the case is flawed in a number of ways. First, the second quotation conflates a predictability criterion with the issue of whether such invariants exist (" . . . enable the consequent to be calculated . . . "). Second, we do not need to include the whole environment in the causal antecedent, for many parts of that environment—in fact, almost all of it—will be causally irrelevant to the effect, as our intended interpretation of the ceteris paribus clause suggests. The color of a filing cabinet makes no difference to its dynamic properties, and that there were 8 million rather than 7,999,999 flies distributed around the forest that day will, in most cases, make no difference to whether the match will light (although one could construct a scenario in which it did). Third, and most important of all, is the fact that in many cases, although again not all, scientific inquiry has drastically reduced the number of *kinds* of potential causal influence that need to be considered. To guarantee that the ticket mechanism of a slot machine will work, it is not necessary to stipulate that there will be no earthquake, no fat man stumbling into the machine, no huge and sudden increase in the earth's gravitational mass under its base, and so on. It is enough, rather, to specify that no force of $>N$ newtons is present, where N is the tolerance limit for the mechanism. This does not make the causal claim logically true, because there is no logical necessity that the mechanism will operate, given the forces acting on it.

The second reason given for the entry of pragmatic features into counterfactual conditionals is the need to choose a suitable contrast case that satisfies the antecedent, and the standard view is that this choice will vary from context to context. Furthermore, the occurrence of the ceteris paribus conditions in the antecedent itself affects the appropriate choice of contrast case. Two things need to be said about this second reason. The first is that we are concerned here only with a choice of contrast cases for causal claims, not for counterfactual claims in general. We devoted a considerable amount of discussion in §15 to the choice of a neutral state as appropriate for probabilistic causality, and I myself find persuasive the reasons given there for adopting that choice. We need not be concerned with what would be the case if, for example, I were Sherlock Holmes, for counterfactual identity claims of that kind are outside the scope of our theory. The second point is that much of the context-dependency involved in causal counterfactuals is not of the kind delineated at the beginning of this section as constituting a subjective component of pragmatic content. Knowing how to set up a particular experimental arrangement that will produce a neutral state with all other factors held constant usually does involve causal knowledge that is specific to the system at hand, and to that extent is context dependent, but that causal knowledge, of the kind discussed in §29, can be objectified.[48]

One final remark on this topic is useful. Van Fraassen ([1980], pp. 125–26) argues that what is salient for one individual ("the" cause as opposed to background conditions) is often different than what is salient for another, that it is the salient feature that constitutes a successful answer to a why-question, and that the answers cannot be combined because each individual "keeps fixed" all but his salient feature, and because what is fixed for one varies for another. This argument is valid in the context of the kind of empiricism held by van Fraassen, which is a sophisticated variety of passive empiricism, dubbed 'constructive empiricism'. But recalling that our arguments for scientific empiricism lead to a separation between the experimental test conditions within which a cause exhibits its effect(s)[49] alone and the nonexperimental ordinary conditions within which each cause is still operating even when the other causes are not controlled, we can see that such combination of causal factors is indeed possible.

A third and a fourth reason that have been put forward as entailing the essentially pragmatic nature of explanations involve, respectively, the choice of a relevance relation and the implicitly contrastive form of explanations. As I mentioned at the outset, I am open to the view that there can be forms of explanation that are not obviously causal in form, and the present work is concerned only with explanatory factors that are causally relevant to the phenomenon to be explained.[50] The fourth reason goes right to the heart of the propositional approach to explanation, and to that I now turn.

§42. Why Ask Why-Questions?

We have seen in §34 how to present causal information so that its diversity and multiplicity is properly represented and, if the information is given in response to a request for an explanation, how that request can be formulated.

---

[48] While one can agree with much of what Polyani and others have said about 'personal knowledge' in the sciences (e.g., Polyani [1958]), one of the striking features of experimental reproducibility is that it enshrines this initially personal knowledge in the apparatus itself. It took a great deal of insight, scientific intuition, and theoretical knowledge to isolate the indicators that are used in home pregnancy kits, but by imposing simple controls, the chance of producing a correct result is remarkably invariant.

[49] Contemporary semantics for counterfactuals are very much like thought experiments, for the similarity relation is used to keep all but a minimal set of circumstances constant.

[50] It is also notoriously difficult to characterize the different kinds of relevance relations. For example, as Kitcher and Salmon (1987) have shown, the characterization given in van Fraassen (1980), chap. 5, §4.3, allows anything to be an explanation of anything else.

It might seem that there are other, equally appropriate ways of presenting that information and of requesting it. For example, it appears that we might have used instead the form 'X because ϕ, even though ψ', as in "This man died because he was exposed to the plague bacillus, even though he was given tetracycline," where X, ϕ, and ψ are sentences describing causes rather than terms referring to them.[51] And, rather than our "What is the explanation of X?" many would prefer "Why is it the case that p?" where again, in the latter, a propositional entity, rather than a term, provides the content of the question.[52] Does anything hinge on our choice of representation, or is it simply a matter of convenience which one we choose?

I believe that it does matter which choice we make. It has become increasingly common to take the why-question format as standard for formulating explanatory requests. Accompanying this has been an increased emphasis on the need for including pragmatic factors in explanatory contexts. The two trends are, I think, connected, and because (as I argued in the last section) pragmatics have no essential role in the kind of objective explanations with which I am concerned, linguistic devices which require their introduction ought to be avoided.

Let me begin with three major claims which Hempel (1965) made at the very beginning of his essay and which go right to the heart of one's conception of explanation. The first was that all scientific explanations may be regarded as answers to why-questions (p. 334). The second was that requests for explanations whose explanandum term is a nondescriptive singular referring device such as a noun make sense only when reconstrued in terms of why-questions (p. 334). The third claim was that every adequate response to an explanation-seeking why-question should, in principle, be able to serve as an adequate response to an epistemic why-question (p. 335). All these claims are connected. I begin with the first two.

The first claim is, of course, a fairly weak one, because it suggests only that we can use the why-question format, not that we must. In making this claim, Hempel was clearly influenced by considerations similar to ours, in that a given explanandum event will usually be multifaceted, and one needs to specify which aspect one needs to explain. Here is Hempel's argument:

> Sometimes the subject matter of an explanation, or the *explanandum,* is indicated by a noun, as when we ask for an explanation of the aurora borealis. It is important to realize that this kind of phrasing has a clear

---

[51] I was myself unconsciously trapped by this in my first paper on aleatory explanations (1981a), where I unthinkingly used the mixed form 'A because ϕ, despite ψ', which requires A and ϕ to be propositional, yet ψ refers to events. I hence slurred over the distinctions by using "despite the fact that" and the alternative "even though" for counteracting causes, thus managing to stay within the propositional form.

[52] I use 'sentence' and 'proposition' as stylistic variants of one another here. No ontological distinction is intended.

meaning only insofar as it can be restated in terms of why-questions. Thus in the context of an explanation, the aurora borealis must be taken to be characterized by certain distinctive general features, each of them describable by a that-clause, for example: that it is normally found only in fairly high northern latitudes; that it occurs intermittently; that sunspot maxima with their eleven-year cycle are regularly accompanied by maxima in the frequency and brightness of aurora borealis displays; that an aurora shows characteristic spectral lines of rare atmospheric gases, and so on. And to ask for an explanation of the aurora borealis is to request an explanation of *why* auroral displays occur in the fashion indicated and *why* they have physical characteristics such as those indicated. Indeed, requests for an explanation of the aurora borealis, of the tides, of solar eclipses in general or of some solar eclipse in particular, or of a given influenza epidemic, and the like have a clear meaning only if it is understood what aspects of the phenomenon in question are to be explained; and in that case the explanatory problem can again be expressed in the form 'Why is it the case that p?' where the place of 'p' is occupied by an empirical statement specifying the explanandum. Questions of this type will be called *explanation-seeking why-questions*. (P. 334)

It is evident, however, that one can meaningfully request an explanation without resorting to the why-question format. When John Snow discovered the principal cause of cholera in 1849, he wrote, "While the presumed contamination of the water of the Broad Street pump with the evacuations of cholera patients affords an exact explanation *of the fearful outbreak of cholera in St. James's parish,* there is no other circumstance which offers any explanation at all, whatever hypothesis of the nature and cause of the malady be adopted" (Snow [1855], p. 54, emphasis added).

A more recent example from molecular biology comes from Crick and Watson: "[Wilkins et al.] have shown that the X-ray patterns of both the crystalline and paracrystalline forms is the same for all sources of DNA ranging from viruses to mammals. . . . It seemed to us that the most likely explanation *of these observations* was that the structure was based upon features common to all nucleotides" (Crick and Watson [1954], p. 83, emphasis added).

Here we have terms "the fearful outbreak of cholera in St. James's Parish" and "the X-ray patterns of both the crystalline and paracrystalline forms of DNA," which associate properties with systems (in the first case, at a particular time; in the second, at all times) in the way suggested by our ontology, and the appropriate accompanying question in each case would be, "What is the explanation of X in S (at t)?" There are many more examples. It is common, and I believe meaningful, to ask for an explanation of such things as the increase in volume of a gas maintained at constant pressure, of the high incidence of recidivism among first-time offenders, of the occurrence of paresis in an individual, of the high inflation rate in an economy, of an eclipse of the sun, and of an influenza epidemic in a population. Indeed, even some requests couched in terms of Hempel's forbidden format appear to be meaningful and legitimate.

It appears to be appropriate for an individual to have asked Galileo or Newton for an explanation of the tides, or a meteorologist for an explanation of the aurora borealis. In the first case, what is being requested is an explanation of the periodic movements of the oceans on earth; in the second, an explanation of the appearance of bright displays in the atmosphere in the northern latitudes. In each of these cases, and in each of the previous examples, the explanation requested is usually explicitly, sometimes implicitly, of the occurrence or change of a property associated with a system, and this, rather than the particular linguistic representation, is the important feature. So ordinary usage will not decide between the why-question approach and the one suggested here.[53]

However, a review of some well-known problems accompanying the propositional approach should make us extremely wary of adopting it without being aware of these problems. First, within causal explanations, a propositional representation of the effect (explanandum) will also require a propositional representation of the causes. (A mixed ontology is theoretically possible, but given that most effects are also causes of further phenomena, and vice versa, a symmetrical treatment seems advisable.) This then makes the causal relation one holding between propositions, and as Davidson's (1967) well-known adaptation of a Fregean argument shows, given referential transparency of causal contexts plus substitution salva veritate of logical equivalents, propositional causal relations would turn out to be truth functional, which is obviously false. Next, consider what happens when the propositional approach is embedded in a nomological-inferential treatment of causation, as Hempel's was. As Kim (1973a) argued, it is extremely difficult to control propositional descriptions of events so that all and only the appropriate inferences are made. Let $(x)(Fx \rightarrow Gx)$ be any true law which subsumes the cause-proposition Fa and the effect-proposition Ga. Let Hb be any true proposition. Then Hb, $H(\imath x(x = b \ \& \ Fa)$ are both propositions describing the same event, i.e., b is H. But then $(x)(Fx \rightarrow Gx)$ together with $H(\imath x(x = b \ \& \ Fa)$ allows us to derive Ga, so Hb causes Ga, according to the subsumption account. This is clearly unacceptable.

---

[53] As one might have expected. An earlier debate about linguistic evidence for and against factlike entities as effects proved inconclusive. See Vendler (1962) and the accompanying papers by Bromberger and Dray. For the arguments that these debates are inconclusive, see Shorter (1965), especially p. 155. I am not suggesting here that Hempel was influenced by considerations of what ordinary-language constructions would allow. The argument is against those who appeal to linguistic evidence as the primary source of insights into explanation.

Next, recall Kyburg's example of the hexed salt discussed in §40C above: "All samples of hexed salt stirred in warm water dissolve. This sample of hexed salt was stirred in warm water. Hence this sample of salt dissolved." This satisfies all the criteria of adequacy for a deductive-nomological explanation yet is seriously misleading. Again, excess content which is causally irrelevant needs to be excluded from a propositional description in order to avoid this problem. Similar difficulties motivate some of Salmon's counterexamples to the inductive statistical model of explanation ([1971], pp. 33–40), although in others all the information given in the explanans is causally irrelevant, as is the case when the spontaneous evolution of a process is accompanied by irrelevant intervention. (Salmon's example of administering vitamin C to cold sufferers, also discussed in §40C, fits this case.)

Each of these cases hinges on the difficulty of keeping out causally irrelevant information from propositions, and we discussed how to avoid the analogous problem for events in §40C above. But the problems are not in fact peculiar to propositional representations of explanation, because similar difficulties infect nominalization of sentences. Consider Dretske's (1973, 1979) use of emphasis to produce terms referring to event allomorphs. Although his examples involved combinations of relevant and irrelevant causal information, we can construct parallel examples which involve a mixture of different kinds of causes. Consider

(1) The Afghan guerrillas' *surprise attack* after sunrise (caused)(explains) the crumbling of the defenses.
(2) The Afghan guerrillas' surprise attack *after sunrise* (caused)(explains) the crumbling of the defenses.

Given conventional military wisdom, (1) seems clearly to be true, while (2) is false. Compared with an attack with advance warning, a surprise attack increases the chances of victory and is a contributing cause to it. Compared with an attack before sunrise, a postdawn attack lowers the chances of victory and is a counteracting cause of it. What is occurring here, as Dretske noted about his examples involving relevant and irrelevant factors, is that stress markers pick out different aspects of spatiotemporal event descriptions and that far from being a pragmatic feature of ordinary discourse, these aspects are genuine features of the world.

The existence of sentential allomorphs has been used in a rather different way by van Fraassen ([1980], pp. 127–28) as the basis of an argument for the implicit contrastive form of why-questions. For example,[54] if one asks, "Why does the earth orbit the sun in an ellipse?" by stressing, in turn, "the earth," "orbit" "the sun," and "ellipse," we can, apparently, generate four distinct requests for explanation, as when we might be interested in why the

---

[54] The example is mine, not van Fraassen's.

earth, rather than the moon, orbits the sun, or, differently, why the earth's orbit is elliptical rather than circular. Van Fraassen concludes from the potential ambiguity of the original why-question that the implicit logical form of the question is a comparative one—Why is it the case that P in contrast to other members of a contrast class X?

Now if this argument were valid, it would introduce another element of pragmatic dependence into explanations, for the choice of a contrast class would ordinarily not be determined by any factual criteria but would be a function of the questioner's interests and knowledge. But the conclusion does not follow. It is true that some requests are for comparative explanations, and the request may be implicit rather than explicit, but it follows neither that the potential ambiguity of most why-questions is a result of an implicit appeal to different contrast cases nor that noncomparative why-questions are essentially ambiguous or illegitimate. It is at least as plausible to suggest that this issue is another facet of the deficiencies of propositional representations of explananda and that the ambiguity of many of these examples is a result of different aspects of the spatiotemporal events being selected as the subject of explanation. To take one of van Fraassen's own examples, in asking, "Why did the sample (of copper) burn green?" in focusing on the greenness of the event instead of the burning that was proceeding simultaneously, we pick out the property of the complex physical event that we want explained. Furthermore, what I want explained is the green color of the event, not why it was green rather than red. I may indeed want to know why the earth's orbit is elliptical rather than hyperbolic, a substantive scientific question whose answer relies on the relationship between the initial distance from the sun and the initial velocity of the earth, on the one hand, and the mass of the sun, on the other. (See §23 for details.) But I may just want to know why the earth's orbit has the property of being elliptical, and, to reemphasize the crucial point here, the potential ambiguity of why-questions does not entail that they are comparative in form.[55]

Indeed, this ambiguity is often a result of allowing the questioner to fix the format of the explanandum description through the use of some particular why-question. This is a dangerous practice, for it fails to make allowance for the important fact that the explainee ordinarily knows less about the explanandum event than does the explainer. By presenting the explainer with a fixed explanandum sentence, the explainer must tailor the explanation to fit the

---

[55] As mentioned in n. 50, Kitcher and Salmon (1987) have shown that there are serious difficulties involved in allowing the relevance relation that is used in an explanation to be left unfixed by the theory of explanation. Since the context-dependency of the relevance relation is the second major source of the pragmatics of explanation for van Fraassen (the first being the context-dependence of the contrast class), if the arguments given above against the implicit contrastive nature of why-questions are correct, then both pragmatic components of that theory are suspect.

description, thus, in many cases, making it difficult to take advantage of the epistemic superiority that he, the explainer, has. For example, the explainee will often describe the phenomenon in an incomplete, ambiguous, or misleading way, and unless the explainer is allowed to reconstrue this description in a way that properly reflects the actual structure of the phenomenon, the possibility for effective explanation will often be lost. Erotetic logic does make some concession in this direction by allowing an explainer to reject a why-question that has a false presupposition, but this is not enough. None of these arguments precludes an explainee from selecting a particular property of an object to be explained, but it does prevent the content of the explanation from being fixed by the description chosen by someone who is all too likely to be ignorant of what is a causal effect and what is not.

This is particularly important in those cases where the questioner is the same individual as the (eventual) respondent. Many scientific discoveries are made by scientists asking themselves why a particular phenomenon occurred that nobody else had thought to question. Frequently, the initial description of the explanandum will be crude and misleading, and it will only be as scientists' knowledge of the phenomenon increases that they will realize which aspects of the effect are the important ones and set up the why-question in the appropriate way. This does not mean that the initial request for an explanation should have been rejected; the request was appropriate but had to be reformulated.

It should by now be clear what the common problem is with all these cases. Mere truth of the explanans and explanandum sentences will not prevent a conflation of relevant and irrelevant factors, or of contributing and counteracting causes, and simple successful reference to multiaspectival events will also allow such conflations. The most direct way to avoid such problems is to select a linguistic form which directly mirrors the separate structure of causal influences. There may be forms other than the one I have chosen, but it will, I think, do the trick.

§43. Explanatory Knowledge

If the assessment of causal explanations given here is anywhere near the truth, it leaves us with a final question. Exactly what kind of knowledge does a causally based explanation of the kind I have suggested convey? The themes which I have been propounding—multiplicity, diversity, incompleteness, the unimportance of probability values, invariance, the reality of causal structures, the primacy of nonlinguistic explanations—all these must be fitted into a coherent conception of how epistemic gains are made by means of the discovery and conveyance of explanations.

It will be recalled that I have not yet discussed Hempel's third major claim, which was that every adequate response to an explanation seeking why-questions should, in principle, be able to serve as an adequate response to an epistemic why-question. Now although Hempel took great care to separate epistemic why-questions, whose answers give some grounds for believing in the truth of a proposition, from explanatory why-questions, whose answers presuppose that the questioner already has some justification for asserting the explanandum sentence, the symmetry of logical structure between answers to the two types of questions, which paralleled the original symmetry of prediction and explanation in Hempel's model, together with the third claim that an adequate answer to an explanatory question provides sufficient conditions for an adequate answer to the associated epistemic question, means that the kind of knowledge provided by answers to Hempelian explanatory questions has an intimate connection with justificatory knowledge.

Recall that for Hume, the effect of a regularity was to generate an habitual association of ideas, so that whenever the cause was observed, a psychological expectation of the effect was provoked. The modern logically based versions of the regularity view allow something similar. By providing an individual with the correct law statements and statements of particular fact, that individual can, in the case of sufficient causes, deduce that the effect will occur. Then, relative to the causal information provided, a purely a priori process leads to an expectation of the effect. By virtue of placing the regularity in an objective law statement, the inference itself is objectified as logical, and it provides a ready device with the aid of which any individual with sufficient logical acumen can generate for himself the exact analogue of Hume's psychological expectation. Thus, although Hempel made it quite clear that the expectability of the explanandum on the basis of the explanans was one of *nomic* expectability, the consequent arousal of psychological expectability is an important element in an empiricist's account of causal understanding. (It is likely that resistance to accounts of probabilistic causality and to low probability explanations which do not require such expectability stems from a reluctance to give up this aspect of Humean causation.) Because this expectability is present in both causal and noncausal regularities, the only way to deny its explanatory force in cases which are answers to epistemic why-questions but not to explanatory why-questions is to deny that it is a *nomological* expectation. Thus, in order for inquirers to have causal explanatory knowledge, their psychological expectation must have been induced by the right kind of source—a law rather than a mere regularity. And hence the whole burden for distinguishing between answers to epistemic why-questions and answers to causal explanatory why-questions falls on an ability to distinguish between lawlike regularities and nonlawlike regularities.

To see this, consider an example discussed by Hempel ([1965], pp. 374–75). The appearance of Koplik's spots (small whitish spots on the linings of the cheeks) can serve as a predictor of the onset of measles rash, and if one were asked to justify one's claim to knowing that an individual was to have the rash, the response "The individual has Koplik spots, and almost all those who have the spots later have the rash" would justify the claim. Hence the quoted sentence would be an adequate answer to an epistemic why-question. The appearance of the Koplik spots does not explain the appearance of the rash, as Hempel acknowledges, and indeed, this is simply another example of the spurious causation problem (§27A), with both the spots and rash being caused by the measles virus. Hempel's reason for denying the explanatory adequacy of the quoted sentence was not this causal one, however.[56] It was rather that the regularity between the appearance of Koplik spots and the later appearance of the rash was not a universal law because the spots might appear without the rash. Yet it is clear that the mere failure to be universal cannot be sufficient to prevent a regularity from serving as part of an answer to an explanatory why-question; otherwise, no statistical explanation would be possible.

Hempel and others, of course, have made systematic efforts to distinguish between lawlike and nonlawlike regularities, none of which, I think it would be generally agreed, have been entirely successful. Indeed, those who have cast the problem in the nomenclature of 'lawlike' versus 'accidental' regularities and considered this division to constitute an exhaustive partition have muddied the issue. Regularities are not accidental if there is an explanation of them, and in the case of regularities produced by a common causal factor, such as the regularity that if any arbitrary subscriber to an academic journal receives a copy on day x, then any other arbitrary subscriber will receive a copy on day $x \pm 4$ with probability .95 is not in the least an accidental regularity. But neither is it a law.

We, however, do not need to distinguish between laws and nonlaws but between causal and noncausal sequences. Yet because, as we have noted, noncausal sequences can equally well produce a justified expectation and because many cases of low probability aleatory explanations would not have produced an expectation at all, we must drop this neo-Humean approach.

What, then, do we have to replace the traditional account of explanatory knowledge? It is not propositional knowledge in the way that the connection between knowing-why and knowing-that is forced on propositional accounts of explanation that retain a connection between answers to explanatory and epistemic why-questions. Nor is it *de dicto* knowledge, shaped by the descriptive form of the linguistic apparatus that is the starting point for most contemporary theories of explanation. It is *de re* knowledge, often incomplete

---

[56] Although his discussion of the example is completely consistent with adopting a causal approach, Hempel himself allowed that one could produce the spots by a local inoculation with a small amount of measles virus and that this would not lead to the rash's appearance. We note also that appearance of the spots can often be prevented, while allowing the rash to appear, by administering low doses of gamma globulin.

knowledge of the causes that contributed to the effect, gained in a cumulative manner, coupled with the discovery of previously unknown structures that pushes the moving boundary of the observable even further from ordinary experience and allows us to become acquainted with finer and finer details of how the world works. When we know of all the causes, then we shall know all there is to know of the kind with which we are concerned, for all that will be left is pure chance, and chance is, as I have said, literally nothing.

Covariance Measures

The basic relationship is that of covariance between two variables. All the relations which are used below in causal modeling can be constructed as functions of covariances.

DEFINITION 1. $\text{Cov}(X, Y) = E[(X - E(X))(Y - E(Y))]$.

The motivation behind the definition of covariance is easy to describe: if $\text{Cov}(X, Y)$ is positive, variations in X and Y away from any reference points tend, *on the average*, to be in the same direction, whereas if $\text{Cov}(X, Y)$ is negative, those variations, on average, are in opposite directions. No causal concepts are involved in this definition, and it is not dependent upon the form of the probability distributions governing the variables, in that it requires only that a joint distribution for the variables exists. (Estimation procedures, with which we are not concerned, may, in contrast, require the assumption of a particular distributional form.)

The covariance is a symmetric functional, linear in both arguments, i.e.,

$$\text{Cov}(X, Y) = \text{Cov}(Y, X),$$
$$\text{Cov}(aX + bZ, Y) = a\text{Cov}(X, Y) + b\text{Cov}(Z, Y).$$

Also, for any constant c, $\text{Cov}(X, c) = 0$. From these last two properties it immediately follows that $\text{Cov}(X - c, Y) = \text{Cov}(X, Y)$. Hence taking any point on the measurement scale as a reference point for covariance measures will not affect either the sign or the value of the covariance. It is thus often convenient to take the variable means to be 0. We can now define a number of other important quantities in terms of covariances.

The variance, a quantity whose value is a measure of the degree to which a variable fluctuates or is undetermined, is simply the covariance of a variable with itself.

DEFINITION 2. $\text{Var}(X) = \text{Cov}(X, X) = E(X^2) - (E(X))^2$.

$\text{Var}(X)$ will often be denoted by $\sigma^2(X)$. $\sigma(X) = (\text{Var}(X))^{1/2}$ is the standard deviation of X.

An important notion is that of a standardized variable, one which is measured from the mean of the original variable and which has unit variance.

DEFINITION 3. $X_s = (X - E(X))/\sigma(X)$.

Standardization has a potentially serious drawback, however, in that because the units of variation are defined in terms of $\sigma(X)$, covariance measures on standardized variables can be transferred only to populations with identical variances to the original.

Standardization allows us to define the widely used (Pearson) correlation coefficient, rho.

DEFINITION 4. The correlation coefficient ρ is the covariance between two standardized variables X_s, Y_s.

Hence correlation coefficients are simply special cases, albeit important ones, of covariances.

We can also define the regression coefficient of Y on X.

DEFINITION 5. The regression coefficient of Y on X, b_{yx}, is:

$$b_{yx} = \text{Cov}(Y, X)/\text{Var}(X).$$

We thus have from Definitions 4 and 5 the relationship $b_{yx} = b_{xy} = \rho_{yx}$ for standardized variables.

Finally, regression coefficients applied to standardized variables are called path coefficients, and we have, when $E(X) = E(Y) = 0$:

DEFINITION 6. $p_{yx} = b_{yx} \, \sigma_x/\sigma_y$

Extension of the Basic Quantitative Theory

The apparatus that was developed in §13, simple as it is, can be extended to serve as the causal basis of a cluster of techniques that are widely used in the social sciences, among which are multiple linear regression, structural equation models, and path analysis.[1] There are two things to mention about the brief discussion below. The first is that it deals with only the most basic features of what is by now an enormous and detailed literature on these techniques. The second is that, as before, issues of statistical estimation are not our concern here, despite their importance to practicing scientists.[2] The purpose of this limited discussion is to allow us to focus on issues of causal interpretation and to assess the principles that are involved in that interpretative enterprise, while keeping those principles separated as far as possible from assumptions that are introduced primarily for legitimating particular statistical estimation techniques or for dealing with important but nevertheless auxiliary concerns, such as the imprecision of measures for particular variables.

This is not to deny that such things as biased estimators and measurement error can lead to incorrect inferences. Indeed such biases can arise from violations of either specifically causal assumptions, such as Assumption B below, or of more general statistical or measurement assumptions, such as Assumption C below. For this reason, practicing social scientists may well argue that there is no real separation that can be made between the two kinds of assumption because they can both lead to erroneous causal conclusions. An interesting defense can probably be made for that view, but in the context of a philosophical treatment of causation, I believe that it is appropriate to emphasize those assumptions that *directly* affect the causal interpretation of these models, such as A and B below, rather than those that indirectly affect the causal inferences through violation of a statistical or measurement as-

[1] Others include factor analysis, ANOVA, and the generically named 'causal models'. Accounts of the first can be found in Harmon (1967) and in Glymour, Scheines, and Spirtes (1987); of the second in Bock (1975) and many other texts on applied statistics; of the third in Blalock (1971).

[2] Thus, all parameters, distributions, and probabilities will be those of the system and not sample estimates.

sumption, such as C below. This is in conformity with our stated intention of dealing primarily with ontological issues and only secondarily with epistemological ones.

Although terminology in these areas is not always uniform, the following definitions are consistent with widespread usage. Employing the same ontology and terminology as is used in §12 and appendix 1, we have:

> DEFINITION. Multiple linear regression analysis applies to cases where all the variables are directly and perfectly measurable (observable), there is exactly one endogenous variable and more than one exogenous variable, and the primary emphasis is on prediction of the endogenous variable from the exogenous variables.

> DEFINITION. Structural equation models consist in a set of regression equations within which an explicit distinction is made between exogenous and endogenous variables,[3] and these variables may be either observable or unobservable. If the equations are hierarchically ordered, so that there is no reciprocal causation between variables (i.e., only lower numbered variables can cause higher numbered variables, and not vice versa), then the model is called *recursive*.[4]

We shall henceforth consider only recursive systems of structural equations.

> DEFINITION. Path analysis is the theory of structural equation models within which all variables are standardized.

A fourth category, generically named 'causal models', is often added to the above three categories, the difference being that in causal models the emphasis is supposed to be on falsification of structural equation models, whereas in the first three categories the primary focus is on the estimation of the structural coefficients, once the appropriate model has been selected. ('Causal models' are often associated with the work of Hubert Blalock and Herbert Simon.) However, as Blalock ([1971], p. 73) has noted, this difference is one of emphasis rather than substance, and we shall hence count causal models here as part of the structural equation apparatus.

Consider now the general case $Y_j = \sum_{i=0}^{n} b_i X_i + U_j$, where the variables Y_j, X_i may themselves be embedded in a network of (nonreciprocal) causal relationships. Although a number of assumptions need to be made about these variables, their relationships, and their probabilistic properties for statistical

---

[3] I shall not make the further distinction here that is sometimes made in the econometric literature between exogenous and lagged endogenous variables.

[4] Not to be confused, needless to say, with the use of 'recursive' in the theory of computation. Recursive models have the desirable property that they are identifiable; i.e., the value of each regression (structural) coefficient is uniquely estimable from the data.

estimation purposes, there are two key assumptions that are made specifically for causal purposes and one for measurement purposes.[5]

ASSUMPTION A. The regression coefficients (structural coefficients, path coefficients) b_i are the same for each individual system, i.e., b_i is a constant and is not a function of any of the X_i's, although, of course, $b_i \neq b_j$ for $i \neq j$ in general.

ASSUMPTION B. The variables X_i and the error variables U_j are mutually probabilistically independent, both within and across equations.

ASSUMPTION C. The variables are assumed to be measured without error, or one can correct for measurement error using an auxiliary measurement theory.

As mentioned earlier, I shall not discuss this last assumption in any detail but shall instead focus on the first two.

Assumptions A and B play a key role in fixing the correct interpretation of the causal claims that are based on the three categories of modeling techniques mentioned above. In particular, I want to argue for three assertions on the basis of these assumptions. First, that causal claims arising from these models can properly be applied to individuals rather than to statistical ensembles of individuals. Second, that these models, via Assumption B, adhere to the invariance requirement for causation stipulated in Assumption 2 of §13 taken across all factors omitted from the model, and hence justify the additivity of U_j in the linear models. Third, that in some cases, although not in all, it can correctly be said that exogenous variables contribute directly to the value of the endogenous variable, rather than simply affecting the probability distribution or conditional means of the endogenous variable. Furthermore, it can be explicitly stated in which kind of case the direct contribution to the exogenous variables occurs. We begin with a discussion of Assumption A.

The explicitness with which this assumption is made varies, but those writers who are concerned with interpretation are usually quite clear about it. For example, "The structural coefficients are assumed to be the same for each individual. The set of all units that follow the same causal relationship [is] referred to as the *population*" (Hanushek and Jackson [1977], p. 7), and "The structural form of the model is that parameterization—among the various possible ones—in which the coefficients . . . are not inseparable mixtures

---

[5] A further assumption that is often imposed for estimation purposes is the homoscedasticity of the error variables, i.e., the variance of U_j is the same for each j. This, together with Assumption B (and implicitly A), gives the ordinary least-squares estimator as the best linear unbiased estimator of the regression coefficients. It is worth noting that none of these assumptions depends on the form of the particular probability distribution associated with the variables—in particular, normality is not required (although it is imposed for other purposes).

of the coefficients that 'really' govern how the world works'' (Duncan [1975], p. 151).[6] One reason for insisting upon the constancy of b_i is, of course, to allow the random variable X_i to be sampled from a homogeneous population, but equally important is the requirement that even when repeated observations are made on the same unit, the value of b_i must remain the same, irrespective of what values X_i itself, the other causal variables X_j, or the chance variable U_j may have. It was this functional independence of b_i from X_i, X_j and U_j that allowed us (in § 12) to separate the relatively permanent structural features of a system S from the variable properties connected with S. What must be emphasized here, however, is that the terms 'individual', 'system', and 'unit' all refer to the basic element of causal analysis, even though these elements may themselves be complex arrangements of smaller units, perhaps even whole populations. Multiple trials on replicas of basic elements are required, of course, to generate statistical data in order to estimate the structural coefficients, but it is the basic elements that constitute the objects about which causal claims are made and that serve as the subject of a single trial. The fact that whole populations can serve as a single system allows for the existence of specifically social phenomena that can arise from interactions between individuals in the population, but the population of populations used to calculate frequency estimators must not be confused with the single population upon which causal factors operate.

These distinctions do not, of course, establish our first assertion, that causal claims apply to individuals. To do that, we must evaluate the role played by the stochastic factor in the models, U_j, and this requires an explicit discussion of Assumption B.

EXAMINATION OF ASSUMPTION B

We have formulated this assumption in terms of the probabilistic independence of random variables, which, leaving aside certain technical restrictions,[7] requires that for any event A_i associated with X_i, and any events B_j associated with any of the U_j, $P(A_i \cap \bigcap_{j=1}^{n} B_j) = P(A_i) \prod_{j=1}^{n} P(B_j)$. (It is not assumed here that the X_i are themselves independent: indeed, since some are effects

---

[6] The contrast here is with the 'reduced form' of the system of equations, in which the coefficients are linear combinations of the true coefficients. An argument against the use of such reduced forms is given in Humphreys (1985). A further reason not to use the reduced form is that such a mixture does not provide the detailed differentiation between direct and indirect causes that the unreduced form allows, and thus, in particular, it does not allow a proper analysis of the problem of negative links (q.v., appendix 3).

[7] The exact definiton of the independence of random variables is: the family $\{X_{\lambda_i} \lambda_i \epsilon \Lambda\}$ of real-valued random variables is probabilistically independent if for every finite set of events $\{B_1, \cdots, B_n\}$, $B_i \epsilon \sigma (X_{\lambda_i})$, where $\sigma(X_{\lambda_i})$ is the sigma algebra generated by X_{λ_i}, $P(\bigcap_{i=1}^{n} B_i) = \prod_{i=1}^{n} P(B_i)$. See Ito (1984), § 3.4, or Chung (1968), §3.3, for a detailed exposition of this concept.

of others within the structural equation models, that would be highly undesirable. However, for the purposes of causal attribution, we still need to
impose a full invariance condition, and the various cases examined in §26
should be reviewed in this light.) Thus, in terms of objective chances, the
chance of an event associated with the property[8] represented by X_i is not a
function of the chances of any events associated with the error variables U_j.
It immediately follows[9] from the independence of the random variables that
$E(X_1, U_1 \ldots, U_n) = E(X_1) \prod_{j=1}^{n} E(U_j)$, entailing that the random variables
are uncorrelated. The applied statistical literature often requires only this
uncorrelatedness, which is a weaker condition than probabilistic independence, but the stronger condition is, I think, to be preferred on the grounds
that it makes explicit the lack of probabilistic influence between the variables.[10]
It is not, however, necessary to formulate the condition in terms of *causal*
independence between the error variables and the exogenous variables, although there is no doubt that in order to test whether the independence requirement holds, prior causal knowledge of some kind is required, as discussed
in §29.

Why impose this requirement? How is it to be interpreted? One way to
answer the first question is to refer to a standard result about omitted factors.

> THEOREM: If a new variable X_{n+1} is added to the system, then the
> existing regression (structural, path) coefficients b_i are left un-
> changed if and only if X_{n+1} is uncorrelated with the X_i.

Although this equivalence holds for the uncorrelatedness condition, it is
easily seen that the independence of X_{n+1} from the X_i is sufficient for the
invariance of the structural coefficients b_i, and this result captures in a completely explicit manner the invariance requirement for genuine causation, as
long as we are clear on what the b_i represent. A convenient fiction often
employed in interpreting these models is that b_i is the measure of the direct
effect on Y of a unit change in X_i when all other factors are held constant.[11]
But of course, in nonexperimental contexts (and even in real, rather than
idealized, experimental contexts) the other factors will not be constant, and
worse, to assume that the uncontrollable U_j is held constant is, properly
speaking, unintelligible. Now, we have argued (in §13) that in the quantitative
case a genuine cause produces its effect independently of the action of other
factors, and it is these arguments that allow a specific interpretation of these
models. That is, a unit change in a causal factor X_i produces a change of b_i

---

[8] And, of course, with the system S with which b_i is also associated.

[9] Given that $E|X_i| < \infty$, which we assume holds for all i.

[10] A third requirement sometimes imposed, that the variables be linearly independent, is itself
entailed by the uncorrelatedness condition, but not conversely.

[11] The position that all other variables must be held constant at their mean value is needlessly
restrictive. See Kenny (1979), p. 47, for an example of that view.

units in its direct effect Y_j, whatever other influences are present that leave b_i unchanged. This does not mean that the change due to X_i is directly observable (in any straightforward sense) when other influences are also present, because the quantitative contribution due to X_i may be supplemented, balanced, or more than compensated by one or more coexisting factors X_j. A failure to distinguish between the actual effect of X_i and the net observed effect of X_i together with all other causal influences on Y is an elementary but common mistake. It would not be erroneous if the independence assumption B was not made, for then interaction effects would have to be taken into account, but it is precisely the use of Assumption B that allows X_i's effect to be separated even when not all the causal influences on Y are explicitly included in the model. Of course, to ensure the truth of Assumption B may be epistemically impossible in many or most cases, but our task here is to examine what follows causally from these common assumptions, not whether their use is justified in specific instances.

With this interpretation of the causal role of b_i and X_i, it is evident, with one further fact, what the independence gives.[12] Whether or not a variable that has been omitted from explicit consideration (and hence is a component of U_j) is causally relevant to Y, the attribution of X_i as a contributing (or counteracting) cause of Y will not be undermined[13] if that omitted variable is probabilistically independent of X_i. This establishes our second assertion— that it is possible to view the U_j as an additive factor in the models.

We said that X_i contributes directly to Y under the independence assumption. Yet since $Y = E(Y/\mathbf{X}) + U = \sum_{i=1}^{n} b_i X_i + U$, could we not equally say that X_i contributes to the conditional expectation of Y? To assess these two apparently different alternatives, we need to pay closer attention to the interpretation of U. In causal diagrams, U is often represented as an influence on Y entirely separate from X_i but not of an essentially different kind. Within this basic representation, U can represent some or all of these influences:

1. A stochastic or indeterministic element due to pure chance in the pathways from the X_i to Y but which varies independently of the systematic contribution of X_i to Y.
2. A stochastic element independent of the path from X_i to Y.
3. The varying effects of uncontrolled factors omitted from the model.

---

[12] The further fact is that when U_j is independent of X_i, any Borel function of U_j is also independent of X_i. Thus, if U_j is itself a function of omitted variables $X_{n+1}, \cdots, X_p$, i.e., $U_j = g(X_{n+1}, \cdots, X_p)$ then as long as the operations required to invert g and represent X_{n+1} as a function of U_j, $(X_{n+2}, \cdots, X_p)$ are themselves Borel, the independence of U_j from X_i entails the independence of X_{n+1} from X_i. Because almost any continuous function is Borel, it will be unusual for these restrictions not to be satisfied.

[13] Since the b_i give the degree of causal contribution, this actually provides a stronger result than the mere invariance of the *kind* of causal relevance involved.

(This last source, however, cannot include omitted intervening variables, because those would not be independent of the X_i in whose path it occurred.)

In our discussion above, we considered case 3, where omitted factors compose U. Many accounts of causal models consider the models to be fundamentally deterministic, and there is a natural inclination to believe that any lack of determination of Y by the X_i's must ultimately be accounted for in terms of as yet undiscovered factors lumped together in U. If so, then the conditional expectation $E(Y/\mathbf{X})$ has to be interpreted for each unit system in an epistemic way, as resulting from a lack of knowledge, and there is no genuine chance involved. In that case, X_i does contribute directly to Y for each unit and not, in any real sense, to $E(Y/\mathbf{X})$. But we ought to allow that there is in some models a genuine, irreducibly chance element to U, and in that case, influences 1 and 2 must be considered. It might appear that those two cases are different. Yet here there is a serious danger of being misled by the notation or the mode of representation in the causal diagram. To represent U as a random variable that is separable from X_i in case 1 is to run the risk of confusing a mathematical separability with a real separability. Unlike the X_j, pure chance is uncontrollable even in an ideal experimental context, and in case 1 the contribution of X_i is, when it occurs, inextricably mixed with U. The problem with claiming that X_i makes a direct contribution to Y in case 1, then, is that it gives rise to the misleading picture of X_i first influencing Y, and then chance contributing its share. Rather, what X_i does is to contribute to Y through its probability distribution via the intermediary of its mean.[14]

In case 2, we must separate the situation where U is operating simultaneously with X_i from the case where the operation of X_i precedes the (separate) operation of U. In the latter, there is no question (assuming case 1 does not also hold)—X_i contributes directly to Y. The former situation further subdivides. When U is due to a separate properly probabilistic factor X_{n+1}, that factor can, at least in principle, be removed by reducing it to its neutral state, and with its removal we would remove the chance element as well. Hence in that case X_i would contribute directly to Y, and by virtue of the invariance condition, we must consider that it contributes directly to Y in the actual situation where X_{n+1} is also present. But when U is purely chancelike, the situation is exactly analogous to case 1, and we must consider X_i as contributing to $E(Y/\mathbf{X})$ rather than to Y directly.

There are thus situations on which it is proper to consider X_i as a causal influence on Y and situations in which it is proper to consider X_i as a causal influence on $E(Y/\mathbf{X})$. But it must be kept in mind that in those latter cases

---

[14] For any distribution function whose support is in a finite interval (i.e., the corresponding probability measure is not spread out over the whole real line), that distribution function is uniquely determined by its moments (expectations of all integral orders).

the causal effect is a deterministic one on the probability characteristics of the systems, and the chance itself still has no causal role.

We have thus established our third assertion, that in some cases it can correctly be said that X_i contributes directly to Y, and the discussion of the three cases should make it clear when this is appropriate. We can now assess the status of our first assertion, that causal claims can be made about individuals on the basis of these models. Taken together with the second assertion, our discussion of cases 1, 2, and 3 for the third assumption allows us to make sense of the claim that X_i directly contributes to the value of Y in individual systems in situations where X_i's action on Y is deterministic. In order to make a similar claim in cases where X_i is irreducibly chancy in action, one must accept the intelligibility and existence of single-case chances and, concomitantly, that the relative-frequency interpretation of probability that so often accompanies these models and probabilistic causality in general is unnecessary and misleading. I refer the reader to §§22, 24–25 for the relevant arguments.

Transitivity and Negative Links

In their paper "Probabilistic Causality and the Question of Transitivity," Eells and Sober (1983) provide a set of sufficient conditions under which probabilistic causality is transitive. By employing the general apparatus of our theory, a much shorter proof of transitivity can be given. The important issue of how strong are the conditions needed to obtain the result is also discussed here.

THE RESULT

If A causes B and B causes C, does A cause C? Consider this apparatus:

1. Causes and effects are *variables*, and for X to be a contributing cause of Y means that increases in X produce increases in Y when all other causal influences on Y are held constant.
2. We represent causal relations by a *path diagram*.

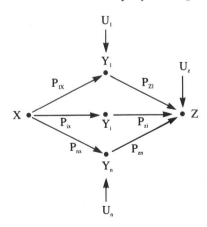

3. Each causal path from a Y_i to Z is given by

$$Z = p_{zi}Y_i + p_{zu}U_z$$

and from X to Y_i by

$$Y_i = p_{ix}X + p_{iu}U_i,$$

where the U_i's represent all other factors (not necessarily causal) associated with Y_i. Now assume:

4. All variables are standardized, i.e., have zero mean and unit variance.
5. Each U_i is uncorrelated with any causal factor occurring to the left of it in the path diagram, and with any other U_j, $j \neq i$. Then we have:

$$Z = \sum_{i=1}^{n} p_{zi}Y_i + p_{zu}U_z,$$

and substituting for Y_i, we have

$$Z = \sum_{i=1}^{n} p_{zi}(p_{ix}X + p_{iu}U_i) + p_{zu}U_z.$$

Multiplying through by X and taking expectations we obtain

$$E(ZX) = \sum_{i=1}^{n} p_{zi}p_{ix}E(X^2) + p_{zi}p_{iu}E(XU_i) + p_{zu}E(XU_z).$$

By Assumption 4 above, $E(X^2) = 1$, and by Assumptions 4 and 5, $E(XU_i) = E(XU_z) = 0$ for all i. Hence

$$E(ZX) = \sum_{i=1}^{n} p_{zi} p_{ix},$$

and using Assumption 4 again we have

$$\rho_{zx} = \sum_{i=1}^{n} p_{zi} p_{ix}.$$

PROOF OF TRANSITIVITY FOR BINARY PROBABILISTIC CAUSALITY

Call $R(A, B) = P(A/B) - P(A/-B)$ the *relevance difference*. For transitivity of (binary) probabilistic causation we thus require the conditions under which $R(B, A) > 0$ and $R(C, B) > 0$ entail $R(C, A) > 0$. Recall this central result of §14: if I_A, I_B are the indicator variables of the events A, B, respectively (i.e., $I_A = 1$ if A occurs; $I_A = 0$ if $-A$ occurs), then $R(A, B) = b_{I_A I_B}$, where $b_{I_A I_B}$ is the regression coefficient of I_A on I_B.

We have thus reduced the problem to one in terms of regression coefficients for variables; i.e., we require that $b_{I_B | A} > 0$ and $b_{I_C | B} > 0$ entail $b_{I_C | A} > 0$.

Suppose $R(B_i, A) > 0$ and $R(C, B_i) > 0$ for every i. Then (i) $b_{I_{B_i} I_A} > 0$ and $b_{I_C | B_i} > 0$ for every i by the central result. Now consider the standardized forms of the indicator variables I_{A_S} etc. (These standardized forms will not themselves be indicator variables, and the transformations are used solely to preserve the signs of the associations.) Since for any variables X, Y, $\text{Cov}(X_S, Y_S) > 0$ if and only if $\text{Cov}(X, Y) > 0$, from Definition 5 of Appendix 1: (ii) $b_{Y_S X_S} > 0$ if and only if $b_{YX} > 0$. Furthermore, (iii) $p_{YX} > 0$ if and only if $b_{YX} > 0$ from Definition 6 of appendix 1 (a transformation of the mean of a variable to 0 also leaves the regression coefficient unchanged).

Hence, employing our path-analytic result together with (i), (ii), (iii), we have that $p_{I_{C_S} I_{A_S}} > 0$. Thus $b_{I_{C_S} I_{A_S}} > 0$ (see appendix 1), and using (ii) again, $b_{I_C | A} > 0$. Hence $R(C, A) > 0$ by the central result.

The path-analytic apparatus can also be used to prove a result that was first shown in Humphreys (1980). This demonstrated that within simple binary Markov chains, it is possible to have a chain in which the initial event is positively relevant overall to the eventual outcome but which is linked to it by a chain in which an even number of links are negative and, more generally, that the overall relevance of the initial event to the final event in a chain connected by n links is a product of the signs of the relevance difference for each link. (This result is discussed in Good [1980].) It is easy to see from the path-analytic result proved earlier, together with the connections between the signs of the relevance difference and its associated path coefficient, how the result follows for a two-link chain. I leave it to the reader to extend the result to chains of arbitrary length.

THE PROBLEM OF NEGATIVE LINKS

The problem of negative links, which was first raised by Deborah Rosen and discussed in Suppes (1970), is peculiar to nondeterministic causation. The issue is this: suppose that one event is connected to a second by a chain of intermediate links and that at least one of those links is of negative probabilistic relevance. Does this preclude the first event from being a (contributing) cause of the second? One can show (see above, p. 155) that it is possible for the first to be positively relevant to the second if there is an even number of such negative intermediate links and if the chain, as we shall assume henceforth, is Markov. The simple example that has served as a focal point of discussion is this: an expert golfer takes his swing (A), uncharacteristically slicing the ball (B); it hits a tree branch (C) and ricochets into the hole (D). What, if anything here, was a cause of the ball's going into the hole?

There has been a great deal of dispute about the correct answer to this question, with some holding that because it is possible to trace a continuous process from A to D, each part of the sequence is causal, while others, noting that at least A is negatively relevant to B, insist that this link cannot be causal, and (hence) neither can the chain as a whole. It is hopeless to rely on 'intuition'[1] in cases where there is so much disagreement, so we use a theoretical strategy instead. First, ask: what exactly are the events that constitute the nodes of the chain? Here we need to use the method of detailed specification of events.[2] Second, ask: what is the correct contrast case for each event? Third, note that this is a singular sequence, and the causal or anticausal claim must reflect that. Fourth, ask: can we claim invariance here?

Let us begin by asking whether there are in fact any negative links in the chain. Is C negatively relevant to D? Using the first, second, and third tactics cited above, we have that C involves a ball with a specific linear and angular momentum involved in an impact with a not perfectly elastic stationary object. D involves the same system, with different values of the same variables, being in a specified region. Two contrast cases exist for C—the ball with zero angular momentum and the ball with zero linear momentum. It is unlikely that we can calculate the exact chances involved here, and we may not be able to state with certainty whether the impact is a deterministic interaction or not. But we can say that having the value of the linear momentum that it did at the time of impact increased the chance over the neutral state of that variable. It may even be true that having that exact linear momentum and no other was required, and perhaps the angular momentum played a role (a more detailed specification would be needed to determine that), but what must not be done is to compare, perhaps implicitly, this situation with the *average* case of golf balls going in holes—$P(D/C)$ compared with $P(D)$. We have said why this is inadvisable (§15), and I suspect that this comparison is responsible for some judging that C is negatively relevant to D. So C is, as it was, positively relevant to D, as it occurred.

[1] This is only the second time this term is mentioned in this book. It is an evil word, for in its modern use it serves as a substitute for argument and thought.

[2] For reasons that seem uncharacteristically unconvincing, Salmon rejects the method of detailed specification of events for this example, and presumably for others like it ([1984], pp. 194–95).

For exactly similar reasons, B is not negatively relevant to C: presumably the branch is off to the side, and had the ball not been sliced, the chance of its hitting the branch would have been 0. But perhaps A is negatively relevant to B. No idealization is necessary to allow a state of zero golf skill, and hence the property of having a high skill level, as indicated by a low handicap, is negatively relevant to a sliced shot. What of our fourth question—are these various relevance relations invariant? To establish this would require specification of the absence of some further factors, such as lateral forces and lubricants on the branch, but not many. Remember, all we need is an increase (or decrease) in the chance, not the same invariant value, and certainly not certainty. So we can, I think, claim that C was a contributing cause of D and B of C, modulo specification of these other factors in C and B. That A invariantly counteracts B is perhaps not so straightforward, but in order to focus on the main issue, perhaps the reader will allow me to assume that it does.

Given all this, and there is a good deal of it, we can say this: Despite the golfer's having a high level of skill, the ball went into the hole as it did because it was sliced and hit the tree branch in the particular way it did, where "as it did" and "in the particular way it did" are concessions to ordinary language but ones that refer to actual events which happen to be radically underdescribed yet could be specified in further degrees of detail. Thus on our account A did not cause B, and A did not cause D, yet we can still explain D by virtue of B and C.

Here, then, is a general conjecture about the problem of negative links. To give an explanation of an event is to tell (part of) the causal story that led up to that event. To tell the story of a chain involves listing each link in the chain, keeping separate positive from negative links. Contributing causes are transitive, but counteracting causes are not, and so although one may, perhaps through ignorance of intervening nodes, combine positive links without trouble, if an overall positive link turns out to be due to a succession of negative links, that overall positive link is not a contributing cause of the phenomenon. Aleatory explanatory chains are thus always dangerously defeasible and require much closer attention to the specifics of what actually happened between the initial and final phases of the process than do deterministic explanations.

I believe that this conjecture will provide the correct answer to genuine examples of the problem of negative links. I have no doubt taxed the reader's patience by going on in such detail, but attention to detail is, nevertheless, the key to a successful account of scientific causation and explanation.

REFERENCES

Achinstein, P. 1983. *The Nature of Explanation.* Oxford: Oxford University Press.

Armstrong, D. 1968. *A Materialist Theory of the Mind.* London: Routledge and Kegan Paul.

Asquith, P., and Giere, R., eds. 1981. *PSA 1980, Volume 2.* East Lansing, Mich.: Philosophy of Science Association.

Asquith, P., and Hacking, I., eds. 1981. *PSA 1978, Volume 2.* East Lansing, Mich.: Philosophy of Science Association.

Asquith, P., and Kitcher, P., eds. 1985. *PSA 1984, Volume 2.* East Lansing, Mich.: Philosophy of Science Association.

Asquith, P., and Nickles, T., eds. 1983. *PSA 1982, Volume 2.* East Lansing, Mich.: Philosophy of Science Association.

Austin, J. 1961. "Performative Utterances." Chap. 10 in *Philosophical Papers.* Oxford: Clarendon Press.

Barrow, J., and Tipler, F. 1986. *The Anthropic Cosmological Principle.* Oxford: Oxford University Press.

Bass, T. 1986. *The Eudaemonic Pie.* New York: Vintage Books.

Beauchamp, T., and Rosenberg, A. 1977. "Critical Notice of *The Cement of the Universe.*" *Canad. J. Phil.* 7:371–404.

Bennett, J. 1987. "Event Causation: The Counterfactual Analysis." In *Philosophical Perspectives, 1,* edited by J. Tomberlin. Atascadero, Calif.: Ridgeview Publishing.

Bhaskar, R. 1975. *A Realist Theory of Science.* London: Humanities Press.

Blalock, H. 1962. "Four Variable Causal Models and Partial Correlations." *Amer. J. Soc.* 68:182–94. Reprinted in Blalock (1971), pp. 18–32.

———, ed. 1971. *Causal Models in the Social Sciences.* Chicago: Aldine Publishing.

Bleaney, B., and Bleaney, B. 1965. *Electricity and Magnetism.* 2d ed. Oxford: Oxford University Press.

Bock, R. 1975. *Multivariate Statistical Methods in Behavioral Research.* New York: McGraw-Hill.

Born, M. 1962. *Atomic Physics.* 7th ed. London: Blackie and Sons.

Brody, B. 1973. "Towards an Aristotelean Theory of Scientific Explanation." *Phil. Sci.* 39:20–31.

Bromberger, S. 1966. "Why-Questions." In Colodny (1966), pp. 86–111.

Bunzl, M. 1979. "Causal Overdetermination." *J. Phil.* 76:134–50.

Campbell, D., and Stanley, J. 1966. *Experimental and Quasi-Experimental Designs for Research*. Chicago: Rand McNally.

Cargile, J. 1967. "The Surprise Test Paradox." *J. Phil.* 64:550–63.

———. 1975. "Newcomb's Paradox." *Brit. J. Phil. Sci.* 26:227–39.

Carnap, R. 1928. *Der logische Aufbau der Welt*. Berlin: Welkreis-Verlag.

———. 1950. "Empiricism, Semantics, and Ontology." *Revue Int. de Philosophie* 11:208–28.

Cartwright, N. 1979. "Causal Laws and Effective Strategies." *Noûs* 13:419–37.

———. 1980. "Do the Laws of Physics State the Facts?" *Pac. Phil. Quarterly* 61:75–84.

Chaitin, G. 1987. *Algorithmic Information Theory*. Cambridge: Cambridge University Press.

Chung, K. L. 1968. *A Course in Probability Theory*. New York: Harcourt, Brace and World.

Church, A. 1940. "On the Concept of a Random Sequence." *Amer. Math. Soc. Bull.*, ser. 2, 46:130–35.

Cohen, L. J., ed. 1980. *Applications of Inductive Logic*. Oxford: Oxford University Press.

Collingwood, R. 1940. *An Essay on Metaphysics*. Oxford: Oxford University Press.

Colodny, R., ed. 1966. *Mind and Cosmos*. Pittsburgh: University of Pittsburgh Press.

Cook, T., and Campbell, D. 1979. *Quasi-Experimentation: Design and Analysis Issues for Field Settings*. Boston: Houghton Mifflen.

———. 1986. "The Causal Assumptions of Quasi-Experimental Practice." *Synthese* 68:141–80.

Creary, L. 1981. "Causal Explanation and the Reality of Natural Component Forces." *Pac. Phil. Quarterly* 62:148–57.

Crick, F., and Watson, J. 1954. "The Complementary Structure of Deoxyribonucleic Acid." *Proc. Roy. Soc., A.* 223:80–96.

Davidson, D. 1967. "Causal Relations." *J. Phil.* 64:691–703. Reprinted in Sosa (1975).

Davis, W. 1988. "Probabilistic Theories of Causation." In Fetzer (1988), pp. 133–60.

Demopoulos, W., and Friedman, M. 1985. "Bertrand Russell's *The Analysis of Matter*: Its Historical Context and Contemporary Interest." *Phil. Sci.* 52:621–39.

Dretske, F. 1973. "Contrastive Statements." *Phil. Rev.* 82:411–37.

———. 1979. "Referring to Events." In French et al. (1979).

Duncan, O. 1975. *Introduction to Structural Equation Models*. New York: Academic Press.

Earman, J. 1987. *A Primer on Determinism*. Dordrecht: D. Reidel Publishing.

Eberle, R., Kaplan, D., and Montague, R. 1961. "Hempel and Oppenheim on Explanation." *Phil. Sci.* 28:418–28.

Eells, E., and Sober, E. 1983. "Probabilistic Causality and the Question of Transitivity." *Phil. Sci.* 50:35–57.

Ellis, B. 1970. "Explanation and the Logic of Support." *Austr. J. Phil.* 48:177–89.

Ferguson, M., and Joanen, T. 1982. "Temperature of Egg Incubation Determines Sex in Alligator Mississippiensis," *Nature* 296:850–53.

Fetzer, J. 1981. *Scientific Knowledge*. Dordrecht: D. Reidel Publishing.

———. 1986. "Methodological Individualism: Singular Causal Systems and Their Population Manifestations." *Synthese* 68:99–128.

———, ed. 1988. *Probability and Causality*. Dordrecht: D. Reidel Publishing.

Forster, M. 1988. "Unification, Explanation, and the Composition of Causes in Newtonian Mechanics." *Stud. Hist. and Phil. Sci.* 19:55–101.

French, P., Uehling, T., and Wettstein, H., eds. 1979. *Contemporary Perspectives in the Philosophy of Language*. Minneapolis: University of Minnesota Press.

Friedman, M. 1974. "Explanation and Scientific Understanding." *J. Phil.* 71:5–19.

Gardiner, P. 1952. *The Nature of Historical Explanation*. Oxford: Oxford University Press.

Geach, P. 1961. "Aquinas." In *Three Philosophers*, by G. Anscombe and P. Geach, pp. 69–125. Ithaca: Cornell University Press.

Giere, R. 1980. "Causal Systems and Statistical Hypotheses." In Cohen (1980).

Gibson, Q. 1983. "Tendencies." *Phil. Sci.* 50:296–308.

Glymour, C., Scheines, R., and Spirtes, P. 1987. *Discovering Causal Structure: Artificial Intelligence, Philosophy of Science, and Statistical Modeling*. Orlando, Fla.: Academic Press.

Good, I. J. 1980. "A Further Note on Probabilistic Causality: Mending the Chain." *Pac. Phil. Quarterly* 61:452–54.

Goosens, W. 1979. "Causal Chains and Counterfactuals." *J. Phil.* 76:489–95.

Gorovitz, S. 1965. "Causal Judgements and Causal Explanation." *J. Phil.* 62:695–711.

Gottlieb, M., et al. 1981. "*Pneumocystis Carinii* Pneumonia and Mucosal Candidiasis in Previously Healthy Homosexual Men." *New Eng. J. Med.* 305:1425–31.

Gottlieb, M., et al. 1983. "The Acquired Immunodeficiency Syndrome." *Ann. Int. Med.* 99:208–20.

Greenberg, O., and Mohapatra, R. 1987. "Local Quantum Field Theory of

Possible Violation of the Pauli Principle." *Phys. Rev. Letters* 59:2507–10.

Hacking, I. 1965. *The Logic of Statistical Inference.* Cambridge: Cambridge University Press.

Hanushek, E., and Jackson, J. 1977. *Statistical Methods for Social Scientists.* Orlando, Fla.: Academic Press.

Harmon, H. 1967. *Modern Factor Analysis.* Chicago: University of Chicago Press.

Harper, H. 1975. *Review of Physiological Chemistry.* 15th ed. Los Altos, Calif.: Lange Medical Publications.

Hart, H., and Honore, A. 1959. *Causation in the Law.* Oxford: Clarendon Press.

Hausman, D. 1986. "Causation and Experimentation." *Amer. Phil. Quarterly* 23:143–54.

Hempel, C. 1965. "Aspects of Scientific Explanation." Chap. 12 in *Aspects of Scientific Explanation and Other Essays in the Philosophy of Science.* New York: Free Press.

———. 1968. "Maximal Specificity and Lawlikeness in Probabilistic Explanation." *Phil. Sci.* 35:116–33.

Hesslow, G. 1976. "Two Notes on the Probabilistic Approach to Causality." *Phil. Sci.* 43:290–92.

Hill, T. L. 1960. *Introduction to Statistical Thermodynamics.* Reading, Mass.: Addison-Wesley.

Hood, W., and Koopmans, T., eds. 1953. *Studies in Econometric Methods.* New York: John Wiley and Sons.

Hume, D. [1739–40] 1888. *A Treatise of Human Nature.* Edited by L. A. Selby-Bigge. Oxford: Oxford University Press.

———. [1748] 1955. *An Enquiry Concerning Human Understanding.* Indianapolis: Bobbs-Merrill.

Humphreys, P. 1980. "Cutting the Causal Chain." *Pac. Phil. Quaterly* 61:305–14.

———. 1981a. "Aleatory Explanations." *Synthese* 48:225–32.

———. 1981b. "Is Physical Randomness Just Indeterminism in Disguise?" In Asquith and Hacking (1981).

———. 1981c. "Probabilistic Causality and Multiple Causation." In Asquith and Giere (1981), pp. 25–37.

———. 1983. "Aleatory Explanations Expanded." In Asquith and Nickles (1983), pp. 208–23.

———. 1984. "Why Propensities Cannot Be Probabilities." *Phil. Rev.* 94:557–70.

———. 1985. "Quantitative Probabilistic Causality and Structural Scientific Realism." In Asquith and Kitcher (1985), pp. 329–42.

———. 1986a. "Philosophical Issues in the Scientific Basis of Quantitative

Risk Analyses." In *Biomedical Ethics Reviews: 1986,* edited by R. Almeder and J. Humber. Clifton, N.J.: Humana Press.

———. 1986b. Review of Salmon (1984). *Found. Physics* 16:1211–16.

Hurwicz, L. 1950. "Prediction and Least Squares." In Koopmans (1950), pp. 266–300.

Ito, K. 1984. *Introduction to Probability Theory.* Cambridge: Cambridge University Press.

Jeffrey, R. 1971. "Statistical Explanation vs Statistical Inference." In Salmon (1971), pp. 19–28.

Kendall, M., and Stuart, A. 1961. *Advanced Theory of Statistics.* London: Charles Griffin.

Kenny, D. 1979. *Correlation and Causation.* New York: John Wiley and Sons.

Kibble, T. 1966. *Classical Mechanics.* New York: McGraw-Hill.

Kim, J. 1971. "Causes and Events: Mackie on Causation." *J. Phil.* 68:426–41. Reprinted in Sosa (1975), pp. 48–62.

———. 1973a. "Causation, Nomic Subsumption, and the Concept of Event." *J. Phil.* 70:217–36.

———. 1973b. "Causes and Counterfactuals." *J. Phil.* 70:570–72. Reprinted in Sosa (1975), pp. 192–94.

———. 1976. "Events as Property Exemplifications." In *Action Theory,* edited by M. Brand and D. Walters. Dordrecht: D. Reidel Publishing.

Kitcher, P. 1981. "Explanatory Unification." *Phil. Sci.* 48:507–31.

———. 1985. "Two Approaches to Explanation." *J. Phil.* 82:632–39.

Kitcher, P., and Salmon, W. 1987. "Van Fraassen on Explanation." *J. Phil.* 84:315–30.

Knuth, E. 1966. *Introduction to Statistical Thermodynamics.* New York: McGraw-Hill.

Kolmogorov, A. 1956. *Foundations of the Theory of Probability.* New York: Chelsea Publishing.

Koopmans, T., ed. 1950. *Statistical Inference in Dynamic Economic Models.* New York: John Wiley and Sons.

Kruger, L. 1976. "Are Statistical Explanations Possible?" *Phil. Sci.* 43:129–46.

Lehman, H. 1972. "Statistical Explanation." *Phil. Sci.* 39:500–506.

Lewis, D. 1973. "Causation." *J. Phil.* 70:556–67. Reprinted in Sosa (1975), pp. 180–91, and in Lewis (1986a), pp. 159–72.

———. 1979. "Counterfactual Dependence and Time's Arrow." *Noûs* 13:455–76.

———. 1986a. *Philosophical Papers.* Vol. 2. Oxford: Oxford University Press.

———. 1986b. "Postscripts to 'Causation.' " In Lewis (1986a), pp. 172–213.

Loeb, L. 1974. "Causal Theories and Causal Overdetermination." *J. Phil.* 71:525–44.

Lombard, L. 1986. *Events.* London: Routledge and Kegan Paul.

MacKenzie, D. 1981. *Statistics in Britain, 1865–1930.* Edinburgh: Edinburgh University Press.

Mackie, J. 1974. *The Cement of the Universe.* Oxford: Clarendon Press.

Maddala, G. 1982. *Econometrics.* New York: McGraw-Hill.

Mandl, F. 1957. *Quantum Mechanics.* 2d ed. London: Butterworths.

Martin-Lof, P. 1969. "The Literature on von Mises' Kollectivs Revisited." *Theoria* 35:12–37.

Masur, H., et al. 1981. "An Outbreak of Community-Acquired *Pneumocystis Carinii* Pneumonia." *New Eng. J. Med.* 305:1431–38.

Mellor, D. H. 1976. "Probable Explanation." *Austr. J. Phil.* 54:231–41.

Mill, J. S. [1843] 1874. *A System of Logic.* 8th ed. New York: Harper and Brothers.

Montague, R. 1962. "Deterministic Theories." In *Decisions, Values, and Groups,* vol. 2, edited by D. Willner. Oxford: Pergamon Press. Reprinted in Montague (1974), chap. 11.

———. 1974. *Formal Philosophy: Selected Papers of Richard Montague.* Edited by R. Thomason. New Haven: Yale University Press.

Nagel, E. 1961. *The Structure of Science.* New York: Harcourt, Brace and World.

Niinuluoto, I. 1981. "Statistical Explanation Reconsidered." *Synthese* 48:437–72.

Nozick, R. 1981. *Philosophical Explanations.* Cambridge: Harvard University Press, Belknap Press.

Otte, R. 1981. "A Critique of Suppes' Theory of Probabilistic Causality." *Synthese* 48:167–89.

———. 1985. "Probabilistic Causality and Simpson's Paradox." *Phil. Sci.* 52:110–25.

Polanyi, M. 1958. *Personal Knowledge.* Chicago: University of Chicago Press.

Popper, K. 1957. "The Propensity Interpretation of the Calculus of Probability, and the Quantum Theory." In *Observation and Interpretation,* edited by S. Korner, pp. 65–70. London: Butterworths Scientific Publications.

———. 1959a. *The Logic of Scientific Discovery.* London: Hutchinson.

———. 1959b. "The Propensity Interpretation of Probability." *Brit. J. Phil. Sci.* 10:25–42.

Porter, T. 1986. *The Rise of Statistical Thinking, 1820–1900.* Princeton: Princeton University Press.

Prior, E. 1984. *Dispositions.* Aberdeen: Aberdeen University Press.

Putnam, H. 1980. "Models and Reality." *J. Symb. Logic* 45:464–82.

———. 1983. "Why There Isn't a Ready-Made World." Chap. 12 in *Realism and Reason: Philosophical Papers,* vol. 3. Cambridge: Cambridge University Press.

Quine, W. 1960. *Word and Object.* Cambridge: MIT Press.

———. 1969. "Natural Kinds." Chap. 5 in *Ontological Relativity and Other Essays.* New York: Columbia University Press.

———. 1970. *Philosophy of Logic.* Englewood Cliffs, N.J.: Prentice-Hall.

———. 1985. "Events and Reification." In *Actions and Events,* edited by E. Lepore and B. McLaughlin. Oxford: Basil Blackwell.

Railton, P. 1978. "A Deductive-Nomological Model of Probabilistic Explanation." *Phil. Sci.* 45:206–26.

Redhead, M. 1987. *Incompleteness, Nonlocality, and Realism: A Prolegomenon to the Philosophy of Quantum Mechanics.* Oxford: Oxford University Press.

Reichenbach, H. 1956. *The Direction of Time.* Berkeley: University of California Press.

Rosen, D. 1980. "A Probabilistic Theory of Causaal Necessity." *Southern J. Phil.* 18:71–86.

———. 1982. "A Critique of Deterministic Causality." *Phil. Forum* 14:101–30.

Russell, B. 1913. "On the Notion of Cause." *Proc. Arist. Soc.* 13:1–26. Reprinted in Russell (1918).

———. 1918. *Mysticism and Logic.* London: Longmans, Green.

Ryan, A. 1970. *The Philosophy of John Stuart Mill.* London: Macmillan.

Ryle, G. 1954. "Formal and Informal Logic." Chap. 8 in *Dilemmas.* Cambridge: Cambridge University Press.

Sakurai, J. 1973. *Advanced Quantum Mechanics.* Reading, Mass.: Addison-Wesley.

Salmon, W. 1971. *Statistical Explanation and Statistical Relevance.* Pittsburgh: University of Pittsburgh Press.

———. 1973. "Reply to Lehman." *Phil. Sci.* 40:397–402.

———. 1980. "Probabilistic Causality." *Pac. Phil. Quarterly* 61:50–74.

———. 1981. "Causality: Production and Propagation." In Asquith and Giere (1981), pp. 49–69.

———. 1984. *Scientific Explanation and the Causal Structure of the World.* Princeton: Princeton University Press.

Schiff, L. 1968. *Quantum Mechanics.* 3d ed. New York: McGraw-Hill.

Shorter, J. 1965. "Causality, and a Method of Analysis." In *Analytic Philosophy,* 2d ser., edited by R. J. Butler. Oxford: Basil Blackwell.

Simon, H. 1953. "Causal Ordering and Identifiability." In Hood and Koopmans (1953) pp. 49–74. Reprinted in Simon (1977), pp. 53–80.

———. 1977. *Models of Discovery.* Dordrecht: D. Reidel Publishing.

Skyrms, B. 1977. "Resiliency, Propensities, and Causal Necessity." *J. Phil.* 74:704–13.

———. 1980. *Causal Necessity.* New Haven: Yale University Press.

Snow, J. 1855. *On the Mode of Communication of Cholera.* 2d ed. Reprinted in *Snow on Cholera.* New York: Commonwealth Fund, 1936.

Sober, E. 1982. "Frequency Dependent Causation." *J. Phil.* 79:247–53.

———. 1985. "Two Concepts of Cause." In Asquith and Kitcher (1985), pp. 405–24.

———. 1987. "Explanation and Causation." Review of Salmon (1984). *Brit. J. Phil. Sci.* 38:243–57.

Sosa, E., ed. 1975. *Causation and Counterfactuals.* Oxford: Oxford University Press.

Stegmuller, W. 1973. *Personnelle und statistische Wahrscheinlichkeit.* Berlin: Springer-Verlag.

Strawson, P. 1985. "Causation and Explanation." In *Essays on Davidson: Actions and Events,* edited by B. Vermazen and M. Hintikka, pp. 115–36. Oxford: Clarendon Press.

Suppes, P. 1970. *A Probabilistic Theory of Causality.* Amsterdam: North-Holland Publishing.

———. 1984. "Conflicting Intuitions about Causality." In *Midwest Studies in Philosophy,* vol. 9, edited by P. French et al. Minneapolis: University of Minnesota Press.

Suppes, P., and Zanotti, M. 1981. "When Are Probabilistic Explanations Possible?" *Synthese* 48:191–99.

———. 1984. "Causality and Symmetry." In *The Wave-Particle Dualism,* edited by S. Diner et al. Dordrecht: D. Reidel Publishing.

Swain, M. 1978. "A Counterfactual Analysis of Event Causation." *Phil. Studies* 34:1–19.

Toulmin, S. 1961. *Foresight and Understanding: An Inquiry into the Aims of Science.* Indianapolis: Indiana University Press.

Truett, J.; Cornfield, J.; and Kannel, W. 1967. "Multivariate Analysis of the Risk of Coronary Heart Disease in Framingham." *J. Chronic Disease* 20:511–24.

van Fraassen, B. 1978. Review of Stegmuller (1973). *Phil. Sci.* 45:158–63.

———. 1980. *The Scientific Image.* Oxford: Clarendon Press.

Vendler, Z. 1962. "Effects, Results, and Consequences." In *Analytic Philosophy,* edited by R. J. Butler, pp. 1–15. Oxford: Basil Blackwell.

von Mises, R. 1957. *Probability, Statistics, and Truth.* 2d English ed. London: Allen and Unwin.

———. R. 1964. *Mathematical Theory of Probability and Statistics.* Edited by H. Geiringer. New York: Academic Press.

von Wright, G. 1974. *Causality and Determinism.* New York: Columbia University Press.

White, M. 1965. *Foundations of Historical Knowledge*. New York: Harper and Row.

Woodward, J. 1988. "Understanding Regression." In *PSA 1988, Volume 1*, edited by A. Fine and J. Leplin, pp. 255–69. East Lansing, Mich.: Philosophy of Science Association.

Yule, G. U. [1911] 1950. *An Introduction to the Theory of Statistics*. 14th ed., with M. G. Kendall. London: Charles Griffin.

INDEX

accidental generalizations, 140
Achinstein, P., 99n, 101n, 115n
additivity: of causes, 28, 103n, 128n; of error terms, 147, 150. *See also* linearity
aleatory explanations, 114–16, 118, 120, 133n, 157
allomorphs: event, 136; sentential, 136
Armstrong, D., 64n
asymmetry problem, 118
Austin, J. L., 54

Beauchamp, Thomas, 12n
Bennett, J., 107n
Berkeley, G., 108n
Bhaskar, R., 56, 56n
Blalock, H., 27n, 146
Brody, B., 99n, 124
Bromberger, S., 135n
Bunzl, M., 12n

Campbell, D., 92
Cargile, J., 11n
Carnap, R., 54n
Cartwright, N., 78n, 79n, 80, 85n, 121n
catalysts, 93
causal contribution: measure of, 19–20; principle of, 9. *See also* cause: contributing
causal empiricism, 91
causal generalizations vs. singular causal claims, 75
causal models, 146
causal power, 20, 65
causal processes, 95–97
causation: population dependence, 88; quantitative, 5
cause: conditions versus, 128–29; contributing, 15, 16, 28, 74, 75–80, 82–83, 88, 93, 95, 100, 102, 104, 108, 114; counteracting, 15, 16, 19, 74, 79, 94–95, 100, 102, 124; counterfactual analysis, 12n; incomplete, 6, 8–9; insufficient, 6; multiple, 6–8, 13, 27, 88, 128; overdetermining, 10–12; potentially overdetermining, 86–87; predisposing, 93; sine qua non, 12–13, 15–16;

sufficient, 9–12; triggering, 93. *See also* probabilistic causality
central result, 34, 155
ceteris paribus, 129–32; definition, 130
chance, 15, 18–21, 35–36, 55, 61–65, 73–74, 104, 113–14, 141, 151–52; as relational, 61–62, 88
"chicken counter's fallacy," 76–77
cigarette smoking, 43
coexistence: laws of, 123–24
Collingwood, R., 77n, 128, 128n
common cause, 81, 119; principle, 66–70
conceptual analysis, 3, 4
context-dependency. *See* pragmatics
contrast case: 37–45, 128n, 129–32, 156; choice affecting relevance, 41, 45; complement of cause as, 43–44; mean value as, 42–43; natural state as, 43; normal level as, 43. *See also* neutral state
Cook, T., 92
correlation coefficient, 144
counterfactual: analysis of cause, 12n, 92; conditionals, 129–130; definiteness, 97; dependence, 89
covariance, 143

Davidson, D., 99n, 135
Davis, W., 42, 85
de re knowledge, 140; vs. *de dicto*, 140
definitions: explicit, 89; implicit, 54; inductive, 89; recursive, 90
Demopoulos, W., 54n
dependent variables, 22
depression, 113
detailed specification of events, 10, 84, 85, 85n, 107–8, 122, 156
determinism, 50, 116, 151
discontinuous processes, 76; and indeterminism, 77
discovery: of explanations, 98, 138
dispositions, 62–64. *See also* propensities; tendencies 'dormitive virtue', 64
Dray, W., 119, 135n
Dretske, F., 136

Ducasse, C. J., 128, 128n
Duncan, 0., 148

Eells, E., 36, 153
Ellis, B., 125n
empiricism, 4, 47; causal, 91. *See also* passive
    empiricism
endogenous variables, 22, 146
epistemology, 3
ERNIE, 18
error terms, 27n, 147–52
essential properties, 23
event, 25, 25n; definition, 24, 104; distinguish-
    ing marks, 10–11; nomologically insepara-
    ble, 82; spatiotemporal regions, 103. *See
    also* detailed specification of events
event aspects, 25
event identity, 97
event types, 24
examples, principal: AIDS, 6; air conditioner,
    105–6; airliner, 8; alligator gender, 95; an-
    gular momentum of earth, 102; aurora bo-
    realis, 133–35; barometer, 119; birth control
    pills, 82–83, 120; bubonic plague, 100, 115;
    car skid, 39, 50; carcinogens, 15, 36–37,
    43, 111; chocolate, 105; chocolate, poi-
    soned, 107; chocolate machine, 95–96;
    cholera, 134; Civil War, 113; defoliant, 121;
    DNA, 134; enzyme-catalyzed reaction, 7, 9,
    101; firing squad, 108; flagpole, 118; flash
    freeze, 14, 88; food poisoning, 66; galactic
    red shift, 118; golf, 156–57; heart attack,
    7–8; hexed salt, 120, 136; induced emis-
    sion, 62, 88; inflation, 76; Koplik's spots,
    139–40, *Lancastria*, 18n; Lotus 7, 63; mari-
    juana, 122; Maxwell-Boltzmann law, 67;
    mimics, 87–88; motorcyclist, 17; orbital
    motion, 68, 137; paresis, 44, 93, 112, 122,
    125; radioactive decay, 19–20, 68, 70–72,
    121; surprise attack, 136; thermionic emis-
    sion, 40; thrombosis, 82–83; tug-of-war,
    56–57; vitamin C, 120
exogenous variables, 22, 146
experimental analysis of causation, 90–91
experimental contexts, 48, 55–58
explanations: causal, 99; complete, 116; con-
    junctive, 115; covering law, 109, 114; de-
    ductive-nomological, 99, 118, 119n, 120;
    deterministic, 105–6; how-possibly, 116;
    ideal, 116; incomplete, 6, 102, 111–12;
    inductive-statistical, 99, 111, 123, 136;
    multiple alternative, 113; objective, 98; of
    natural and artificial phenomena, 7; pro-

babilistic, 19; quantitative, 5; statistical-
    relevance, 109–10, 121, 122. *See also* alea-
    tory explanations
explanatory requests. *See* questions

facts, 25
Fetzer, J., 88, 109n
formalism, 54
frequency-dependent causation, 87–88
Friedman, M., 54n
future events: explaining, 126

Galileo, G., 7
Gardiner, P., 119n
generating conditions, 52–53, 55
Giere, R., 87

Hacking, I., 53n
Hart, H.L.A., 129n
Hempel, C., 99, 101n, 109n, 111, 113n, 114,
    116, 119n, 123, 127, 133, 139–40
Hesslow, G., 82
homoscedasticity, 147n
Honore, A., 129n
Hume, D., 18, 18n, 20, 36n, 47, 47n, 48, 49n,
    52, 52n, 106n, 108n, 139
Humphreys, P., 55n, 109n, 113n, 114, 133n,
    148n, 155
Humphreys, W. C., 18n
Humphreys, W. E., 18n
Hurwicz, L., 67

ideal science, 116
independent variables, 22
indeterminism, 16–18, 35, 63, 76, 88, 96,
    117–18; as psychological prejudice, 17; and
    sine qua non analyses, 12n, 16
indistinguishability of particles, 40n
inductive definition: of causation, 89–92
inevitable events, 85
instrumentalism, 67–69
'intuition', 156
invariance condition, 28, 31, 72–75, 79, 114–
    17, 130; applied to regression, 147–52
irrelevant factor problem, 120

Jeffrey, R., 112n
joint effects problem, 119

Kant, I., 13–14n
Kenny, D., 149n
Kim, J., 13n, 74n, 99n, 104n, 135

Kitcher, P., 132n, 137n
Kolmogorov, A. N., 24n, 53, 53n, 70
Kruger, L., 117
Kyburg, H., 136

laws, 56–57, 70–72, 139–40
Lehman, H., 122
Lewis D., 12n, 13n, 14n, 107–8, 108n
linearity, 30–31
linguistic form of explanations, 98, 100–103,
    105–6, 133–38
logical analyses of causation, 92

Mackie, J., 12n, 14n, 52n, 95, 97
Maddala, G., 26n
manipulability theory of causation: circularity
    of, 91–92
manipulations, 48, 69, 92, 123; logical vs.
    causal, 51
Markov processes, 77; vs. non-Markov, 77
Marschak, J., 67
Martin, C. B., 64
maximal specificity conditions, 80n, 110, 114
mechanisms, 95–97
Mellor, D., 125n
Michaelangelo, 57
Mill, J. S., 29, 48n, 56, 57n, 72–73, 77n, 128
Mill's Methods of Experimental Inquiry, 48,
    49n

necessary conditions, 93; noncausal, 87
necessity: natural, 65
negative links: problem of, 126, 148, 155–57
negative relevance, 121–22
neutral state, 38–41, 44–45; non-Boolean na-
    ture of, 44
nomic expectability, 119n, 139; vs. psycho-
    logical, 139
nonadditive causes, 28–29
nondiscrimination problem, 125
nonlinear phenomena, 103n
Nozick, R., 116

ontology, 3, 22–25, 103–4
ordinary language: arguments against, 4–5,
    98–99, 108, 129, 131, 135n
Otte, R., 78n, 83–84, 85n, 93n

passive empiricism, 47–50, 56, 89, 92, 132
path analysis, 145–46
path coefficient, 144
Pearson, K., 49n

Peirce, C. S., 55n, 116
pendulum: elastic, 123; rigid, 123
place-selection function, 51, 53
Polanyi, M., 132n
Popper, K., 53n
pragmatics, 126–32, 133; in counterfactuals,
    130–32; definition 126–27
predictions, 37, 115
probabilistic causality, 14, 18, 46–47, 54; as-
    sumptions for, 27–31; binary case, 34–37,
    41; nonbinary case, 41–42; quantitative,
    26–33
probabilistic model of explanation, 110–11,
    114
probability, 25n; interpretation of, 55; pure,
    113
probability values: as predictors, 37; relation
    to cause, 19–20; relation to explanation, 19,
    37, 109–17, 123
propensities, 20, 62–64, 85n, 121

quasi-experimentation, 92
questions: comparative, 117, 136–37; epistemic
    vs. explanatory, 133, 139–40; how-possibly,
    121; rejection of, 124–25; why-questions,
    6, 132–38
Quine, W., 64, 67, 103n

Railton, P., 109n
randomness, 51–52, 80, 111
realism, 66–69; causal, 4
recursive models, 146
reduced form of equations, 148n
reference class, 45, 70, 109n; homogeneous,
    45, 80n, 110, 111, 121
regression: coefficient, 144, 147; constancy of,
    147–48; linear, 145–46
regularity analysis of causation, 50, 55, 92,
    119
Reichenbach, H., 49, 66
relative frequencies, 45, 50–51, 53, 57, 65,
    70, 74, 111n, 115, 121, 152
relativization of explanation, 127
relevance difference, 34, 154
relevance relation, 45, 137n
residuals. See error terms
Rosen, D., 46, 83, 155
Rosenberg, A., 12n
roulette, 53n
Russell, B., 50–51 77n, 130–31
Ryan, A., 49n
Ryle, G., 101n

Salmon, W., 66n, 91n, 101n, 109n, 109–10,
    115, 120, 120n, 121–22, 132n, 136, 137n,
    156n
secondary analysis, 49, 57
Shorter, J., 135n
Simon, H., 146
single case: problem of, 50, 109n
Skyrms, B., 79n, 80, 80n
Snow, J., 134
Sober, E., 36, 87, 153
spontaneity, 14, 19–20, 88
spontaneous emission, 116
spurious causation, 81–82, 84, 119, 140
standard deviation, 143
standardized variable, 143–44
state description, 80
Stegmuller, W., 117
stock-market analysis, 53n
Strawson, P., 99n
structural equation models, 145–46
structures, 58–61, 67–70; basis of chance, 20,
    62
Suppes, P., 4n, 49, 54, 54n, 70, 79n, 84n, 155
symmetry thesis: prediction vs. explanation,
    114–15, 139
system, 22–23

tendencies, 57n
theoretician's dilemma, 69
transitivity: of probabilistic causes, 153–55
trivialization problem, 50–53

unconditionality. *See* invariance condition
understanding, 101n, 127
universal causation: principle of, 20, 75, 88

van Bendegem, J. P., 29n
van Fraassen, B., 117, 122n, 124–25, 127,
    129n, 132, 132n, 136
variance, 143
Vendler, Z., 135n
verisimilitude, 115n
von Mises, R., 51, 53, 53n, 70
von Wright, G., 94n

White, M., 128n
Woodward, J., 27n, 34n, 36, 40

Yule, G. U., 49

Zanotti, M., 70